ALONE

In The Night

Lighthouses of Georgian Bay, Manitoulin Island and the North Channel

Written by:

ANDREA GUTSCHE
BARBARA CHISHOLM
RUSSELL FLOREN

This book was made possible through the assistance of the following organizations:

Huronia Museum, Midland, Ontario

Department of Canadian Heritage, Museum Assistance Program

The McLean Foundation

The Charles H. Ivey Foundation

Jackman Foundation

Copyright © 1996 by Lynx Images Inc.
P.O. Box 5961, Station A
Toronto, Canada M5W 1P4
Web Site: http://www.lynximages.com

Editor: Barbara D. Chisholm
Cover illustration and design: James Flaherty
Typesetting and layout: Heidy Lawrance Associates
1st Edition, June 1996

Printed and bound in Canada by Metropole Litho Inc.

Canadian Cataloguing in Publication Data

Gutsche, Andrea, 1964-
    Alone in the night: lighthouses of Georgian Bay

Includes bibliographical references.

ISBN 0-9698427-4-0 (set)
ISBN 0-9698427-5-9 (book)
ISBN 0-9698427-6-7 (videocassette)

1. Lighthouses - Ontario - Georgian Bay - History.
2. Lighthouses - Ontario - Manitoulin Island - History
I. Floren, Russell, 1965-   . II. Chisholm, Barbara, 1962-   .
III. Title.

VK1027.O5G88 1996   387.1'55'097131509   C96-931006-4

*This book is dedicated
to the lightkeepers and their families,
and to those keepers of history
who have preserved the stories
while much of the official record
has been lost.*

TABLE OF CONTENTS

---✦---

PREFACE

✛

Lighthouses capture the imagination. There is an obvious appeal in the romantic image of lights as beacons of strength and protection, but the fascination goes beyond that. Pass one of the silent towers and an eerie presence beckons – of untold stories and forgotten memories. The inevitable questions surface, "what would it have been like to live there? Who were the keepers and what exactly did they do? How did the lights work?"

We became intrigued with the subject during the production of *Ghosts of the Bay*, the focus of which was the history of Georgian Bay. Our early research efforts were stymied, however, when we realized that there has been little, if any, research or literature on the lighthouse service in Georgian Bay. There are several books on Great Lakes lighthouses, but they all deal with lights south of the border. Scant Canadian records remain, save the memories and photo albums of keepers and their families. When they are gone, their history will be lost.

As their stories unfolded, the silent towers developed individual characters. Some rang with tales of heroic struggles, others with the sounds of family life, while others throbbed with loneliness and isolation. As the project progressed, we gained new respect and appreciation for these keepers of the lights. Many of the locations are isolated, they are very hard to land on, let alone to imagine living on. And while we understand why the lights are deemed to be obsolete, we also had occasion to be glad that some were still there. One late September night we found ourselves navigating in heavy seas, heading for the shelter of Tobermory as have countless vessels before us. Seeing the lights at Cove and Flowerpot Islands in the distance reassuringly confirmed our position. In the pitch dark they took on an intensely personal note, adding warmth to a potentially frightening scene.

The fate of many Canadian Great Lakes and coastal lighthouses currently swings in the balance. One by one they are being torn down. With the destruction of each one, a piece of our heritage is lost. The urgency to document the lights and their keepers and to secure for them a place in our history motivated us in this project. The need for public action to save the remaining lights is equally urgent.

INTRODUCTION

✛

The history of lightkeeping on Georgian Bay, Manitoulin Island, and the North Channel is one of which we can be justly proud. Faced with the need to light one of the longest stretches of waterways in the world with little money, Canadians used remarkable initiative, innovation, drive and vision to respond to the challenge. Why have Canadians not heard more about this remarkable part of their history? Perhaps because those involved were practical people, or, as marine historian Thomas Appleton suggested, people "to whom the day's work has been more important than the telling."

But without their stories we are on the verge of losing an integral piece of our marine heritage. This project is designed to try to address that problem. It is intended to paint a portrait of the life and times of lightkeepers from the 1850s to 1991 when the last keeper was removed from Cove Island. The book is not intended to be a comprehensive history. Rather it is a scrapbook of anecdotes and personal histories gathered from hundreds of people. We have attempted as much as possible to identify each keeper's tenure, and to describe the original characteristics of the lighthouses. Where appropriate, we have included later developments. Ideally, this book will provide the basis and stimulus for further research.

From an official perspective, there has been no incentive to preserve the lightkeeping records. Nor is there any compelling reason for the Coast Guard to preserve the lighthouses. Its mandate is the safety of shipping, and with modern navigational equipment, lighthouses are no longer considered necessary. On the Great Lakes, all the lights have been destaffed, and many have been demolished for the most part during the last thirty years. Where there once were over fifty lighthouses on Georgian Bay, Manitoulin Island, and the North Channel, there are now half as many, and their numbers continue to dwindle. The reason? They are considered liabilities and their potential historic and aesthetic value has not been identified or taken into account.

These proud lighthouses encapsulate the unique spirit of a neglected era. In the United States, they are protected monuments. Even the most remote tower attracts thousands of visitors each year and provides welcome income for local communities. Can we not emulate their concern and enterprise? As one American aware of the situation put it: "why do Canadians always see things as problems? Why don't you see their potential?"

PART I

LIGHTHOUSE BASICS

Fresnel lens
— Marine Museum of the Great Lakes at Kingston

ORIGINS

Lightkeeping has ancient roots, and through the millenia has been perceived of as the mark of a civilized society. In sixteenth-century England, it was considered an act of Christian charity. Along the English coasts, monks tended the lights in church towers. The British Trinity House's original charter names the "Master Wardens and Assistants of the Guild Fraternity or Brotherhood of the most glorious and undivided Trinity and of St. Clement, in the Parish of Deptford Strong, in the county of Kent," a group that existed in the reign of Henry VII as a religious house with certain duties connected with pilotage, and was incorporated during the reign of Henry VIII. In 1565 it was given rights to maintain beacons, and in 1680 began owning lighthouses. After that date it began purchasing most of the ancient privately-owned lighthouses and erected many new ones. An act of 1836 gave the corporation control of English coastal lights with supervisory powers over other local lighting authorities.

In 1805, following the English model, a corporate body known as the Quebec Trinity House was created with "the power and authority, to make, ordain and constitute such and so many Bye laws, Rules and Orders, not repugnant to the maritime laws of Great Britain or to the laws of this Province . . . for the more convenient, safe and easy navigation of the River Saint Lawrence, from the fifth rapid, above the city of Montreal, downwards, as well by the laying down, as taking up of Buoys and Anchors, as by the erecting of Light houses, Beacons or Land marks, the clearing of sands or rocks or otherwise howsoever." In 1832 a Montreal Trinity House was instituted with jurisdiction upriver from Montreal. That jurisdiction eventually passed over to the Department of Marine and Fisheries.

Why Were They Built?

—✛—

To experience a Georgian Bay storm is to understand the need for lighthouses. Few early nineteenth-century sea captains would have traded places with their upper Great Lakes counterparts. When savage weather hit Georgian Bay, captains did not have a wide ocean and the option of running before the storm. Instead they had to manoeuvre through narrow, uncharted passages with no navigational aids. Seasoned captains could only rely on memory and instinct or, as the saying went, could only navigate 'by ear, by nose and by God.'

Since water transportation was the most practical means of carrying goods and people on these upper lakes, the British Admiralty in 1819 commissioned Admiral Henry Wolsey Bayfield to chart the islands and shorelines of Georgian Bay and the North Channel. This gruelling task took four years to complete, but even then hundreds of shoals lurking just beneath the water's surface remained hidden and unmarked. The only way to determine depth was to drop a lead measuring line.

Adding to these problems was that of poorly built and badly maintained ships. In 1837, the travel writer Anna Jameson complained that Georgian Bay's first steamer, the *Penetanguishene,* was "a dirty little boat . . . the upper deck to which I have fled from the close hot cabin is an open platform with no defense or railing around it." Another ship which came in for criticism was the *Kaloolah,* a 188-foot side-wheeler. William H.G. Kingston in his travel book, *Western Wanderings,* commented, "had we been told that the vessel . . . was built of pasteboard, we might almost have believed it." He continued, "one is apt to fancy a lake an ornamental and harmless bit of water, but I would a hundred-fold rather have been in a tolerably good ship in a heavy gale of wind in mid-ocean, than where we then

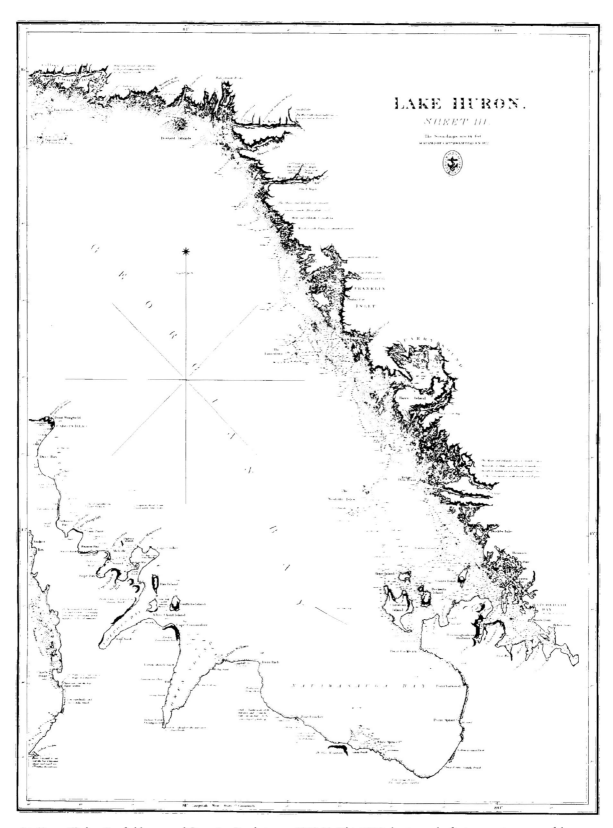

Lt. Henry Wolsey Bayfield surveyed Georgian Bay between 1819-22. This 1828 chart was the first accurate survey of the shores and islands of Georgian Bay but did little to point out the shoals and rocks beneath the water's surface.
— Archives of Ontario

Lt. Henry Wolsey Bayfield, 1795-1885. This skilful, imaginative nautical surveyor who surveyed Georgian Bay and the North Channel over a gruelling four year period, 1819-1822, began his service in the Royal Navy at the age of 11. The massive job was only one piece of his grand project to survey from the head of Lake Superior to the western shores of Newfoundland. It took him forty years to accomplish his ambitious goal.
– Discovery Harbour, Penetanguishene

floated on board the *Kaloolah.*"

These difficulties did not slow the flow of traffic. Records show that the Great Lakes in 1850 were congested with 969 schooners, 203 propellers, 147 steamers, 86 brigs, 62 barques and 15 sloops. The naval and military base at Penetanguishene had to be served, as did the burgeoning communities of Collingwood and Owen Sound and the growing number of settlers. Between the years 1854 and 1856, four dramatic developments occurred adding to the explosion in shipping. With the opening of the Bruce Peninsula for settlement, more people began to pour into the area. A free trade agreement with the United States removed duties on Canadian resources such as furs and lumber, both of which were transported by water. In 1855, a larger U.S. shipping canal opened at Sault Ste. Marie, and most consequential, the first railway to hit the shores of Georgian Bay opened between Toronto and Collingwood. Collingwood was now an important transshipment centre with immigrants and supplies flowing west while grain and wood products

were off-loaded and sent east to the Atlantic ports and international markets.

As the economy grew, so did the number of collisions, fires and groundings. The toll grew worse when steam vessel owners increased night travel in the mid-1850s in order to maximize profits. At a few villages, seamen's lanterns were suspended from poles to guide ships into the harbour. Needless to say, they were woefully inadequate. It was becoming painfully obvious that these waters had to be lit. There were lighthouses on the lower Great Lakes, and in 1847 one had been built at Goderich on southern Lake Huron. But as of November 27, 1854, there were no lighthouses above that point on the Canadian Great Lakes.

An anticipated rise in shipping had propelled the initiation of a lighthouse building project, but stories such as the fate of the *Bruce Mine* added fuel to the pressure being put on the authorities to act. On November 27, 1854, the ship was caught in a fierce storm off Stokes Bay in Lake Huron and after hours of stress sprung a leak. Captain Fraser ordered the crew to toss the cargo overboard but that did nothing to stop the

Author Anna Jameson travelled on Georgian Bay's first steamer the Penetanguishene *in 1837 and complained bitterly about the deplorable conditions.*
– Metropolitan Toronto Reference Library

The Kaloolah, *renamed the* Collingwood *ended her days aground near Michipicoten Island, Lake Superior. One passenger complained, "had we been told that the vessel . . . was built of pasteboard, we might almost have believed it."*
— *Metropolitan Toronto Reference Library*

gushing water. A fire broke out and though the crew worked frantically through the night, by dawn the ship was at the mercy of the waves. When the carpenter threatened to abandon ship, the captain pulled out two pistols, cocked them, and screamed at the wild-eyed crew, "I'll shoot the first of you who gets into the lifeboat before I order it!"

No sooner had he spoken these words than the doomed *Bruce Mine* sank. Miraculously, the entire deck was torn off, forming a perfect platform from which to launch the lifeboats. Had it happened any other way, the disbelieving crew knew they would have been sucked under with the ship. One lifeboat carried nine crewmen and the Mate, Duncan McGregor Lambert. The other carried the remaining fifteen and the

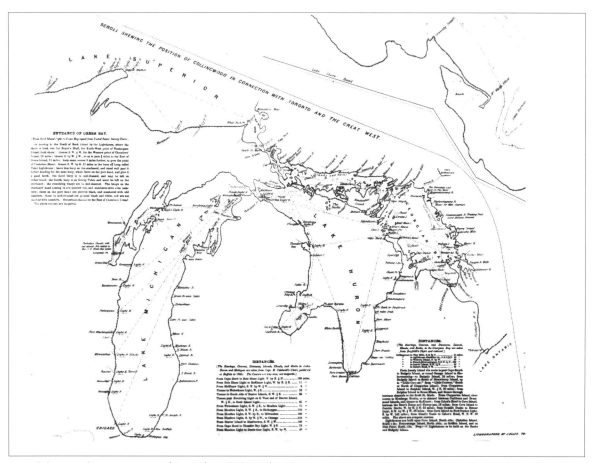

Detail showing the 1858 Course of Trade from "Chart of Collingwood Harbor and its Connections" by William Gibbard. The "northern route" to the Georgian Bay railheads was faster than shipping grain east via southern Lake Huron.
— *National Archives of Canada NMC24034*

Captain. The carpenter tried to jump into one of the lifeboats but missed and vanished into the churning water.

Each boat was supplied with only one pair of oars. It was nearly 10 p.m. when they landed approximately twenty-four kilometres from where the ship had gone down, Lambert's group on Devil Island and Captain Fraser's on nearby Russel Island. By daybreak the two groups had reunited on Devil Island. The odds of being discovered this late in the shipping season were slim; they were faced with starvation and hypothermia. There were no roads on the Bruce Peninsula, and the closest community was Collins Harbour (Tobermory), only a handful of abandoned fishing shacks in winter.

The decision was unanimous. They would have to row all the way to Owen Sound. Despite the winds and the cold, the soaked men took turns rowing and bailing with the Captain and Mate cheering them on. They passed Cove Island where five years later there would be an impressive limestone lighttower. Relying on his memory, the Captain guided them past Cabot Head, Cape Croker, and Griffith Island – all sites of future lighthouses.

Saturday, December 2, four days after leaving Devil Island, the Captain's boat landed at the Owen Sound wharf. They should have been jubilant, but the men were so cold and exhausted

they could only stare blankly at the curious townspeople. Fires were lit along the shore to guide the second boat in. Finally, at three o'clock Sunday morning, they heard a shout. Lambert's group had arrived.

The following year, 1855, the provincial Board of Works finally began the largest lighthouse building program yet seen in Canada. In 1858, Duncan McGregor Lambert, who had led his men to safety, would be appointed the first lightkeeper of Chantry Island on Lake Huron and would serve for forty years. Chantry was one of the six Imperial lighthouses built on Lake Huron and Georgian Bay.

THE IMPERIAL TOWERS

The First Wave of Lighthouse Building

When the decision was made to build the towers, the question remained: who could do the job? The Board contracted John Brown, a Scottish stone mason from Thorold, Ontario to erect eleven lighthouses on Lake Huron and Georgian Bay. Though he had never built a lighthouse, Brown was an experienced contractor whose quarry and skills had been used for all the replacement locks on the Welland Canal. He was also wealthy, a key determining factor, as his reserves could help him weather the financial risks involved in this project, which was far from straightforward.

It was a huge undertaking – build eleven tall stone towers in a near wilderness, accessible only through little known, dangerous waters. To begin, Brown had dolomite limestone quarries opened at three locations, including the western escarpment of Owen Sound. That stage went relatively smoothly. Transporting the cut stone to the sites was a different matter. Four supply boats went down with their loads before even

Duncan McGregor's son William became Chantry Island's most famous lightkeeper. Seen here holding a watch presented to him after rescuing crew from the schooner Nettie Woodward *in 1892.*
– Bruce County Museum and Archives

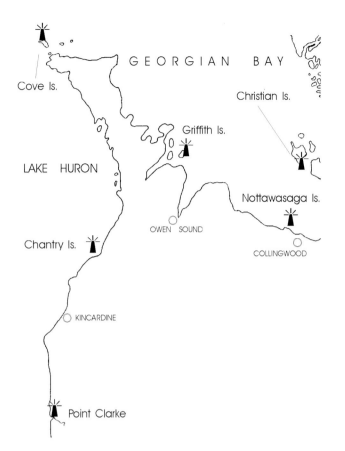

GEORGIAN BAY

Cove Is.

Christian Is.

Griffith Is.

LAKE HURON

Nottawasaga Is.

OWEN SOUND

Chantry Is.

COLLINGWOOD

KINCARDINE

Point Clarke

*List of the 11 planned towers
of which only the first six
were completed:*

1 Point Clark
2 Chantry Island
3 Cove Island
4 Griffith Island
5 Nottawasaga Island
6 Christian Island
7 White Fish Island
8 Mississagi Strait
9 Isle St. Joseph
10 Clapperton Island
11 Badgeley Island

*John Brown, contractor for the six Imperial towers – a job
that proved to be more than he had bargained for.*
– *Woodward Grant and Co. Lith.*

reaching the sites. One was sunk by an ice floe, and countless times materials were swept off the decks. Because of the constant delays, workers sat idle, a situation doubly vexing to Brown because he had had to pay dearly just to induce these men to step foot on these remote, blackfly-infested shores. It quickly became apparent that the estimates of the costs involved had been grossly underestimated, and a depression in 1857 ensured that no more provincial funds were forthcoming. Of the eleven towers planned, only six were actually built: Chantry Island and Point Clark on Lake Huron; and Cove Island, Griffith Island, Nottawasaga Island and Christian Island on Georgian Bay.

The keepers' houses were completed first, presumably to provide shelter at each site. Both the dwellings and the towers are testament to Brown's unwavering standards. The craftsman-ship of the exterior stonework is exceptional. Only the best limestone was chosen so that little maintenance would be required. Foundations were built securely, and walls at the base of the towers were about six feet thick. Mortar was processed on site, undoubtedly to the highest standard, for Brown had earlier won awards for the quality of his masonry cement.

The finest French Fresnel lenses were ordered from Paris, but were delayed because of a backlog resulting from a massive U.S. lighthouse building program. In the meantime, keepers were installed to provide temporary lights on the towers. Despite Brown's financial reserves, he was losing 1,500 pounds on each tower and was near bankruptcy. He petitioned the Governor

Second order Fresnel lens similar to one used at Cove Island
— National Archives of Canada PA143613

Decorative bronze water-spouts adorned all the Imperial tower lantern rooms.
— Courtesy of Robert Square

Above: Nottawasaga Island lighttower and house — infamous for being damp and uncomfortable
— Mazur Collection/Huronia Museum L995.0003.0001

General for more funds, citing unforeseen delays and the "boisterous state of the weather" among other uncontrollable circumstances. He concluded his letter with the entreaty: "he [the petitioner] does not seek for profit whatever but trusting to your Excellency's justice that the public benefits to be immediately derived from these important works will not be obtained at his cost and ruin."

Finally in 1858, the order for lenses was filled. Specially trained French technicians came to Canada to install the cast iron lantern rooms and complex lenses. William Scott, the head engineer, described the triumphant moment the Cove Island light burst into life:

Coat of Arms of Dominion of Canada

> The effect from a distance is grand beyond description as it seems to gather together, rolling itself up into a dark cloudy night and then bursting out into a brilliant flame that illuminated the whole horizon; and cannot be better illustrated, than by the sudden appearance of a brilliant sun breaking out of a dark rolling cloud.

Cove, Nottawasaga and Griffith were lit late in 1858, Christian the following spring. Each had distinctive lights. Cove and Nottawasaga had strong "second order" lenses — Cove because it marked the entrance to Georgian Bay and had to be seen from a great distance, and Nottawasaga because Collingwood was developing into an important harbour. Griffith was given a slightly less powerful third order lens, and Christian, a still weaker fourth for local traffic. The final cost of the six towers was so prohibitive that none of their kind were ever built again on Georgian Bay.

CONFEDERATION

The Second Wave of Lighthouse Building

After Confederation in 1867, emphasis was put on lighting the waterways as quickly as possible in order to assist the increased traffic on the upper Great Lakes. While stone lighthouses were preferable in the years that whale, coal oil and other flammable fuels were in use, they were too expensive for the nascent Dominion of Canada. Subsequent towers, even their lantern rooms, would have to be built of wood which was in plentiful supply. This emphasis on economy and simplicity was set out by the Canadian Lighthouse commissioner in the 1872 Department of Marine and Fisheries' Annual Report:

> . . . in this country the extent of sea coast, lake and river shores to be lighted up is so enormous, that in order to secure sufficient light to make our shores approachable with safety, it became absolutely necessary that a cheap but efficient system of lighting should be adopted, in respect both to construction and maintenance, as it is of no importance to the shipping navigation around our shores, whether the lighthouses are built of wood or stone, so long as the light is brilliant, and is maintained with efficiency and regularity.

The first lighthouses were built between 1866 and 1867 in the Manitoulin Island area. These were simple frame lights at Little Current, Clapperton Island, Spider Island and Killarney. By the 1870s, shipping on Georgian Bay and the North Channel was expanding rapidly and the region's economic backbone continued to strengthen with the growth of farming, timbering, and fishing. All around the Bay, lights were coming on to guide vessels into harbours, mark shipping passages, and to warn of hidden dangers. Lonely Island was built in 1870 to mark the shipping route up to the North Channel; Red Rock, built in 1870, guided vessels into Parry Sound; and in 1875, Gin Rock facilitated schooner traffic in and out of Penetanguishene and Midland.

Giants Tomb lighthouse, 1939
– National Archives of Canada PA182838

Six years after Confederation, members of the Trinity House, the English lighthouse authority, made an inspection tour of Canadian lighthouses. They were amazed by what they saw. Not only had the job been done, but it had been done for a fraction of what it would have cost in either the United States or Britain. A coastal lighthouse that would cost $100,000 in Britain could be erected in Canada for $8,000. The lights on Georgian Bay were being erected for even less, between $300 and $2,000. Whereas British and American lights were constructed of expensive stone, were fitted with sophisticated lenses, and burned expensive oils, the Canadian lights were built of wood, used simple but effective reflectors, and burned an inexpensive fuel – coal oil or kerosene. Invented by a Canadian, kerosene had proved to be so much cleaner and brighter than conventional oils that it actually made up for the inferior lighting apparatuses. Eventually, Britain and the U.S. switched over. The Trinity praised these towers as

being "admirably adapted for the wants of a young and rapidly improving country." (The Department of Marine and Fisheries 1872 *Annual Report*)

Small isolated communities began to dot the shores while the larger ports hummed with activity. The unceasing demand for wood kept the forests ringing with the sound of axes and saws. Fleets of schooners, some carrying 600,000 feet of lumber squeezed in their holds or piled precariously on their decks, filled the horizon. Two-masted brigs and three-masted barques carried other bulk freight such as coal, stone and grain, while the steamers carried passengers, livestock and package freight. Fuel gradually switched over from wood to coal, sidewheelers increased in size, and with the increasing demand, the steam lines began offering travel to more destinations.

But this boom activity was not without problems. The competition was so intense that there was always pressure to sail when prudence would have suggested otherwise. Grain schooner captains coming from the Lakehead or the grain ports of Lake Michigan such as Chicago or Milwaukee began taking more and more chances

Above: Steamers vying for space in Owen Sound Harbour, c. 1890.
– County of Grey-Owen Sound Museum

Right: Once filling the horizon with their billowing sails, schooners began to lose ground to iron-hull ships which were disdainfully dubbed "iron ships run by wooden men". Their captains were barred from membership in the sailor's union by the schooner captains.
– Thunder Bay Historical Museum Society

as they raced to be the first into the elevators at Collingwood, Owen Sound, and Midland, for to be second could mean delays of up to a week if elevators were full or trains delayed. Despite the successful lighthouse building program, the scene was set for numerous disasters. Often ships ran late into the season when the weather was the most dangerous and often they were overloaded and undermanned. More and more ships were wrecking on unmarked shoals and ledges or being lost in the brutal fall weather. The *Waubuno* went down in November 1879 with all hands lost. The *Regina* sank September 1881 and the *Jane Miller* (November 1881) wasnever found. Crushing losses to the communities, they were to culminate in the *Asia* – the worst disaster ever on Georgian Bay.

Georgian Bay captains like 'Black Pete' Campbell were local celebrities. He was described as a man with a lurid vocabulary but a warm heart.
– Courtesy of Jamie McMaster

Captain J.N. Savage survived the sinking of the Asia but later died in one of the life boats.
— County of Grey – Owen Sound Museum

The worst marine disaster ever on Georgian Bay, the steamer Asia disappeared September 14, 1882, leaving only two survivors.
— Archives of Ontario

The *Asia*

14 September, 1882. After loading fuel and hay, the *Asia* left Presqu'ile at about four in the morning. Pressed to reach French River and to continue the run to the Sault, Captain Savage ignored the brewing storm and the exceedingly low barometric reading. As the storm gathered force, the old Welland Canal propeller boat laboured its way towards French River under a heavy load of logging equipment, provisions, horses, other livestock and passengers. Already by 9 a.m. she was in serious trouble, listing badly, but when she came out into the "gap" two hours later, she was no longer protected by the Bruce Peninsula and was hit by the full force of the storm racing across Lake Huron.

Among old-timers, the hurricane force winds were unprecedented. Watching the storm from near Killarney, one sailor reported that when the wind changed and the two seas met, a column of water shot twenty or thirty feet in the air. The *Asia*'s steering was always difficult in bad weather and now winter stores filled the lower deck, with

William and Mary Greenfield on their wedding day before embarking on the doomed Asia, *September 1882.*
— Through the Years, *January 1986*

the overflow piled high on the hurricane deck. Worse, there were not enough life rafts or life preservers for the over one hundred passengers crammed on board. She was supposed to carry only forty passengers and should have been detained in Collingwood before ever embarking.

It was believed that heavy seas shoved in the ship's gangways, forcing her on her side and causing the upper works to separate. Some passengers were able to cling to wreckage, and a few managed to haul themselves into lifeboats, but the lifeboats were quickly swamped. In the end, of about one hundred and twenty-five passengers, only two teenagers survived the ordeal, Christy Anne Morrison and D.A. (Duncan) Tinkis.

J.G. Boulton, R.N., having served as assistant on the Newfoundland Survey was appointed head of the coveted survey of Georgian Bay.
– County of Grey – Owen Sound Museum

The Georgian Bay Survey

People were at the breaking point. Four hundred and seventy lives had been lost in shipping disasters on the Great Lakes between 1879 and 1882 alone. And now the *Asia*. Something had to be done. An inquest was held, and even though it was determined that the ship did not founder on an unmarked shoal, the disaster brought attention to the extreme need for accurate charts of Georgian Bay. Under pressure, the Canadian government announced it would undertake its first major hydrological survey – the Georgian Bay Survey.

While Bayfield's chart (produced by the British Admiralty) had plotted the shoreline and islands, a thorough survey of water depths was needed, one which would pinpoint the location of underwater rocks, reefs, banks and shoals.

First Bayfield *Sounding Crew, 1884. Soundings were taken by dropping lead lines.*
– County of Grey – Owen Sound Museum

Survey boat the first Bayfield. *The Georgian Bay Survey marked the beginning of the Canadian Hydrographic Service.*
– County of Grey – Owen Sound Museum

Because at that time there were no Canadians trained in this work, the experienced surveyor Staff Commander John G. Boulton of the Royal Navy was appointed to head the survey and to train a team of hydrographers. Boulton, a veteran of the Newfoundland survey, had been hoping for this assignment because to him the Georgian Bay survey was the ultimate challenge. The survey began in 1883, less than a year after the *Asia* went down, and took eleven seasons.

Time and again, Boulton found it necessary to defend the length of time taken. He spoke of the storms and "fresh" weather that impeded his progress and in his report on the Georgian Bay Survey for the Season of 1889, he wrote: "work on [the northeast shore] of Georgian Bay must necessarily be slow, for a more broken up coast line it is impossible to conceive, and the same up-and-down character of the bottom is extended to sea for two or three miles in the shape of many dangers very hard to find . . ." In the following year's report (1890), referring to the work between the Limestone Islands and Moose Deer Point he wrote:

these unsurveyed waters, with many sunken rocks in them render navigation extremely hazardous, and only the unceasing vigilance, powers of observation, retentive memories and dexterity of handling their vessels enable the masters of the passenger and mail steamers on this coast to avoid the dangers as well as they do.

To effectively silence opposition, he concluded his 1889 report with the addition: "the United States Government completed the survey of their shores of the Great Lakes in 1881, taking 40 years, with a staff three times as large as mine, and spending $2,977,000 over it." The Georgian Bay survey was completed in 1894 at a total cost of $215,000.

POST-*ASIA* LIGHTHOUSES

The Third Wave

The *Asia* disaster also brought attention to the need for more lighthouses. By the 1880s the Bruce Peninsula was well settled, and commerce in Georgian Bay communities was strong. Lights were built at Big Tub (Tobermory) in 1885, Cabot Head in 1895, Flowerpot in 1897, and at many other locations around the Lakes. Steam fog alarms were introduced at major stations,

Western Island Lighthouse, 1909. Erected in 1895, the lighthouse was part of the third wave of lighthouse building undertaken after the loss of the Asia. *Note keeper standing on wooden steps leading to the water.*
– Huronia Museum 1947.0144.0155

while other navigational aids were added where necessary.

At the turn of the century the Department of Marine and Fisheries was in a strong position. The most important lighthouses had been built and it was now adequately funded and could boast a trained staff. In 1903 the Department established the Dominion Lighthouse Depot at Prescott, Ontario. It was a centre for experiments in navigational technology such as the testing of illuminants to determine which ones would perform best under Canadian conditions. Here, too, lightstation equipment was designed, manufactured and repaired, thus reducing Canada's former dependence on foreign suppliers. An agency was established at Parry Sound in 1905 to carry out the region's operations from a more accessible base.

Facilities continued to be upgraded and advanced technologies in lighthouse construction introduced new shapes and materials such as steel skeleton towers. In 1906 a major advance was made with the introduction into Canada of reinforced concrete for lighthouses. The second tower built at Cape Croker in 1909 was one of the earliest experiments in this material. At the time, reinforced concrete was not at all widely accepted. A paper read to the Royal Institute of British Architects in 1903 had observed that "owing to many unpleasant experiences," there was a feeling among architects and builders that it was a "treacherous and unreliable material." (*Canadian Architect and Builder*, Vol. 17 (Dec. 1904), pp. 202-3.)

Inevitably changes in the economy of the Georgian Bay region were felt as the twentieth century progressed. The famous steam barges or "lumber hookers" that once plied the waters were rarely seen by the time of the First World War. The passenger and freight trade to way-

ports along Georgian Bay's shores declined in the 1920s with the developing network of roads. As the lumber industry and fish stocks dwindled, and as the Depression took hold, many once prosperous communities struggled to survive. Some lighthouses like French River presided over ghost towns. In 1936 the federal government created the Department of Transport with jurisdiction over the country's major transportation systems. For the first time, navigational aids, railroads and canal systems were under one roof. This would prove useful during World War II when the demand for essential raw materials exploded and the need for shipping grew once more.

After the war, the pace of economic and social change quickened, and lighthouse life was irretrievably altered. In the late forties, radio beacons were installed at key stations, giving keepers more access to the outside. Slowly, diesel generating plants were installed at the larger stations providing electricity to power the lights and the dwellings. In the late '50s and '60s separate houses were built for the assistants.

The large bulk carriers were gradually ceding Georgian Bay's waterways to pleasure boaters, but the opening of the St. Lawrence Seaway in 1959 largely finished off the job. Sea-going ships could now sail all the way from the Atlantic Ocean to Thunder Bay or Duluth on Lake Superior. No longer did they have to enter Georgian Bay to transship their goods via railroad. This development sounded the death knell for many of the lighthouses. In 1962 the Coast Guard was formally created under the authority of the Department of Transport and it was handed the job of gradually automating the stations. This was followed by their inevitable destaffing, and for many, their eventual destruction.

WHAT THEY LOOK LIKE

✢

Imperial Towers 1855-1859

Construction of lighthouses in the Georgian Bay, Manitoulin, and North Channel area spanned a period from 1855 to the First World War. There were three waves: the first during the expansion of shipping in the 1850s, the second following Confederation in 1867, and the third in response to a growing number of shipwrecks, culminating in the sinking of the *Asia*. Each wave can be distinguished by the architecture of its towers.

The six Imperial towers built between 1855 and 1859 are tall, round and tapered and made of white dolomite limestone, "hammer-dressed" to give a beautifully rusticated appearance then set in level rings. Originally left in its natural state, the stone began to be whitewashed sometime during the 1870s.

Round-headed doors, narrow windows staggered around the circumference, and a slight corbelling below the lantern complete the design. The tower's form and texture is so striking it needs little decoration. Atop each tower is a red polygonal cast iron lantern enclosing rows of rectangular window panes. The lantern is surmounted by a dome topped by a ball pinnacle, and is encircled by a round gallery with iron railing. Bronze lion head rain spouts around the lantern combine practicality with elegance. (They can still be seen at Cove Island.)

– National Archives of Canada

The walls are made of two concentric rows of stone filled with rubble. At the base, they are five to seven feet thick but only two to three feet thick at the top. This creates a uniform interior space of ten feet six inches in diameter. The inner structure is of heavy timbers. A steep stairway leads up through a metal fireproof floor to the lantern room. The floor is laid on "I" beams and lengths of railway iron mortared into the stonework. On this is set the pedestal for the light. The cast iron lantern room is bolted to a high ring of strong granite through which a doorway leads to the outside gallery. This gallery facilitates the cleaning of the lantern glass on the outside.

Ventilation

To facilitate good combustion (in the years when flammable oils were used) and presumably to prevent keepers from being overcome by the heat, adjustable ventilators are set into the gallery door. The metal trap door covering the stairs, and the ball pinnacle on the roof also provide air flow.

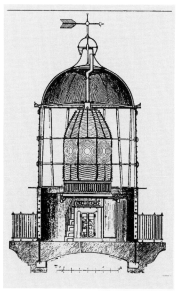

Drawing of lantern room similar to Imperial Tower design.
— National Archives of Canada

Dwellings

The dwellings are styled after a simple Scottish cottage design and constructed with the same heavily rusticated limestone walls as the tower. Placed adjacent to the towers, the two structures complement each other, providing a pleasing composition. Doors, windows, and chimneys are symmetrical. Originally, the roofs were slate. Using Cove as an example, the ground floor consists of an open room with a large hearth, a small parlour and a small bedroom, with other bedrooms upstairs. A kitchen was a later addition at the rear.

Cove Island dwelling.
—Spears Collection/Huronia Museum L995.0017.0008

NEW DOMINION OF CANADA

Wooden Towers From 1867 On

The earliest wooden towers like the first one built at Killarney, were freestanding, short, square and box-like. In the 1870s the style changed to a square tapering tower set on a stone foundation with square walkway around a polygonal lantern. They were generally short, economical to build, easy to move, and sturdy enough to withstand the battering of wind and waves. Some were freestanding like Presqu'ile (1873); the Bustards

Killarney West, the first new light to be lit on Georgian Bay after Confederation, July 1867.
— Courtesy of Dorothy Hoyland

Big Tub, Tobermory, erected 1885.
— County of Grey – Owen Sound Museum

(1875); and French River (1875); and others had attached dwellings like Janet Head in Gore Bay (1879); and Strawberry Island in the North Channel (1881). The towers with attached dwellings were generally three stories with the dwelling one and a half to two stories. They were one of the most picturesque lighthouse styles created by the Department of Marine and Fisheries design office, and generally built at the more important or most isolated locations. Amazingly, the original lanterns on many of these towers were of wood and were only replaced by safer metal lanterns as funds permitted.

After the *Asia* shipping disaster in 1882, a tapering polygonal tower became popular for its strength, durability, and aesthetic appeal. The few examples in this region are the hexagonal tower built at Big Tub Harbour at Tobermory in 1885; the Westerns (1895); and Lonely Island's new octagonal tower in 1907.

In the mid-1890s yet another style emerged: a frame dwelling with a short tower on the roof (Jones and Snug Islands, 1894; Cabot Head, 1895-6; and Flowerpot Island, 1897.)

The height of the towers varied according to need and topography. Towers built high on cliffs were shorter than usual so that they would not be obscured by fog. If needed to be seen from a great distance, taller towers were built on low lying sites or some offshore islands. For local navigation shorter towers on low lying rocks were sufficient.

Strawberry Island, North Channel built with tower and dwelling attached, 1881.
— Courtesy Vicki Raisbeck

Badgely Island Lighthouse, built in the 1890s style, where the tower extends from the dwelling roof.
— Huronia Museum L995.18

Dwellings

The earliest frame residences were either attached to the towers where there was living space in both the tower and the dwelling, or were simple cottage designs. After 1900, the Department built dwellings of a two-story "foursquare" design. With little ornamentation and little wasted space, they were functional and easy to maintain. Floors were painted grey. This austerity was softened by wainscotting and by pastel yellow, blue, green or pink walls. One of these dwellings still stands on Flowerpot Island. In the late 1950s and 1960s bungalows were built at many of the stations so that keepers and assistants could have separate dwellings.

Fog Alarm Buildings

Fog plants were simple utilitarian wood-frame buildings. Their main features were: double doors facing the water large enough to admit heavy machinery; big windows to ensure good light; and a single roof dormer on which to mount a fog horn.

Lion's Head Lighthouse section and elevation, 1911.
— National Archives of Canada NMC19907

Great Ducks fog alarm building.
— National Archives of Canada PA195253

Lonely Island dwelling, erected 1907 — a practical frame foursquare design.
— National Archives of Canada PA182869

New Building Technologies
The Twentieth Century

The twentieth century ushered in new ideas in lighthouse construction — steel skeleton towers and reinforced concrete. The first steel skeleton tower in the area was erected at Pointe au Baril early in the century. After the 1950s an army of them would march in and begin to replace many of the remaining lighthouses.

Cape Croker was one of the first lights in Canada to be erected of reinforced concrete. It is short and octagonal in design. The other reinforced concrete tower in the region, the Great

Constructing the new Cape Croker tower, 1909.
— National Archives of Canada PA195250

In 1910 Pointe au Baril's old wooden back range was moved to Owen Sound.
— National Archives of Canada PA172472

Its base is a large steel cylinder and while the concrete upper portion appears to be cylindrical, it is actually a flattened oval with two straight sides. Perhaps this shape was mothered by desperation after conventionally-designed towers were swept off the rocks by the force of the Bay. The addition of a helicopter pad on Red Rock's roof was another essential adaptation.

Ducks, was built in 1918. Despite wartime austerity, it is a beautiful, soaring, tapered octagonal tower, its height accentuated by a classically-inspired exterior incorporating the traditions of base, shaft and cornice with pedimented windows and door. It is the tallest tower in the region.

Sometimes, necessity dictates design. Red Rock's tower near Parry Sound is most unusual.

Cape Croker's second light tower.
— Courtesy of Nancy Armstrong

Keeper and his family, Janet Head Lighthouse, Gore Bay.
— National Archives of Canada PA172483

Michigan lightkeepers standing at attention, early 20th century.
— Courtesy U.S. Coast Guard

Early American keepers were well-trained, well-paid, properly housed and uniformed. In Canada, they were none of the above. Whereas in the States, two to three men were appointed to tend a light, in Canada, a keeper's family was often expected to provide the assistance.

WHO KEPT THE LIGHTS?

✢

Canada could rightfully take pride in the success of her efforts to build light-houses quickly, efficiently and at minimum cost. The results had even gained favourable recognition from Britain's powerful lighthouse authority, the Trinity House. But when it came to setting up an organization for staffing those lighthouses, Canada fell far short. Unlike the United States where two to three keepers were appointed by the government to tend a light, Canada usually appointed one. The American keepers were well-trained, well-paid, properly housed and uniformed. In Canada, they were none of the above.

From the very beginning the keepers seemed to have been left to their own devices. As soon as the Imperial Tower was completed at Cove Island in the fall of 1858, the Head Engineer Mr. Scott and his 27 technicians departed, leaving the first keeper, George Collins, and his assistant alone to face the bleak winter and to solve the mysteries of the light through trial and error.

In 1859, Vesey C. Hill, the second keeper at Griffith Island, was quite direct about this lack of supervision: "as we have neither received sufficient practical or verbal instructions, I deem it necessary that you send us printed instructions for our guidance as the lights require the greatest care possible." Instructions were eventually drawn up which minutely detailed the manner in which the many tasks of managing lights and fog horns should be carried out, and it concluded with the warning, "the breach of any of the foregoing Rules and Instructions will subject the Light-house Keepers to dismissal, or to such other punishment as the nature of the offence may require." Despite a rather lax attitude toward training, the Department of Marine and Fisheries looked for conscientious men who would run the site with military precision, and who would understand the importance of never failing to maintain a bright light, to wind the weights for the rotating mechanism as often as every three hours, and to run the fog horn whether for a stretch of one hour or seven days.

The 1901 *Regulations For the Admission of Light-Keepers into the Service of the Dominion of Canada* required prospective keepers to be between 19 and 40 years old, to produce a good reference from their last employer, plus certificates of physical health, marital status, and their ability to operate an open boat. A certificate was also required from a clergyman, magistrate, or schoolmaster confirming the candidate's ability to read and write, to have a fair knowledge of arithmetic and to be of good moral character. Apparently age was not a critical factor as John Smith, hired at Tobermory in 1912, retired fourteen years later at the age of 81. Many others managed lights well into their 80s. What seemed to be more significant was whether the keeper had a wife and children. It was believed a family man would have greater support and be more content with the isolation and his job than a single man. Although not publicly stated, it was tacitly understood that family members would provide unpaid labour thus eliminating the need for an assistant — one reason why isolated light-towers were built with attached dwellings large enough to accommodate a big family.

Jack Kennedy, former Superintendent of the lights, describes the type of lightkeeper they sought in later years — men with mechanical aptitude, who liked the life, and who were stable, "like if the guy said he was going to write a book, we'd go 'oh yeah'. We didn't want anyone who thought a light station was a romantic place." Local ex-fishermen were ideal as they knew the waters intimately and were comfortable in the environment.

Although the first Imperial tower keepers wintered on the lights, subsequent keepers would arrive in early March before break-up, walking or sleighing over the ice, bringing with them their dry goods, provisions, and often chickens and a cow. At the end of the navigation season, it was their responsibility to get themselves off the lights in the government-issue open sailboats, no matter what weather conditions prevailed. During the season, babies were born, illnesses endured, broken legs set, and vaccinations administered, all without outside help. According to Pat Johnston (85), who spent his childhood on a light, "the attitude was clear. They paid your wages and then didn't want to hear from you again." By the 1920s, there was nominally more official support. A supply ship would visit twice a year to replenish coal and kerosene stocks but other necessities such as food and medicine were the responsibility of the keeper and his wife. If they miscalculated about how much they would need for nine months, they were out of luck.

Particularly on the outer islands, isolation and loneliness often took their toll but they could be most oppressive in the spring and fall when families were on the mainland. Jim Keith remembers being left alone with his assistant Jerry Emery on the Western Islands until mid-December. As winter descended, ice would cover the dwelling making it extremely dim inside and the monotony of carrying out the same routine day after day would become even harder to combat. As Keith put it, "lightkeepers were like hermits — only hermits were better off: they desired isolation, preferred loneliness, and didn't have the pressure and responsibility."

The one issue the government seemed to continually ignore was salaries. John Frame, Griffith Island's first keeper, sent his bill to the authorities with this plea, "Sir, as I have received no salary, I do not know what I am to receive . . . please inform me if my receipt is correct." For the most part the salaries were meager, so

After both world wars, lightkeeping positions were reserved for war veterans like Jim Keith.
— Courtesy of the Keith family

Thomas and Ethel Foley. Thomas became keeper at Nottawasaga in 1924 after spending one year in the Gravenhurst Sanitarium recovering from exposure to gas warfare.
— Archer Collection/Huronia Museum L995.0002.0007

meager that keepers often took to supplementing their income with other jobs. On Nottawasaga alone four of the keepers worked as: musician (Thomas Bowie), barber (Samuel Hillen), flame cutter (Jim Keith), and in the case of Thomas Foley, shoe repairman. Nevertheless, lightkeeping positions were coveted as they promised security and after 1924, a pension.

Sometimes jealousy of those holding these jobs made people act in a cruel way. During the Depression, Foley's family had to keep the curtains drawn as people in Collingwood were constantly spying to see if Thomas was at home rather than tending the Nottawasaga light. On one occasion when he was in town, someone smashed a hole in his boat. He was reported missing from the light and lost his job of eight years.

Especially in the early years, lightkeeping appointments were sometimes political. In one of many instances, Hope Island lightkeeper Thomas Marchildon was replaced by Charles Vallee in 1898 when the Liberals won the Federal election, only to be reinstated as keeper in 1911 when the Conservatives returned to power. Politics undoubtedly played a part as well in the decision following both world wars, to reserve these civil service jobs for returning war veterans. From the Department's viewpoint, men with military training were desirable, as they would (and did) make reliable keepers. For some like Jim Keith (Nottawasaga, Westerns) this policy greatly eased his transition back into civilian life. On his return, he had been told by his former employer that there was no record of his having been employed (wages had conveniently been paid in cash.) Thankfully, lightkeeping was an available option. For those veterans whose lungs had been damaged by gas or who had contracted tuberculosis, the fresh air associated with a lightkeeper's life proved an ideal environment in which to recuperate.

During the Second World War, lightkeeping had been designated an essential job. The safety and smooth passage of grain and mineral ore boats was a high priority. Arnold Wing who was lightkeeping at the Westerns remembers telling Department of Transport officials of his desire to join the Navy. "They looked at me and said, young man you're not going anywhere. You're staying on that light." Somehow their deep concern did not extend to his pay cheque for when his nine-month salary was broken down by his twelve-hour shifts, seven days a week, he received approximately fifty-six cents an hour.

Over the years working conditions slowly improved including building separate dwellings for the keeper's and assistant's families, but it was not until the early 1970s that a union was formed to help set pay schedules, uniform performance standards, etc. Ironically, this happened just as lighthouse keeping was entering a period of decline, and in some ways, this development actually accelerated the process of destaffing.

LIGHTKEEPERS AND ASSISTANTS

Good Company, Troubled Company

When the Imperial Towers were constructed in 1858, the government took on the job of hiring assistants but gave little thought to whether they would be compatible with the keepers. Very quickly it discovered that perhaps it had made a wrong decision. Letters filled with conflicting complaints descended on the agency. George Collins, Cove Island's first keeper wrote the Secretary of Public Works, Thomas Begley, to vent his frustration with his assistant:

> . . . this last two weeks he had refused to obey my orders by saying he was hired by Government —it is then unpleasant and unsafe to be with such a man for he said that if I discharged him he wants to smash my head. I told him that such conduct would not do that I should discharge him by the end of his month 5th.

A month later, another letter arrived on Secretary Begley's desk, further illuminating the situation. William Scott, one of the engineers who installed the Imperial tower lanterns said this about the keeper:

> Mr. Collins the Light Keeper has made himself so obnoxious to all persons who have come in contact with him by his demanding, selfish and unkindly spirit & to all who may be under him, that there is no person out of all those who have worked on the island, would stay with him as his assistant.

Soon after, the government eased itself out of the business of hiring assistants. Unfortunately for the keepers, the increased harmony was offset by decreased wages as the government covered

William Wallace (Hope Island 1917-1940) experienced the tension of the Depression first-hand when his assistant tried to have him fired.
– *Wallace Collection/ Huronia Museum L995.0007.0004*

had to get along." Sometimes they didn't. Jack Kennedy recalls having to act as a 'Father Confessor' on some of his inspection trips.

> You go out there and they haven't spoken to each other for two or three months. They'd have a little notebook with everything listed that was a problem. I'd have coffee with one guy, I'd have coffee with the other guy – when I'd leave they'd be arm in arm waving good-bye. Most of it you could settle so easily it was ridiculous – but I guess they needed a facilitator.

Although most keepers and assistants got on well there was a strong underlying frustration with the way the Department handled certain situations especially after they again resumed responsibility for the hiring of assistants in the early 1960s. Frank Rourke, keeper at Great Ducks, had an excellent helper, Earl Martin, who loved the lighthouse, was at ease with boats and was skilled with machinery. Best of all the Martin and Rourke families enjoyed each other. Therefore when Frank received a memo from the Parry Sound Agency informing him that the government would thereafter be hiring assistants by competition, he was not particularly worried. Logically, the Department would defer to Frank Rourke's strong recommendation and rehire Martin. It was not to be. The Rourke's were sent an assistant who lacked even the most basic skills necessary for working at an important station like the Ducks.

In 1967, one keeper wrote the Department complaining about his assistant:

> He is not capable of doing the work that is required, even the minimum amount of work . . . after all this time here he still does not know what he is supposed to do in regard to changing engines, putting the light on, and he cannot

only half an assistant's wages. Lightkeepers were expected to subsidize the other portion and pay for the assistant's food. One lightkeeper put it frankly:

> [the government] took five or six years of my life, and decapitated my earnings [by requiring that I pay for my assistant.] You could be as lucky as blazes that you wouldn't come out in the hole by the end of the season. But we couldn't bargain. Times were tough. I was just back from overseas and I needed a job, and jobs were hard to find. What they did to us was criminal. They kept promising raises that never came.

This situation did not change to any degree until the union arrived in the 1970s.

Although there were qualifications for hiring keepers, there seemed to be none for hiring assistants. At Flowerpot in the 1930s, William Spears' father, "just found someone who wanted work, took him out there and tried him to see if he worked. If the guy didn't like it he wouldn't stay. Wages were poor. You weren't paying a decent wage so you couldn't get a good man. It's like this – its just two men in one building – they start the fog engines. He will not sleep on his time off, as he should be awake for the night shift, so it is obvious that he is sleeping at night. He will not make any entries in the log books. And you cannot get him to do any cleaning up either in the house or round the station.

Two weeks later he again wrote:

[The assistant] informed me that he had a light heart attack the night before last. And he did not inform me until this morning. I am calling Wiarton to advise me whether to have a boat come out from Tobermory for him, or get a Dept. boat for him, to take him to a doctor.

After several exchanges – including one in which the assistant claimed he had never mentioned a heart attack – an official letter was sent from the Parry Sound base to the assistant explaining that the keeper had agreed to take him back for the remainder of the season "but we do not want any more reports of heart attacks, and we do want you to keep the best watch possible . . . and to get along with the chief lightkeeper."

Part of the problem lay with the government's oversight in not outlining a clear hierarchical relationship between keeper and assistant. This confusion was exacerbated when assistants were classified as lightkeepers. Numerous departmental memos attempted to clarify the situation:

March 13, 1963
. . .We want to correct two erroneous impressions held by many of our employees: firstly, some chief lightkeepers seem to think that assistants are provided to do all the manual work on the station and to stand shift as well. This is not so. Secondly, some assistant lightkeepers feel that because they are Civil Servants they are on equal status with the chief lightkeeper and should not have to take orders from him. This, too, is not so.

Doris Keith, daughter Susan, and Jerry Emery (Assistant) at the Westerns. Jerry is in a new coat, a birthday present from the crew of the lighthouse tender the St. Heliers.
– Courtesy of Keith family

Gradually the Department became more responsive to the keepers' concerns and started to hire more local men as assistants. After the Rourkes' first failure with their government-appointed employee at the Great Ducks, they were sent Jim Rumley from Manitoulin Island whose father, William, had been lightkeeper of the Ducks in the thirties. Jim became a second son to the Rourkes, and a lasting friendship developed. One of Juanita (Rourke) Keefe's fondest memories is the sound of Jim's music as he played the fiddle in the lighthouse tower. On the Westerns, the assistant came with the island. In the early forties, Arnold Wing had hired Jerry Emery. Though mentally disabled, Jerry was excellent at his job and after the Wings left, he stayed to assist three other lightkeeping families. He performed his job with pride and expertise and was considered one of the family.

Women and Families

At stations like Badgeley and Brebeuf, light-keepers were not offered extra half wages to hire an assistant, the assumption being that the wife or children would do the work. And at one time or another, they did perform most of the

Adam Brown (at right) tended Red Rock lighthouse for 40 years.
– Parry Sound Library

tasks required at a light. On Griffith Island, Kathleen Thornley recalled one occasion when the hand cranked fog horn had to be kept going all night. Although she was only eight or nine, she went with her father to ensure he did not fall asleep, and mid-way through the night, she took over the cranking so that he could have some hours of rest. On Flowerpot Island Audrey Coultis' sons were his workforce. While at Nottawasaga, Samuel Hillen's wife often kept a vigil for fog, signalled the ships, or lit the light on those evenings when it was too rough for Samuel to return from his day job in town.

In an emergency, the women filled in. When the assistant on Great Ducks had to leave because of his brother's death, Juanita (Rourke) Keefe recalls, "I was the only alternative. Frank couldn't do twenty-four hours a day for seven days – and that's how the fog horn sounded – for seven days. I knitted to stay awake. I thought 'this is nice, I'll make something out of this season,' but the

assistant didn't give me any of his wages for watching the light for seven nights – awful!"

Despite being contrary to official policy, at least seven women are known to have become keepers. They all took over after their husbands died. The Bay's first female lightkeeper was Mrs. Tizard, who maintained Hope Island until December, 1886, following her husband Charles' death in August. Elizabeth Martin kept Boyd Island for at least eleven years; Esther Harvey managed Thessalon from 1915-40; and Emma Borron ran the French River and Bustards range lights for eighteen years, despite complaints from ship captains about a woman holding such a position. Emmaline Madigan of Pointe au Baril (1978-83) was the last female lightkeeper on Georgian Bay.

Every lightkeeping family has bittersweet memories of the life they led. On the one hand there was the ever present danger of water and at times a certain tedium, a certain sameness about the routine. Psychologically, there was no way to get away from the job. On the other hand, there was often an exhilerating sense of freedom. For children like Dorthea Herron, growing up at a lighthouse was magical – she still has the turtle she adopted 31 years ago. For Emmaline Madigan, Pointe au Baril brings back fond memories of always knowing her children's whereabouts as they thought up innumerable ways to make their own fun. And so the same isolation which could magnify their stress when a child fell ill or an emergency arose, actually strengthened their bonds of togetherness.

With school-age children, families had to make a difficult decision. Some mothers like Lillian Wing on the Westerns (1938-46) chose to teach her children at home through correspondence – a major commitment on top of all the other daily chores. Others felt it important that the children attend public school. For them the choice was to have the mother stay on the mainland with the children during the school year, leaving the father alone on the light, or to send the children to the mainland while both parents stayed at the light. Either decision brought wrenching feelings of guilt. Being with her husband at the Great Ducks while he recuperated from a heart attack, Juanita (Rourke) Keefe remembers: "I had moments – like one Easter Sunday, it was snowing – Lake Huron was really heaving and we landed [in the helicopter] in the front yard in this wilderness and you say to yourself, 'what am I doing here?!' I had three children and I worried about them."

For those children who were sent to live with families in town, the memories are still vivid. Jim Wallace, son of William Wallace (Hope Island), was sent to live with fisherman Johnny Weeks, between ages seven and twelve: "Johnny was strict. The first day he said to me, 'I've only had to lick my kids once – when they said no.' I never said no to Johnny." Separation was more frightening for Joanne Paradis, an only child, who lived in Midland while her parents Mary and Clifford tended the Brebeuf light:

around December 15th, the close of navigation, I knew they would be coming off the light. I started getting worried around that time because I knew how they came off. Sitting in class, I actually visualized them [the police] coming to tell me they had been killed. Another year they were late in getting home. I was so scared and I had no brothers or sisters to talk to.

Like all lighthouse children, Joanne fully understood the dangerous power of Georgian Bay.

Those who chose the life of a lightkeeper came from many quarters – the retired sea captains who manned the first Imperial towers, the loners who relished working without direct supervision, the victims of the Depression who welcomed any job, the veterans, and the ones who loved the water and the active life. Most of them mastered their duties and took pride in their ability to meet and overcome hardships and emergencies. They recognized and accepted their role in the maintenance of one of the vital transportation links of their vast country. Though each was unique, they shared the kind of strength and humour that is necessary for such a demanding job and some such as Jim and Dora Keith never lost their zest for life.

My wife wanted to really experience a storm. So I agreed to lash her to this well-secured pole. Well, she disappeared right inside a huge wave, and when it whipped back with all its force, she actually saw the bottom of the lake – 60 feet of water peeled right back bare. Above the roar of the wind and surf, I could hear her laughing and laughing – wet as a fish.

Jim Keith (Western Islands)

Mary Paradis and her daughter Joanne, Brebeuf Lighthouse.
– Courtesy of Paradis family

LIGHTKEEPERS' RECIPES FOR SURVIVAL

---✦---

(Excerpts from Medical Directions for the Use of Lightkeepers, *and* Rules and Instructions for the Guidance of Lightkeepers*)*

Inflamed Eyes:

They will be greatly relieved by the application of the following eye-wash: half as much sulphate of zinc as will lie on a five cent piece dissolved in three wineglassfuls of rain water.

For the sick and convalescent:

Beef-tea is one of the most useful articles of diet in sickness and early convalesence; beef, however, cannot be obtained at many of the stations; moreover, as commonly made, beef-tea is scarcely nutritious at all. When beef can be got, a good essence may be made by putting the lean — cut into small pieces — in a jelly pot, adding enough cold water just to cover the meat, and heating it gently at the fireside for five or six hours, keeping the vessel covered. The essence should then be squeezed out through a cloth and allowed to cool, to remove fat and grease. Diluted with several parts of hot water, this makes a strong beef-tea.

Purifying Water:

At stations where rain water from cisterns is used it may be contaminated with chloride of lead from salt spray resting on any lead or lead paint used in the roofs. This water cannot be freed from the poison either by boiling or by exposure to the air, but by putting some powdered chalk or whiting into the cistern and stirring it up well occasionally after rain has fallen, it will be purified and rendered perfectly fit for culinary and domestic purposes.

Brandy and Egg:

In cases of great weakness, a table-spoonful of brandy, beat up with the yolk of an egg, and a little water, will be found very sustaining. It may be repeated several times in the twenty-four hours.

Vaccination:

The vaccine matter should be carefully blown out upon the end of the blade of a pen-knife. Five or six scratches should then be made on the arm with a needle, over a space about the size of a threepenny piece, and again at the distance of an inch . . . . Rub the vaccine matter over the two scratched surface with the pen-knife and allow it to dry . . . . Advantage may be taken of the vaccination of an infant to obtain matter from the vesicles which form on its arm, by opening them with a sharp knife or lancet eight days after the operation. Matter enough to vaccinate several adults or children may thus be obtained.

Whitewash:

Slake half a bushel of unslaked lime with boiling water, keeping it covered during the process. Strain it and add a peck of salt, dissolved in warm water, 3 lbs. of ground rice put in boiling water, and boiled to a thin paste, half a pound of powdered Spanish whiting, and a pound of clear glue, dissolved in warm water. Mix these well together, and let the mixture stand for several days. Keep the wash thus prepared in a kettle or portable furnace, and when used put it on as hot as possible, with painters' or whitewash brushes.

Long focus catoptric reflector. Installed at Jones Island, Owen Sound, Brebeuf, and Hope in 1916.
— *National Archives of Canada PA195270*

How Did They Work?

---✛---

Early Illuminants

From ancient times until the late eighteenth century, lighthouse beacons consisted of open wood or coal fires set in grates high in a tower or on a hill. In small English coastal villages they were often shown from church towers. The first innovation saw these fires replaced by rings of candles. Although an improvement on the original, the candles also demanded close vigilance, and produced a poor quality light. On occasion, they were even known to endanger ships rather than aid them, for a mariner enticed by such a weak beam could discover too late that his ship was almost on top of the very reef of which he was being warned.

Oil-burning Lamps

Lighting took a significant step forward when an oil-burning lamp with a flat wick was developed and used in lighthouses at Liverpool, England, in 1763. Although the oil came from sources as diverse as olives, rapeseed, coconuts, and animal fats, sperm whale oil was preferred as it did not thicken in cold weather. Whatever the source, these oil shared one characteristic – they smoked and blackened the glass. Poor combustion was often the main problem. This was largely overcome in the 1780s, when Aimé Argand of Geneva developed a burner with a circular sleeve-like wick inside a glass chimney. This created a central current of air which allowed a more perfect combustion of the gas issuing from the wick. The result was a brilliant, steadily burning, non-smoking clear flame – unless of course the quality of the oil was inferior. The first keepers of the Imperial towers on Georgian Bay in 1858 complained bitterly when they were issued sperm whale oil for their Argand lamps that was too old and too thick. Instead of a clear light it produced a smoky, poor quality flame that blackened the glass chimney giving them countless extra hours of polishing.

But fuel was only one of several factors that could affect the quality of a light. Architectural design proved to be another. After fitting the lantern room on the Cove Island lighthouse, the technicians discovered they had a problem. Because of the position of the stairs, a strong current of air was being created in the tower and the sudden gusts caused the flame to shoot up and repeatedly burst the chimney glass of the Argand lamp. Their answer? Install extra doors and a circular staircase underneath the lantern room.

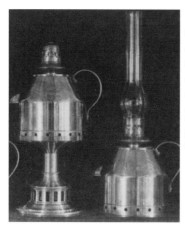

19th-century oil lamps for use with Fresnel lenses (left lamp for 6th order, right lamp for 5th order)
— Department of Transport/ Metropolitan Toronto Reference Library

Colza Oil

As the number of sperm whales decreased throughout the world, the cost of the oil rose to a prohibitive $2.20 to $2.50 a gallon and so in 1860 Dutch or French colza oil was introduced into Ontario lighthouses as an alternative fuel. Colza was classified as a kind of rape-seed oil. In fact, it was manufactured from a variety of Swedish turnip. At $1.69 to $1.85 per gallon, colza was significantly cheaper than whale oil and keepers actually preferred it because of its relatively flicker-free flame and non-clogging properties.

A CANADIAN BREAKTHROUGH

Kerosene

The most important development came with the discovery of "coal oil" or kerosene in 1846 by a Canadian, Dr. Abraham Gesner. Produced from the fractional distillation of coal, the new fuel burned more brightly than either whale or colza oil and was considerably cheaper. However the inefficiency of contemporary lamp designs tended to negate its superior qualities. Nearly two decades would pass before Canadian lights were fitted with flat-wick lamps for use with coal oil. At between 22 and 24 cents a gallon, kerosene promised remarkable savings and so in the spring of 1869 the new Department of Marine and Fisheries called for tenders for 36,000 gallons of coal oil to be used in the lighthouses throughout the Dominion.

Strict rules for the maintenance of these oil supplies were issued by the Canadian Department of Marine and Fisheries:

The oil will be delivered from the supply steamer into tanks, which are to be kept in the oil store, and only the small service cans are to be kept in the lightroom.

The quantity of oil consumed nightly is to be carefully measured, and noted in the lightkeepers daily journal. In dioptric lamps, the unconsumed oil is to be drawn off in the morning, measured, filtered, replaced in the lamp, and the deficiency filled up with fresh oil.

As soon as an oil tank is emptied it is to be cleansed out with hot water, and wiped dry, particular care being taken to handle it so as not to injure the solder, and to see that no water remains inside.

(Excerpts from Rules and Instructions for the Guidance of Lightkeepers in the Dominion of Canada, 1875.)

Even with these rules, determining the appropriate amount of oil required for each lamp was a learned process. Maitland Warder recalls Lion's Head keeper Ivan Butchart had his own unique method:

> There was a mark on the bowl indicating the level for December 21st, the shortest day of the year. At prescribed subsequent dates, a pre-selected smooth pebble was inserted, which displaced some of the oil. More pebbles were added at prescribed intervals until the longest day, June 21st, was reached. Then one by one the stones were removed until December 21st was reached again. Simple but effective.

Coal Vapour

At the turn of the twentieth century, an oil vapour illuminant was produced through the combustion of vapourized coal oil within an incandescent mantle. This advance resulted in a staggering 345 per cent increase in candle power over flat-wick lamps. Major lighthouses on Georgian Bay with revolving lights such as Great Duck Island, the Westerns, and Cove Island were converted to this system. A vapourizer was set on a pedestal inside the lens and covered by a mantle. A small pan filled with alcohol was placed under it and lighted. This gave the vapourizer its initial heat, enough so that when kerosene was pumped under pressure through a tube into the vapourizer, the kerosene turned into gas. The burning vapour made the mantle glow brightly, and was sufficient to keep the tube hot enough so that kerosene continued to vapourize.

There was one drawback as noted by John Adams, Lonely Island's keeper, 1959-65:

> If the tubes plugged up, by the time you got from the house to the tower there'd be streamers [a black cobweb-like substance created by the clogged coal vapour] hanging to the floor. Everything would be black. It would take you two days to clean it all up and paint it.

3 coal oil lamps at right; 3 vapour burners at left.
– Marine Museum of the Great Lakes at Kingston 984.28.734

I tell you, on watch you had your head stuck out the window every fifteen minutes looking to see if there were any flare-ups.

Acetylene

At the same time as coal-oil vapour made its appearance, acetylene gas was developed. It is a poisonous, colourless, highly inflammable gaseous hydrocarbon, produced by the reaction of water and calcium carbide. Because of its explosive nature it was considered more suitable for lighting buoys and beacons than lighthouses. Several accidents resulted from its use such as

Acetylene gas powered light. In November 1905 both the Westerns and Red Rock lighthouses were converted from fixed to oscillating lights illuminated by acetylene gas. These systems were soon replaced by coal oil vapour.
— Marine Museum of the Great Lakes at Kingston 984.28.754

In the early 1900s Canada began installing buoys with automatic water-to-carbide generators for producing acetylene gas. Invented by Thomas Willson of Ottawa in 1904.
— Courtesy of Pat Johnston

The Pilot *after a carbide gas buoy exploded killing Captain Clark, c.1908.*
– Courtesy of the Mosley family

the one that destroyed the *Pilot* killing its captain near Ten-Mile Point.

Eventually the danger in handling the explosive calcium carbide was reduced when dissolved acetylene was placed under pressure in cylinders and so acetylene became the favoured fuel because it produced a bright flame, was easy to transport and to recharge, and would last up to a year or more. For awhile it was used at a few unattended lights like Griffith Island, Red Rock, and Meaford.

World War II
Distillate (or "Desolate"!)

Since coal oil was classified as a valuable commodity during the Second World War the government supplied the lightkeepers with an alternative fuel called distillate. John Adams recalls, "most of us with pressure [vapour] lights ordered kerosene and we would get enough to do us for the lighthouse, but we would use the distillate for oil stoves and lanterns. It was a mixture of something – whatever it was it wasn't good." (It was possibly the less refined furnace oil.) Unluckier stations received inferior fuel for the light as well. Norman Lloyd of Clapperton Island recalls the oil smoked so severely that by morning the whole glass would have to be

replaced because of the black corrosion baked on the lamp chimney. The Great Duck Island lightkeeper had even more difficulty. His low-grade fuel clogged the vapour light and caused countless hours of cleaning the prisms and lantern room interior. A more serious consequence than the extra work was the dimming of the lights due to a thick layer of soot. Complaints poured into the Department and eventually it had to send a supply ship back to replace the vile substance with the real thing.

Electricity

In the late 1800s, electricity was introduced. The first lighthouse in Canada to have an electric light was Reed Point, New Brunswick in 1895. In 1909, Cape Croker became the first station in Canada to have both its light and fog plant electrified. Over the next fifty years, other oil lamps and vapour lights were gradually converted to hydroelectric power. On inaccessible sites like Great Duck Island, diesel generating units were installed to bring electricity with all its conveniences. Today, most lights are charged by solar panels positioned on the towers.

Great Ducks engine room and fog plant with Lister diesel engines. Assistant Earl Martin on left, keeper Frank Rourke on right.
– Courtesy of Juanita Keefe

ILLUMINATING
APPARATUS

Optics: The Eye through the Storm
Catoptric Reflectors

Light escaping in all directions is weak and so in order that beams can be seen far out over the water, they need to be amplified, directed and intensified. Beginning in 1763, experiments were conducted in Liverpool, England with 'catoptric' reflectors (from the Greek *katoptron*, or mirror), a system in which parabolic silvered mirrors concentrate the light rays creating a narrow beam. (It is the same principle used in car headlights and flashlights.) With catoptric reflectors, generally more than one lamp was required and since the system was based on the principle of reflection, it was essential that the mirrors be properly focused and carefully maintained. This inexpensive yet effective system was used extensively in the 1870s and 1880s on Georgian Bay and the North Channel, and continued to be used with the smaller lights.

Dioptric Lenses

Dioptric lenses for lighthouses were invented by the French physicist Augustin Fresnel in 1822. The 'dioptric' system (from the Greek *dioptrikos*, to see through) differs from the catoptric in that it is based on the principle of refraction rather than reflection. Concentric rings of glass prisms set around a single light source refract and bend the light rays into a narrow beam (the desired focal plane.) At the centre, the lens is shaped like a magnifying glass, so the concentrated beam is even more powerful. It was an astounding development, allowing a beam of light to be thrust twenty or more miles out to sea. At first it was limited to revolving lights, but in 1836, the British Trinity House modified the lens design making it applicable to fixed lights.

The first four Imperial towers on Georgian Bay were fitted with dioptric Fresnel lenses manufactured in Paris, France. These lenses came in

Reflector light used in the first Red Rock tower, 1870. (This style used in most Georgian Bay and North Channel lighthouses.)
– Marine Museum of the Great Lakes at Kingston 984.28.668

Nottawasaga 3rd order lens. Note section of lens swung open allowing keeper to light the lamp.
– Marine Museum of the Great Lakes at Kingston 984.28.711

seven 'orders' depending on their focal distance; the first three were for coastal lights, and the last four for smaller harbours or bays. Cove and Nottawasaga received strong second order lenses, Griffith Island a weaker third, and Christian Island a still weaker fourth order. When completed in 1859, Lake Huron and Georgian Bay's Imperial Towers had six of the ten Fresnel apparatuses found anywhere in the Canadas.

Although these lenses were recognized as producing a light five times brighter than the catoptric system, there was no possibility after Confederation of immediately installing more because of the expense, so all subsequent lights were fitted with catoptric reflectors. As funds came available, the Department of Marine and Fisheries upgraded the major lights. A catoptric system was installed at Lonely Island in 1870 when it was first built, and was upgraded to a stronger dioptric apparatus when the lighthouse was rebuilt in 1907.

Specific requirements for the care and maintenance of the refracting lenses of dioptrics were set out in the *Rules and Instructions for the*

Guidance of Lightkeepers in the Dominion of Canada, 1875:

> The glass prisms and lens of a dioptric apparatus are to be cleaned every day when in use, being first freed from dust by using the linen dusters slightly dampened, and then rubbed with perfectly clean and dry chamois skins. If the glass becomes greasy, it should first be washed with a linen cloth steeped in spirits of wine, then carefully dried with a soft linen cloth free from all dust or grit, and finally rubbed with a fine chamois skin.

Following the introduction of electricity and the improvement in the quality of electric bulbs with their concentrated light, the intense refractive qualities of the Fresnel lenses became less important. Most of the older jewel-like fixtures have been replaced by cheap plastic molded dioptric lenses. Although Cape Croker, the Great Ducks, and Cove Island retain their beautiful Fresnel lenses at present, the end of an era is in sight as Cape Croker and the Great Ducks are slated to lose them in the near future.

4th to 7th order dioptric lenses
— Marine Museum of the Great Lakes at Kingston 984.28.705

ROTATING MECHANISMS

Working In Shifts

In Europe, lighthouses with rotating lights became the norm in the 1790s. On Georgian Bay, major lights were upgraded from fixed to rotating as funds allowed. The propulsion system operated on the same principle as the grandfather clock. Weights would be wound to the top of the tower with a hand crank, taking a certain number of hours to fall back through a hole to the bottom. The clockwork had an adjustable governor for the timing. (Over the years the weight-driven mechanisms were replaced with electrical motors.) As rotating lights

Westerns clockwork. Note crank used to wind weights.
— *Marine Museum of the Great Lakes at Kingston 984.28.628*

required a constant watch, assistants were hired so that the light could be manned either in four six-hour shifts, or two twelve-hour shifts. Both the keeper and the assistant had to abide by the *Rules and Instructions for the Guidance of Lightkeepers in the Dominion of Canada*, 1875:

> The machinery employed to operate revolving lights must be kept scrupulously clean. All working parts must be regularly and carefully oiled once a week when in use, and those making quick motions more frequently.
>
> The machinery must be regulated so as to have a uniform motion. The times of revolution must be frequently tested, and in case of deviation, corrected by the regulators.
>
> The cords or chains must be frequently inspected to see that there is no danger of their parting, and the weight must never be allowed to bear on them when the machinery is out of use.

Keepers soon devised ways to keep an eye on the light while maintaining relatively normal lives. Arnold Wing (Western Islands) set up a mirror inside his house that reflected the light's beam onto the kitchen table so that he would immediately be aware of any problem.

Mercury

Friction from the heavy optical apparatus was overcome by placing the rotating portion in a mercury bath. Two concentric ring-shaped troughs were separated by a small quantity of mercury. Two hundred weight (224 Imperial pounds) of mercury is sufficient to ensure the flotation of three tons of lighting apparatus. Current health concerns about mercury vapour is the official reason given for removing the rotating Fresnel lights from the Bay.

Rotating base for heavy optical lens. Mercury between two troughs overcame friction.
— National Archives of Canada PA143585

Fog Alarms

The 1955 *Great Lakes Pilot* carried the following warning:

sound is carried in a very capricious way through the atmosphere. Large areas of silence have been found in different directions and at different distances from the fog signal station, in some instances even when in close proximity to it. A fog often creeps imperceptibly towards the land, and is not observed by the people at a station until it is upon them; whereas a ship may have been for many hours in it. When sound has to travel against the wind, it may be thrown upwards; in such a case, a man aloft might hear it when it is inaudible on deck. Fog can trick a mariner, one should never assume because he hears the fog signal faintly, that he is at a great distance from it, or that because he hears it plainly he is nearby.

Fog Bell

Bells are perhaps the oldest but least efficient fog alarm system as they need favourable conditions for the sound to carry. A mechanical fog bell that rang every seven seconds was used at Flowerpot Island until 1902 when it was replaced by a hand-cranked horn.

Hand Horns

Many Georgian Bay lighthouses had hand-cranked foghorns. Marie Hall, daughter of lightkeeper Frank Fowler (Badgeley Island) described one:

it had a handle on it and we would have to carry it outside. The ships would signal and Dad would run to signal back. It had two holes in the front. One would start to blow and as he pumped, the second one would start to blow too. They would be blowing together only with two different tones.

Hand pump fog horn ready for action on Clapperton Island
— Lloyd Collection/Huronia Museum

Steam Fog Alarms and Whistles

The steam foghorn was invented by Robert Foulis, a portrait painter and engineer living in St. John, New Brunswick. Frustrated by the ineffectiveness of fog bells he was searching for a sound that would cut through the heavy fog of the Bay of Fundy. He found it in an interesting way. Walking home before dinner each evening, he could hear his daughter practicing piano scales. One particularly foggy evening he realized only one note of the scale was audible – the note he would eventually incorporate into a new type of signal. The first steam fog alarm was installed at the entrance to St. John's harbour in the 1850s and its success led to this system being introduced into the most important lightstations on Georgian Bay and around the world. A specific series of long and short blasts distinguished one alarm from another.

Whistle fog horns were employed in the United States, Sweden and Canada. Their most serious short-coming was a resemblance to the sound of a steamer whistle. To overcome this, a distinctive whistle called the "Wildcat" was installed at Mississagi Strait in 1891, but from the description given in the *Sessional Papers*, it must have driven the poor lightkeeper mad. The wildcat was fitted "with a piston that changes the tone of the blast which, beginning low, rises to a screech, and again sinks to a low note at the end. The blasts are of eight seconds duration, with intervals of two minutes between them." The shipmasters however were completely satisfied. The government should have been happy as well for the cost of the wildcat had been a reasonable $111. Fifteen years later in 1906, when it was replaced by a diaphone built by the Canadian Fog and Signal Company in Prescott, the cost was $5,746.90.

The Diaphone

Another important advancement in the field of marine aids came in 1902, when J.P. Northey of Toronto developed the compressed-air diaphone. The diaphone had a distinctive descending note or "grunt" at the end of each blast. Only the larger stations had these plants: Cabot Head, Cape Croker, the Great Ducks, Hope, Cove, and Lonely Islands, Mississagi Straits, and the Westerns.

Pat Johnston whose father kept Caribou light on Lake Superior described the diaphone's engines:

> they were upright internal combustion engines starting on gasoline and switching to the cheaper kerosene. Power was supplied to the compressors from a pulley and flat leather belts. Pulleys rotated the crankshaft and consequently moved the pistons up and down in the cylinder. As the pistons went up air was compressed in the chamber above the piston and passed on to the air tank.

The engines and compressors were cooled by large, open, water tanks. Hot water from the engines would be piped to the top of the cooling tanks, and cooler water from the bottom of the tank would be piped back to the engine – "thermo-cooling." Jim Keith (Westerns) explained the unexpected benefits of running the foghorn for extended periods of time:

> when it got hot the engine would ping and you would turn the water on a bit and it would quieten right down. You wouldn't even hear the engine running – it was beautiful. There were two 500-gallon tanks of water open at the top. Run one four hours and when it got hot shut it down and start the other one. The beauty of it was when you had them going you could crawl into the tank and have a bath. Nice warm water. Best tub in the world. Our only tub!

Although the sound of the diaphone was highly effective, a lightkeeping family could become so used to it that during the day they would not notice when the alarm stopped. At night, it was a different story. Audrey Coultis of Flowerpot Island was known to waken the instant the sound ceased and could tell his assistant the precise time he had switched it off. How to determine when skies were clear enough to shut down the system probably varied from light to light. At Flowerpot, the rule of thumb required that any lake boat heading down Georgian Bay stay in sight for twenty minutes after it had passed the lighthouse.

Acetylene Gun

An automatic acetylene fog gun was developed in 1912 whereby pressurized gas was piped into a gun and flint-ignited by a rotating system of levers. It was not as audible as the diaphone and therefore not as widely used although one was employed on Lonely Island in 1944.

Left: Automatic acetylene fog signal gun
– National Archives of Canada PA195341

Right: Acetylene fog gun house
– Canadian Coast Guard

Interior fog alarm building
– Courtesy of Jack Kennedy

Synchronized Radio Beacon

and Fog Alarms

In the mid-1940s Cove Island and Hope Island were set up with radio beacon towers that sent a signal synchronized with the station's fog horn for distance finding. When there was fog, a group of two radio dashes, short and long, emitted from the radio beacon. This signal was accompanied by two matching signal blasts from the fog alarm. A vessel could determine its distance from the station by observing the number of seconds which elapsed between hearing any part of the distinctive group of radio dashes and the corresponding group of fog horn signals. Dividing the result by five (for statute miles) gave the distance in miles the boat was from the fog plant.

Fog Alarms Today

No fog plants continue to operate in this region. In fact, only three are still standing: Hope Island, Mississagi Straits, and Cove Island. Of these, Cove is the only one with equipment. In their place, automatic videographs were installed which emitted two beams of light to measure visibility up to three kilometres. If the machine sensed fog for more than ten minutes the fog alarm would automatically sound. These too have been almost all phased out. Where there is a demand, the Coast Guard intends to implement a system whereby a mariner will click a specified number of times on a designated marine radio channel and the fog horn will sound for a prescribed length of time.

Repair shop, Parry Sound base, 1909
— Marine Museum of the Great Lakes at Kingston

Hope Island radio transmitter station,
c. 1945
— Courtesy of Howard Warner

PART II

LIGHTHOUSES
OF GEORGIAN BAY

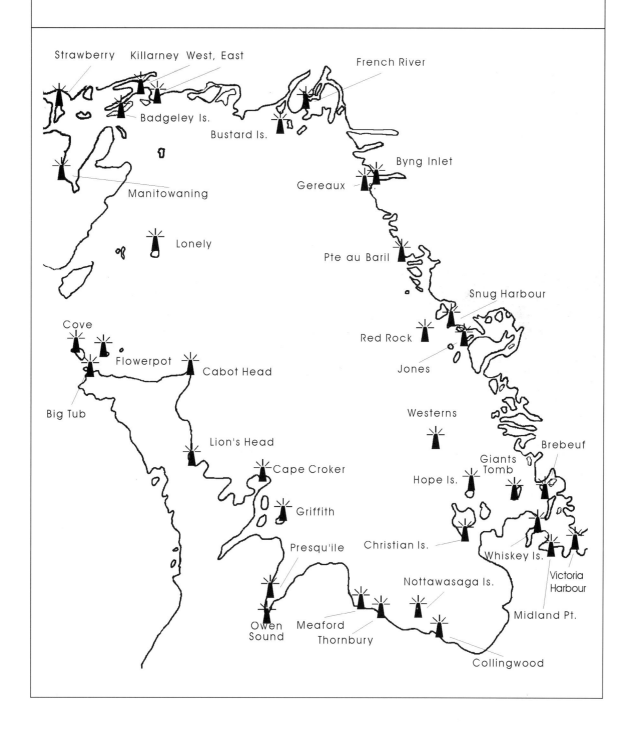

Strawberry
Killarney West, East
French River
Badgeley Is.
Bustard Is.
Byng Inlet
Gereaux
Manitowaning
Pte au Baril
Snug Harbour
Lonely
Red Rock
Jones
Cove
Flowerpot
Cabot Head
Big Tub
Westerns
Lion's Head
Brebeuf
Giants Tomb
Cape Croker
Hope Is.
Griffith
Whiskey Is.
Presqu'ile
Christian Is.
Victoria Harbour
Nottawasaga Is.
Midland Pt.
Owen Sound
Meaford
Thornbury
Collingwood

Cove Island lightstation.
— Halcyon, *April/May 1985*

COVE ISLAND

———————— ✦ ————————

*F*all's breathtaking red and yellow canopied the islands. We were heading out to Cove Island lighthouse in a boat arranged by the Friends of Fathom Five. Our last attempt had been somewhat disquieting. While tied at the dock, the winds unexpectedly changed direction and intensity. At one in the morning a huge roller lifted our 28-foot boat and snapped our heavy stern line like a piece of thread. Casting off into the black night, we plunged in and out of deep swells, the "obsolete" lights from Cove and Flowerpot reassuringly confirming our position.

This time we were dropped off at the island. Once again the wind blew and rollers came crashing up on shore, but now we could enjoy them. Standing in the shaking lantern room our ears filled with the grinding sound of the revolving lens, we were mesmerized by the beam of light as it hit the dark surf. A strange thing happens at night on this lake: everything is magnified; the wind, the waves, the shoals . . . we were glad to have the light as company. It was easy to understand why for so many, lighthouses have a romantic attraction.

Cove Island is the jewel of Georgian Bay lighthouses — perhaps of any on the Canadian Great Lakes. It has the distinction of being both the first lighttower to be lit on Georgian Bay in 1858, and the last to have its keeper removed in 1991. As such, it spans Georgian Bay's entire lightkeeping history. Most of its original buildings still stand and it may be the only light left on Georgian Bay with a rotating Fresnel lens. Within this eighty-five-foot limestone tower lie the roots of this inland sea's lighthouse beginnings.

Cove was the most remote of the six Imperial tower construction sites and the most difficult and expensive to build. The dwelling and first storey of the tower were in place by November of 1855 despite the lateness of the season and the stormy weather. In 1856, seven masons and stone cutters worked the limestone extracted from the island, while ten labourers, one blacksmith, and a foreman concentrated on the tower. One can still imagine the sounds of the scene: the tools shaping the stone ashlar, the shouts of workmen, the horse hooves and carts. Vestiges remain from this time: a set of initials and the year 1856 carved into one of the deep-set tower windows; an iron capstan embossed with the words 'C. Yale, St. Catharines, C.W.' [Canada West] lying half-hidden in the grass behind the boat-house, believed to have been used to haul construction materials ashore; and a collapsed lime kiln with a stand of cedar trees growing out its bowl-shaped centre. By October 1856 the tower had reached its full majestic height, although the cast-iron lantern room and Fresnel lens did not arrive from France for another two years.

In the spring of 1858 the first official light-keeper, George Collins, his wife Sophia and four year old son, Charles, came to the island. For most of the first season Collins lit a temporary lantern on a pole which extended a dim light about half a mile out over the water. Needless to say, there was much jubilation when the Parisian lantern room and light fixture arrived, followed closely by M. St. Aubin and a team of French workmen to install them. Unfortunately the atmosphere turned sour.

On November 2nd, 1858, the engineer, William Scott, reported from Collingwood,

[The lightkeeper] Mr. Collins has contrived to fall out with and gain the ill will of every individual among my own & Mr. St. Aubin's workmen numbering 26 or 27 men, & of whom I can speak of in the highest terms . . . Mr. St. Aubin says decidedly that the keeping up of this light will be a failure if Mr. Collins is left in full charge . . . .

On the 3rd of November, Collins retorted:

. . . the only reason St. Aubin would plot against me is for not giving him Government [sperm whale] oil for his private use. I told him

COVE ISLAND

Location: Northwest tip of Cove Island at the Lake Huron entrance to Georgian Bay
Date: 1858
Description: Limestone Imperial tower and stone dwelling
Height: 85 ft./25.5 m
Light: 2nd order dioptric lens; Argand lamp for whale oil; flat wick lamp for colza and coal oil; coal oil vapour; lightbulb. Revolving and flashing.
Visibility: 13 miles/20.8 kms
Foghorn: 1883 coal fired fog plant, then diaphone; 1947 diesel generators.
Radio: Radio beacon installed in 1940s
Additional: Second dwelling built 1950s, another 1960s
Present: Most buildings remain in very good condition. Light flashes white every five seconds.

KEEPERS:

1858-1859	George Collins
1860-1872	David McBeath
1873-1876	William McBeath
1877-1878	Bryce Millar
1879-1902	George Curry
1902-1903	W. Collier
1904-1912	Kenneth McLeod
1912-1945	W.J. Simpson
1945-1945	William Leslie
1946-1946	Harold Banas
1947-1948	Russell Bothan
1949-1976	William Spears
1977-1981	Robert Nelder
1982-1991	Jack Vaughan

I would measure him off any quantity he requires and report accordingly, and that when he wanted oil to work the new lamp for practice he should have what he requires . . . . The reason the foreman carpenter Mr. Jostlin and his men turned against me was for saying he ought not to allow whiskey be brought on the Island from other islands . . . .

William Scott continued:

> I have the honour to report for the information of the Honorable Commissioners, that I have examined the Isle of Coves light which was finished on Saturday night last, and... found the machinery, lens, and all the apparatus complete in every point and working well, and the whole just up in a most workmanlike and substantial manner.

George Collins who was left to face the bleak winter begged to differ:

> George Collins
> Lightkeeper, Isle of Coves
> 10th November 1858
> This morning every part of the machinery was wet as if it had been in the Lake . . . everything is cleaned and oiled which I do myself with dry clean cloths. But I see no purpose as . . . the damp comes on immediately & freezes again . . . I am using every means in my power to prevent the machine from rusting, but how can it be possible when in an hour or two after cleaning, the inside of the casing & the same is running with water caused by the dampness of the walls.

Climbing the staircase today, one can imagine Collins prying the ice off the lantern room glass and struggling to keep the machinery dry. The original Fresnel lens still rotates, but instead of being powered by weights that dropped through each floor of the tower, it operates by shore power. Out on the narrow railed walkway around the lantern room, the guardian bronze lion's head water spouts still gaze out over the expanse of Cove Island. The fog plant at the north end of the

Captain George Collins, Cove Island's reluctant first lightkeeper, 1858-1860.
– Courtesy Jamie McMaster

complex is the last of its kind on Georgian Bay and the North Channel to retain its machinery. It was built in 1947 after the original 1883 building was destroyed by fire. Inside, two silver-painted boilers once filled with steam to run the fog horn, sit near the back wall, their round bellies sporting rows of bolts like buttons on a uniform. Two Lister Diesel engines lie silent.

Entering through the back kitchen, the interior of the original 1856 limestone dwelling seems haunted. Layer upon layer of tired wallpaper peels and curls away from mottled terra-cotta coloured walls. Creaking wooden stairs lead to the loft where the ceiling is no more than 5'6" high. Keeper Bill Spears' words are recalled: "it was mighty cold in the spring — its all stone. A long time to get it warm, get the bedding warm. And oh was it damp. You couldn't keep wallpaper on the walls." Downstairs, old books are strewn at the foot of the fireplace and stacked on the mantle — each dusty copy bearing a yellowed Upper Canada

Tract Society bookplate, 'with a love of Books and with Books to read no man need be lonely.'

A Father's Choice

It was December 7, 1860. Keeper David McBeath was pacing the shoreline transfixed by the 20-foot sailboat rocking in the heavy swells. The night before he had made his decision — he and his family must leave Cove Island. The sharp crunch of the snow under his feet was nearly lost under the sound of the waves crashing against the frozen shore. Dense clouds rushed over the horizon pushed by biting winds. He turned at the sound of his children's voices and looked back at the house.

On the front stoop, his wife, Mary Jane, was holding the baby and wrapping a scarf around young Margaret. Their other five children huddled around their mother's skirt. They were subdued. David and Mary Jane had rationed their food for weeks. Now only dirt was left on the root cellar floor. The urgent letter sent by ship a month ago had been ignored by the Department of Public Works. Twice he himself had sailed into the shipping lane to flag down other ships. No response. He was desperate for food and supplies for his large family. Winter had them in its clutches, and they would soon be made prisoners by the encroaching ice.

Cove Island from the northwest. Painting the 109 steps involved painting every other step and then waiting a week for them to dry. Inevitably, one evening when it was dark and he was tired, keeper Bill Spears would forget which steps he had painted.
— *National Archives of Canada PA143637*

The children began to walk down the path; the youngest moving stiffly under layers of heavy clothing. Turning away from their bright faces McBeath scanned the churning water beyond Flowerpot Island and then began arranging the sail. It was sixty miles to Lion's Head with only sail and oar to get them there. Was it the right decision?

What McBeath Didn't Know . . .

The *Ontonagan* had arrived at Collingwood December 1 and immediately passed McBeath's desperate message to the collector of customs, John McWatt. McWatt sent a telegram to the headquarters of the Department of Public Works in Quebec City: 'the lighthouse-keeper Isle of Coves has no supplies for Winter — himself and family will starve. Shall the *Rescue* take his supplies — No other boat going there.' When the *Hunter* arrived in port, it too passed on McBeath's message. As telegrams fired back and forth between officials, McBeath's usual supplier took it upon himself to convince a fishing schooner to make the delivery. But the customs officer, McWatt had picked a different boat, the steamer *Rescue*. All the captains in the harbour agreed with his choice — no other could do it. There was one problem — the *Rescue* had not yet returned from the Sault.

There was an anxious buzz among the sailors. The harbour was freezing and many ships, including the American *Ontonagan* were already ice-bound. Then the schooner loaded with McBeath's provisions became frozen in and her captain demanded that McWatt pay for the freight. The customs collector refused as he had never requested the schooner take the provisions in the first place. Tension mounted. If the *Rescue* did not soon arrive he, McWatt, would have the death of the McBeath family on his head.

Nearly a week had passed since the *Ontonagon* first delivered word from McBeath. Finally the steamer *Rescue* was spotted pushing her way through heavy seas. No doubt her Captain was relieved to have reached port safely. He could not have been pleased when McWatt related the dire situation on the Isle of Coves. It was storming, his insurance was cut off, and the lake was beginning to freeze. Nevertheless Captain James Dick agreed. He spent a full day loading fuel, and then set off with his brother, Thomas Dick, another experienced lake captain. On their

Lightkeeper George Currie found Captain Tripp's body and buried him on Cove Island
— *Bruce County Museum and Archives*

arrival, the final report states, the McBeath family "were found about to commit themselves to the Lake upon a very insecure Raft, in the midst of the Storm." The *Rescue* battled back to Collingwood and was safely laid up for the winter.

The Ghost of Cove Island

Before assuming his duties on Cove, each new lightkeeper was trained on the machinery and taught its many quirks. He was also told about the folk-lore that had grown up around the light. Every keeper knew about the ghost, and even non-believers took a second glance when a door slammed suddenly in the still of night. The ghost was said to be Captain Tripp from the schooner *Regina* that had foundered southwest of Cove Island. According to legend, the Captain's body floated onto shore whereupon it was wrapped in a sail and buried on the island by the lightkeeper. A good story but did it match the facts?

As reported in the newspapers September 13, 1881, a group of fisherman spotted something glinting in the waves. They scooped out a clock — its hands frozen at 1:00. After draining the mechanism the clock resumed ticking. Back in Collingwood, the men handed the clock around. It was confirmed to be from the *Regina*. To the seafarers it was evidence of the exact hour and minute the *Regina* had perished.

A day later the surviving crew of the *Regina* arrived at Lion's Head after an arduous sixty-mile row from Cove Island. They claimed the old 'coffin-ship' went down around 10:30 p.m.. They claimed a lot of things — most of it contradictory. The *Toronto Globe* gave one account from the crew:

Cove Island's shipping log from May 12-13, 1881, records with little emotion the foundering off Yeo Island of the schooner San Jacinto *and her crew's subsequent stay on Cove.*
– Bruce County Museum and Archives

. . . At 10:30 p.m. we made a reef in the mainsail to clear the Cove Island light. Finding the vessel labouring heavily and making water fast, we bore up and ran for Cove Island beach. She made water so fast she got beyond control, and was sinking fast. The Captain gave order for the men to take boats to save their lives. All hands succeeded in reaching the boat except the Captain who was at the wheel. He caught the main boom and hung to it but the lifeboat being half full of water and having only one oar we were unable to render him any assistance. We then ran the yawl for Cape Hurd Passage. The Captain, when last seen, was clinging to the wreck and calling for assistance. . .

The crew's account was questioned. The word 'mutiny' was whispered over many a shot of whiskey. A final evaluation of the wreck suggested both vessel and captain could have been saved had the *Regina* been kept afloat a short while longer, but nothing came of the report. On September 27 the Collingwood paper announced that Captain Amos Tripp's body was found and that the tug *Mathan* was bringing him home for burial. So much for the ghost of Captain Tripp haunting Cove Island.

Finding Truth in Lore?

Lightkeeper Bill Spears (1949-1976) was the custodian of the early log books. He refused to allow them to leave the island, but welcomed historian Patrick Folkes to come and look at anything he wanted. There they were – old bound volumes: a personal chronicle written by George Currie; ten volumes of lightkeeper's diaries (1890-1911); nine *Diaries of the Engineer* (1894-1910); and a log book from the wreck of the *San Jacinto* left behind by the crew after the ship foundered off Yeo Island. The entries recounted basic life, passing ships, equipment malfunction, weather, shipwrecks, the *Regina* . . .

> *Sept. 12 [1881]* – Blowing Hard since noon from N.W. First heard today noon of the schooner 'Regina' being wrecked about 2 miles south west of this island in the Gale of Saturday night the 10th her top masts are to be seen above water. The crew are supposed to be all drowned – only one drowned Captain

> *Sept. 25* – Recovered the body of Capt. Tripp who was drowned on the 10th inst. – sewed him up in Canvas and buried him on the west side of this Island. wind slight s.w. – starry night

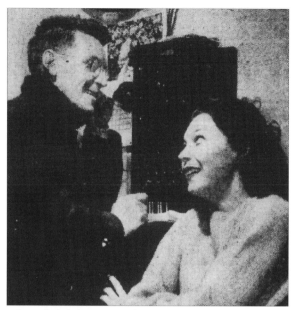

The night lightkeeper Harold Banas and his assistant disappeared was the longest in nineteen-year-old Iris Banas' life. She is seated listening, as Harold assures his mother he is fine after his rescue.
— Sun Times, *April 1946*

Did the crew mutiny on the *Regina*? Does old Tripp haunt Cove Island — the place where he was supposedly buried and later exhumed? Only the lighthouse knows for sure.

Adrift 20 Hours in an April Storm

On a cold morning in April 1946, Flowerpot Island's lightkeeper, Hugh Rumley, sped across the rough seas and tied up at the Cove Island dock just as dawn was breaking. Something was wrong — Cove had been unlit throughout the night. Charging up the walkway he was met by Iris Banas, the lightkeeper's wife. She explained that she first realized something was amiss the day before around 5:00 p.m. after hearing the radio beacon signal but no answering reply from her husband at the radio station. A search of the island turned up neither Harold nor his assistant Alvie Stewart. Then she recalled that around 3:00 p.m. both men had been racing up and

down the shore testing their new twenty-foot boat and motor. Not knowing how to operate the radio she had sounded the fog alarm but it quickly ran out of air. Her only recourse was to draw the attention of the Flowerpot Island lightkeeper by not lighting Cove's light.

Rumley quickly headed off to Tobermory where he knew a visiting American with a seaplane. Within a short time Lawrence Lenz and his friend Tom Sawyers were flying over Georgian Bay. They first made for Fitzwilliam Island, then Club Island where they stopped at the fishing station to alert the men, and then on to Lonely Island. Both men were silent as they buzzed over Half Moon Island on their way back to Tobermory. They had covered 200 square miles with no success.

They refueled and this time Rumley offered a suggestion. They should cover the islands near Manitoulin again. Flying over the exposed rock of Half Moon, at about 1,500 feet Rumley spotted something dark in the water, a gasoline can. Lenz circled four times before he could make out the lines of a partially submerged boat. Suddenly they glimpsed the two marooned men waving from the island. They had fallen asleep, exhausted from their twenty-hour ordeal.

As the plane could not carry more passengers, Harold Banas and Alvie Stewart waited for the lighthouse tender, the *St. Heliers* which had already been dispatched. It arrived at Half Moon at 6:00 p.m. but because of the heavy surf the men had to wade out to meet her. On board, Harold emphatically defended his sunken boat: 'a forty-mile wind and she only shipped a couple of bucketfuls!' Evidently the new engine had broken down but according to the two men it was the faulty oar locks that were really to blame. While rowing back to Cove Island the locks had snapped and they were left to the whim of the seas.

The Last Years

One of Cove's institutions was keeper Bill Spears (1949-1976.) During his twenty-seven-year tenure, Cove Island was a communication hub for several Georgian Bay lights as it had a radio-phone. On a regular daily schedule, Spears contacted other lights, exchanged weather and other information, then transmitted this information to Wiarton. If a keeper did not answer two consecutive calls, it was assumed there was a problem, and someone was dispatched. Even a case of mumps was not allowed to interfere with these regular radio reports and so in 1954 the ill keeper found himself living and sleeping in the fog plant between the two diesel generator engines during a fourteen day period of continuous fog because his assistant was too inexperienced to run the equipment.

1883 fog alarm building, Cove Island. Smoke from a 1947 fire that started in the chimney attracted attention in Tobermory. Unable to reach the island on the radio, the Department of Transport contacted Flowerpot's keeper Hugh Rumley by ship-to-shore telephone and he confirmed their fears. The fog plant was a total loss.
— *National Archives of Canada PA188337*

Spears loved the old fog alarm that delivered a deep resonating bellow which sometimes could be heard as far as Tobermory, six miles away: "when it got foggy we'd say, 'better start up the old sergeant major!' You could really feel the vibration once the old boomer got going." When the fog horns were replaced by automated electric systems, (derogatorily referred to as "car horns") the keepers were forbidden to touch them. Before the Coast Guard could do away with the keepers it had to prove that the automated system would work efficiently. Jack Kennedy, Superintendent of the lights, remembers the night Bill Spears could not take the

Lightkeeper Bill Spears spent 27 seasons on Cove (1949-1976), the second longest tenure in its long history. For a touch of domesticity, he planted roses around the keeper's house in soil hauled from the mainland.
— Halcyon *April/May 1985*

Lou Brandon at the radio transmitter, Cove Island
— *Arthur Collection/ Huronia Museum L995.9.83*

Georgian Bay and the Canadian Great Lakes. Because of Vaughan's diligent care, Cove today is in good shape, but steps will have to be taken if that is to continue. One plan is for the Cove Island lighthouse to be leased by The Friends of Fathom Five.

'Mumford Portable'(!) boilers in Cove Island's first fog alarm building. "People who say this island is quiet should be here when there's a fog. June and July are the worst. Two years ago the foghorn, giving three blasts a minute, was going steadily for only four hours less than a week. We get so used to it we have to stop and listen to see if it's going." (Earl Banas, assistant 1945)
— National Archives of Canada PA148182

J. Benim & W. Croswell, carpenters building new kitchen, 1943
— National Archives of Canada PA182854

puny sound any longer. After a few drinks he pulled the plug and started up the real fog horn, then just sat and listened to its reassuring grunt.

When the last keeper Jack Vaughan took over, the job was primarily one of caretaking the site. In 1991 he was taken off the light, bringing to a close the glorious era of lightkeeping on

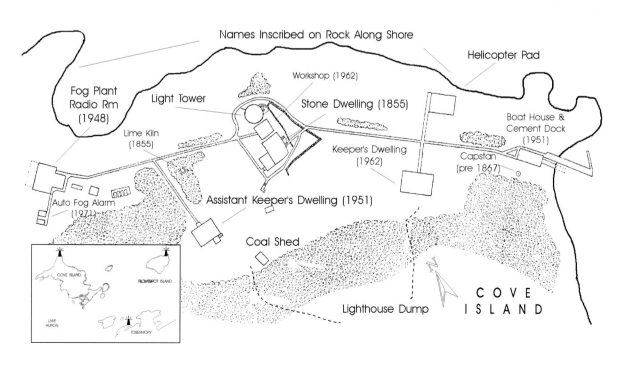

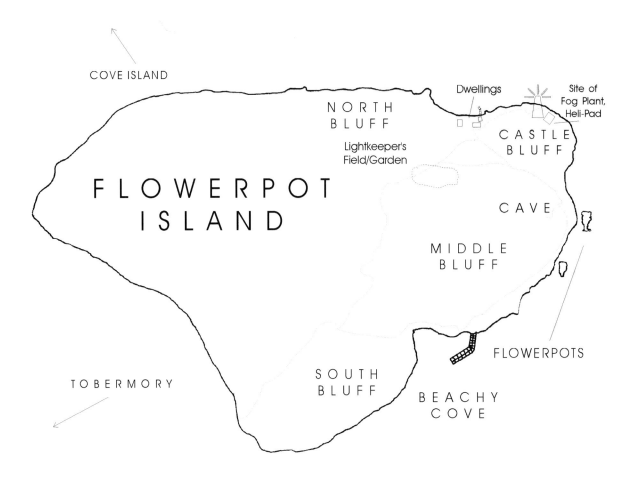

COVE ISLAND

NORTH
BLUFF

Dwellings

Site of
Fog Plant,
Heli-Pad

Lightkeeper's
Field/Garden

CASTLE
BLUFF

FLOWERPOT
ISLAND

CAVE

MIDDLE
BLUFF

FLOWERPOTS

TOBERMORY

SOUTH
BLUFF

BEACHY
COVE

FLOWERPOT
ISLAND

⁌

In 1897, when shipping on Georgian Bay was at its zenith, a lighthouse was perched high on a cliff face at Flowerpot Island to guide traffic through the treacherous Tobermory Islands. Known as Castle Bluff, the cliff is an ancient fossilized coral reef that offers a panoramic view over the waters. In the 1890s several variations of lighthouse styles were designed, all with the tower extended up from the dwelling roof. Flowerpot was one, Cabot Head, Jones and Snug Islands were others. Flowerpot's unique design and setting created a dramatic landmark. It was all the more terrible, then, on that fall day in 1969 when, without warning, the lighthouse was torn down, and burned. The year before a steel skeleton tower had been erected and a cement helicopter pad laid on the site of the fog plant.

Flowerpot Lightkeeper Dan Smith Saves Crew

From his vantage point high on Castle Bluff, lightkeeper Dan Smith sipped his tea and stared through the window at neighbouring Bear's Rump Island. He was uneasy. At that moment, the brooding, sinister sky broke and the wind picked up. A mixture of driving rain and spray blocked the view from the window. Dan Smith put down his cup and turned toward the wooden staircase. It was time to light the light.

As he carefully trimmed the wick something caught his eye — the *Marion L. Breck.* The three-masted schooner, loaded with a cargo of bricks intended for Blind River, was bucking the waves and struggling to get into the shelter behind

Dan Smith (1897-1903) watched the foundering of the Marion L. Breck unfold, but was unable to render assistance for two days.
— Hewers of the Forest, Fishers of the Lake

Marine archaelogist collecting data on wreck. Note the double air tanks enabling them to work under water for longer periods.
— Fathom Five National Marine Parks/Parks Canada

Bear's Rump Island. Dan Smith could only pray; his small sailboat was no match for these seas. The schooner's sails were being shredded by the wind, and Smith could only watch helplessly as the *Breck* was pushed onto the rocks. Throughout the night the crew ran the pumps, trying to stay ahead of the gushing water. Dan Smith hoped the steady beam of the tower was bringing some comfort to the beleaguered men. He sat up all night in the kitchen convinced he could hear their desperate shouts swirling through the howling wind.

As dawn broke the *M.L. Breck*'s bow was awash. Captain Sutherland could do no more. Just as he ordered the exhausted crew ashore, the ship broke apart. Bricks scattered in the breaking surf

In 1909 the 270-foot S.S. Athabaska grounded below Flowerpot light-house. More fortunate than the Marion L. Breck, she was pulled off and repaired.
— Fathom Five National Marine Park/Parks Canada

Flowerpot formation, Bill Spears' favourite look-out spot.
— Author's collection

Dora and Bill Spears following their wedding, May 20, 1937. Although Bill returned to the lighthouse right after the ceremony, someone complained to the authorities that he had left the lighthouse unattended.
— Friends of Fathom Five/National Marine Park

A Boy's Paradise

Bill Spears' lined face had seen more than a few years of Georgian Bay sun. A man of strong opinions, he chuckled as he rolled a cigarette with nimble nicotine-stained fingers and recounted his memories of the island which for him had been a boy's paradise. The son of lightkeeper William Spears (1912-1937), he recalled combing the rocky beach for ship debris after the Great Storm of 1913 and discovering a new cave. To explore it, he made a torch out of a handful of birchbark ("oh it smoked to hell but that didn't matter,") and climbed down the thirty-foot tunnel filled with glistening stalactites. The sea-stacks, or flowerpots as they are locally called were one of Bill's favorite spots. He would lean a ladder against the side, climb on top and sit in his private lookout among the trees. Eighty years later, taking a drag on his cigarette, Bill nodded, "Nice piece of natural work."

Just behind the old house on the beach, there is another cave which still bears the names of former assistants carved in the stone. It was used by generations of lightkeepers for cold storage.

like pebbles. It was another two days before the seas calmed enough to allow Smith to make his way to Bear's Rump to rescue the crew.

The *Marion L. Breck* foundered on October 16, 1900. Over the years, waves scattered the old schooner along a shoal but parts of her hull, capstan and anchor are still visible. She is now among the 21 shipwrecks found within the boundaries of the Fathom Five National Marine Park, a park open to both sport divers and under-water archeologists who are measuring the effects time and currents have on shipwrecks. The Park also encompasses nineteen islands including Bear's Rump and Flowerpot. Flowerpot Island is a treasure-house of rich forests that shelter ferns, mosses, and twenty species of orchids; caves formed during a glacial melt; and the remarkable free-standing limestone pillars that lend the island its name.

The Spears family kept milk and butter inside but no meat because of flies. Bill recalled with a shudder, "We had a cow only one year — the flies were so bad she went crazy — stormed into the water."

The more time Bill spent on the lake, the more he loved it. Watching the boats pass by the lighthouse inspired him to build toy replicas and ships in bottles, and later, 36-footers. The most exciting days were ones when the lighthouse tenders brought supplies. When it was rough, deliveries were made by punt to the beach and then the sacks of coal and barrels of oil were hauled up to Castle Bluff by hand. On calm days when waves could not throw the boat against the cliff, an old winch lifted supplies directly up to the light.

Bill especially remembered the thunderstorms. "Never heard thunderstorms as bad as at Flowerpot," he insisted. There were four bedrooms in the beach house and all eight children were squeezed into one of them. The walls trembled under the force of the terrific thunder that rolled and echoed between the cliffs. "Oh I was scared to death," he nodded with a smile.

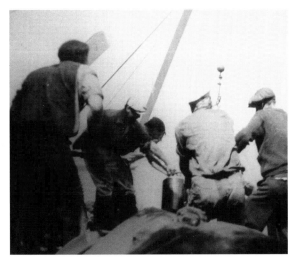

Men and A-frame in front of fog plant used to lift supplies up Castle Bluff on calm days.
— Friends of Fathom Five/Fathom Five National Marine Park

As children, his seven sisters, Viola, Hattie, Stella, Lola, Dorothy, Orma and Joan had somewhat different impressions of living on the island. "My sisters hated it on Flowerpot," Bill recollected. "They spent their days cooking, cleaning and sewing." His mother, too, was not particularly fond of the island. She found the isolation oppressive, feared the water, and

Flowerpot lighthouse with A-frame in front of fog plant.
— Author's collection

constantly worried for the safety of her eight children. She especially hated the fall and spring. For over twenty years she would watch her husband trudge down the road, bundled in his Mackinaw, gloves and toque, with a sack of supplies slung over one shoulder. With his assistant, he would push the eighteen-foot rowboat into the lake which was still dotted with drifting slabs of ice. The journey across was bone chilling and dangerous as the bow was often hit by jagged floes. Several times the men had to climb out and heave the weighty boat over ice banks. The winter journey home was equally arduous. Laden down with belongings, the men would row back to Tobermory through the freezing December weather. With each stroke, more and more ice would coat the boat and oars, making each stroke harder than the last.

A terrible student, Bill escaped to the lighthouse whenever possible and was taught how to tend the light. In 1928 he cheerfully became his father's official assistant and when his father died in 1937, Bill took over as keeper for six months. He married Dora, a childhood sweetheart from neighbouring Tobermory and they honeymooned at their favorite spot — Flowerpot Island.

Bill Spears was replaced at Flowerpot by the World War I veteran and commercial fisherman, Hugh Rumley, who was in turn succeeded by Flowerpot's longest serving keeper, Audrey Coultis. Audrey's son John recalls the day his father "tried to outrun lightning."

It was the late seventies, three years after diesel generators for electricity were installed at Flowerpot. Audrey and John heard an enormous crack and saw a bolt of lightning hit the water just off the dock making the water boil. Audrey believed that lightning always strikes in threes and he began to count. Boom! The second bolt landed in the bushes behind the generating station. Audrey took off like a shot despite the fact

he had a broken leg and was sporting a full leg cast! He had to get to the generating station to kill the power before the lightning zeroed in on the electrical equipment. He was counting aloud as he ran. Bang! The third bolt hit dead on target.

The energy charge was so intense it melted everything together: the control panel, the fuse panel, and the distribution panel. The steel box looked like overheated plastic. "Do you think Dad would get excited?" John mused, "He just took it in stride and set about calmly dealing with the situation, although, after smashing his cast all to hell he did notice his leg hurt a bit." In the aftermath, they had to take turns slowly cranking the enormous overheated Lister diesel engines for five to six hours to prevent their seizing up.

In 1901 a house in the department standard two-storey four-square design was constructed on the beach, as the house on Castle Bluff was too inconvenient for hauling water. Photograph taken in 1908, before veranda was added. Note graffiti on the foundation.
– National Archives of Canada PA182866

Assistant Archie Culham, keepers Brent Skippen and John Freethy.
– Courtesy of Culham family

As calm and cool as Audrey was in a job-related crisis, he became a nervous wreck when his children's health was concerned. Left alone with young John who had measles, he contacted the doctor from Wiarton by radio-phone. He was instructed to give John some rye in order to break the fever by drawing out the measles. Audrey took the advice literally and made sure everything the boy drank included rye: orange juice and rye, apple juice and rye, milk and rye . . . "I was so thirsty!" John laughs, "but was too sick to get my own water. I've never seen my Dad like that, he was a worried man."

Coultis' sons made up his workforce. It was one way to keep four eager boys out of mischief. From the beginning they learned to do things the right way whether it was washing glass chimneys for the kerosene lamps or tending the machinery. The old Wisconsin engines that powered the fog plant were started up with gas, then switched to the more economical kerosene. But before shutting down the engines, gas had to be run through the carburetor to flush it out. "If you ever forgot, the engine would not start. Dad would not be a happy camper. You would have to laboriously drain the engine then clean it, and of course the whole time you would be working the other engine beside you would be running

and the fog horn would be blowing — each time it blew your toes would curl and your hair would stand on end."

Like Bill Spears, the boys felt they owned the island. There was always something to do — swimming, exploring, cowboys and Indians — and only a few rules. The boys could not play behind the house during the afternoon when their father slept, or behind where the assistant slept in the morning. And after five-year-old Danny fell off Castle Bluff (fortuitously landing on a ledge), they were forbidden to go up to the lighthouse while their father was working because he could not keep an eye on them. As they grew older, Audrey, who was also hired by Parks Canada to caretake the park, commandeered them into blazing trails, checking for fires, and removing dead trees.

Over the years, the lighthouse technology had slowly changed. The lamp, (a double flat-wick and then a circular-wick Alladin lamp) had continued to be fueled by kerosene into the 1960s, when Lister diesel generators were installed to provide electricity to the light and the houses. During the 1970s, Mark Coultis, Audrey's youngest son, worked on the Coast Guard tenders that delivered automated equipment to the islands. Having grown up at Flowerpot using wood stoves for heat, kerosene for light and the cave for refrigeration, Mark had mixed feelings as he unloaded the equipment that would displace his father as keeper.

Flowerpot's last assistant, Archie Culham (1982-87), witnessed the decline in the daily shipping count from twelve to fifteen ships a day to only two to four. He would start the engines weekly to ensure they were in good operating condition but there was less and less to do. During the final years, a videograph was installed that emitted two beams of light to measure visibility up to three kilometres. If the machine sensed fog for more that ten minutes, the fog alarm would automatically sound.

The last keeper was John Freethy, assisted by Archie Culham. They have many memories – of the day a storm ripped out the concrete dock and tossed a seven ton rock onto the beach; of the tower magically transformed into an ice sculpture by freezing spray, and of the tragedy of an American sailor. A call from Jack Vaughan, Cove Island's keeper, had sent them through the bush to discover what Jack had spotted washed up on shore. They found a yacht with a dead man on deck still wearing his harness. Evidently on a solo cruise from Detroit to Mackinaw Island, he had suffered a heart attack. The Coast Guard came to retrieve the body while another crew stuffed the sails into a hole in the hull and towed the boat to Tobermory.

It was not easy for the Culhams and Freethy to leave when the light became fully automated in 1987. Freethy used to joke "when we leave, I'll pull out the plug and the island will sink." As reported by Terry Weber in the *Sun Times*, others regretted the passing of the age of light-keepers as well. While stand-ing on the beach, the keepers overheard the commentary of Captain Hugh Campbell on one of the tour boats, "Maybe next year, if you come back, you can go up and talk to the robots."

Memorium

Before the Culhams retired from Flowerpot they left a memorial tablet dedicated to their daughter Lynda and her fiancé Terry. A few days before their planned wedding on Flowerpot Island, Terry and Lynda decided to make a quick trip to Cleveland. Terry was an expert pilot. He had flown for the American Airforce in Vietnam and had run his own flying business for several years. Over Lake Erie they encountered terrific turbulence and radioed for a change in flight plan. They were tracked on the radar for several minutes, then vanished. The memorial which is placed near the foundation of the early light-house on Castle Bluff reads, "In memory of Lynda and Terry, missing over Lake Erie August 26, 1986."

The island may no longer have a lighthouse or lightkeeper but it is still popular. Daily boat tours leave from Tobermory for Flowerpot Island and it is a favourite with campers.

After an unsatisfactory fog bell and hand horn, a fog alarm building was finally built to house a new diaphone system, Flowerpot Island 1908. Note the attractive design of the light-house to the right.
– National Archives of Canada PA148047

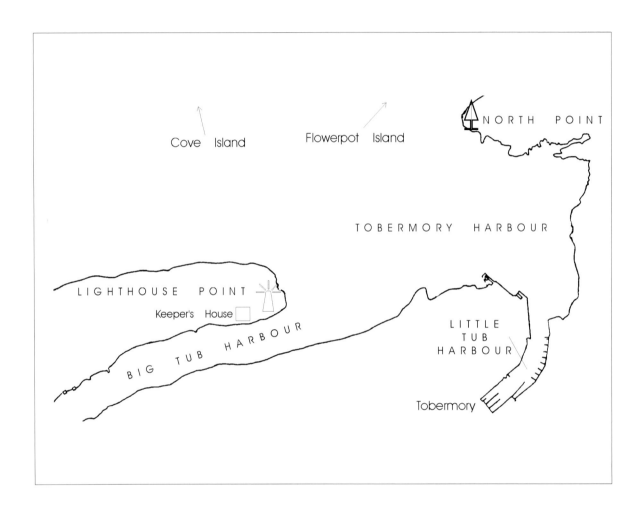

Cove Island

Flowerpot Island

N O R T H   P O I N T

T O B E R M O R Y   H A R B O U R

L I G H T H O U S E   P O I N T

Keeper's House

LITTLE
TUB
HARBOUR

B I G   T U B   H A R B O U R

Tobermory

TOBERMORY

⸸

If most of the files that the Department of Marine and Fisheries maintained regarding lighthouses are routine and rather dull, those of Tobermory read like an ongoing comedy of errors. One can only imagine the apprehension with which correspondence from Big Tub was received by a succession of bureaucrats in Ottawa.

The Feud

The beautiful hexagonal tower on Lighthouse Point at Big Tub Harbour was erected in 1885, four years after Charles Earl was first paid $100 a year to hang a lantern at the same spot. For years he had feuded with a neighbour, Abraham Davis, and their Abbott and Costello-style attacks on each other set the scene for the first of many sideshows that would bedevil the Department over a thirty-year period. Earl is said to have struck Davis on the head with a stick. Davis is said to have responded by pummeling Earl's son, who then threatened to shoot Davis. Then Davis' son is said to have struck Earl's son in the face. Thankfully, a local judge intervened before things went too far. Earl and Davis were given the opportunity to cool their passion in the local jail. Finally, in 1885, Davis won out when he was appointed lightkeeper at the new Big Tub Tower. Ten years later, his tenure ended abruptly and unhappily.

> Kingston *News*, Saturday 9 November 1895
> Probably Drowned
> Tober, Moray, Nov. – On Wednesday night at about ten o'clock, A. Davis, lighthouse-keeper here, left for the scene of the wrecked vessels Owen Sound and Worts in a small skiff, telling his wife he would return about 3 a.m. Davis has not since been seen or heard from, and it is feared he has been drowned . . . Searching parties are now out, but have little hope of finding him.

Before the Department was even aware the position was vacant, Thomas Vail of Owen Sound wrote:

Dear Sir

. . . as I am informed that the Lite-House at tubara-marrie gorgania bay is vakent and if it is vakent I would like to get it at the same salary as desease if a reckamend is required I can give that from Owen Sounds most respected sitisens I have always been use to the watter hoping to hear from you soon I remain yours truly   Thos Vail

Two days later a letter was received from Alex McNeill, local Member of Parliament revealing that:

. . . Davis was an old man on the borders of 80, the night was very dark, there was a good deal of sea running, the boat he had was very small . . . Any doubt that may have existed as to his fate seems to have been put to rest by the discovery of the little scow yesterday at Golden valley . . . It would I think be well that his son Mr. Henry Davis of Tobermory should be appointed lightkeeper . . . .

The Department wasted no time in appointing Henry as keeper at $130 per annum but before the ink was dry, his mother Flora applied for the same position: "I have had a great deal of experience in the work. I humbly pray that you favour one with the appointment." Her application was supported by a petition, signed by a "traveller", a "labourer" and an assortment of mariners, ship masters, fishermen, farmers, engineers, lumbermen, and a minister, from as far away as Kingston and St. Catharines. It was a somewhat surprising endorsement:

. . . she is thoroughly competent and reliable, having performed all the duties for the past five or six years, as her husband was well advanced in years also enjoyed poor health. The light has been faithfully kept and with great satisfaction

to all. We therefore humbly pray that you will give her the appointment and we will ever pray.

Alex McNeill was more cautious:

if you think it advisable to appoint a woman Lightkeeper in such a place as Tobermory, I will Cheerfully withdraw my recommendation of the son . . . But while the poor old woman Could be and I believe has been very useful in helping to trim the lamps, I should very much question the advisability of appointing her Lightkeeper . . . .

TOBERMORY

Location: Lighthouse Point on Big Tub Harbour, west of entrance to Tobermory
Date: 1885
Description: Hexagonal wooden tower, wooden lantern replaced with iron polygonal lantern. Cedar shingle exterior
Height: 43 ft./12.9 m
Light: Fixed red dioptric, 7th order, duplex burner
Visibility: 8 miles/12.8 kms
Fog horn: Hand fog horn, 1910
Automated: 1952
Additional: Wooden dwelling with masonry foundation, 1904
Present: Fixed red harbour light. Friends of Fathom Five and the Township of St. Edmunds have made site accessible by clearing a pathway.

KEEPERS:

1881-1885	Charles Earl
1885-1895	Abraham Davis
1895-1901	Henry B. Davis
1901-1903	Daniel Butchart
1903-1912	Archibald Currie
1912-1926	John Henry Smith
1926-1952	T.A. Hopkins

The Department replied that it was against regulations to place women in such positions, and besides it was too late anyway, as they had already appointed Henry Davis on his (McNeil's) recommendation. When Davis wrote to accept his appointment, he agreed that the lighthouse "neads a man theare that can handle a Bot." For the moment the file was closed.

1898: Farming it Out

In 1898, a local official added a new twist to the story:

> . . . I am instructed to say that Henry Davis who has been keeper of the light house at Tobermory is farming out the work and it is their wish he be forced to resign the position as to endorse such conduct, is against the principals of the Reform Party.

Dutifully, the Department enquired of Davis whether the allegations were true. The first of Henry's replies arrived July 9:

> . . . I hav never went from the light at any time that I cad not return in 30 minets . . . in regards to the farm I had a man looking after it so it das not draw my atencen fom my dutes . . . hopen this will Be sadfactry.

A few days later, he made an about-face:

> my der sir I find that thear are partes that crave for my letle offer So I will resine and give up kepen the lite also I will recemend if you will give the light to mr henry marten he is a trustworthy man he has keep the light for me when I was away and I found true and trust worthy . . . and resine in his favor.

The Deputy Minister rolled his eyes and turned his attention to more pressing matters. Clearly he did not intend to take any action. But two years

Henry B. Davis, wife Mary Ann and son Bill.
– Hewers of the Forest, Fishers of the Lakes

later when the Superintendent of lighthouses, P. Harty, wrote after an inspection of Big Tub:

> . . . the keeper was absent and a man named Henry Martin was in charge. Martin said that the keeper paid no personal attention to the Light but employed him to attend to it giving him nine months pay and retaining three for himself. I understand the keeper lived on his farm source two miles from the lighthouse . . .

the Department resigned itself to the need for replacing Davis. Their only qualification was that he be ". . . able to read and write." The salary would be the tried and true $130 per annum. A shudder must have gone through the Deputy Minister when he shortly received correspondence from both the new keeper, Daniel Butchart, and his predecessor. Davis wrote, "letter received dismissing me as light keeper. Butchart on lake fishing advise what to do;" while Butchart's plea was, "Gents – will you allow me the Privelage of letting Mr. Harry Martin attend the light for the ballance of the season as he has been attending it for the last three years can I fish at the harbor for wages and keep the light as it is a small salary." The Superintendent recommended the acceptance of Butchart's request on the basis that conditions at the light were not good – the assistant keeper was living in a small house formerly used as a cow shed. The Department relented but warned that in future Butchart must give personal attention to his duties as lightkeeper or resign.

During the summer of 1902, Superintendent Harty inspected the station, only to report that Butchart had not been there even once, since his appointment. The light continued to be tended by Henry Martin. By this time the Tobermory file was covered with red annotations and a terse summary was sent to the local M.P. with the observation that "it is subversive of all discipline to allow such a condition of affairs to continue." The Minister clearly believed in stating the obvious.

Matters had not improved by 1903. The exasperated Superintendent reported the Tobermory lightstation was ". . . suffering for the want of a keeper" and recommended an increase in salary to an unprecedented $250 for a reliable man. He argued that the light was an important one, with its harbour being one of the best refuges on the Great Lakes. In September, the Department hired Archibald Currie with the emphatic proviso that he not absent himself from the light station and he was further instructed to deliver a dismissal letter to his predecessor. In Currie's reply, he first mentioned the fact he was unable to deliver the message because Mr. Butchart was absent fishing on the North Shore and then he seized the opportunity to request permission to spend time at his farm occasionally until his affairs were settled. He added for effect, that of course the light would always have his personal attention. It was a bad case of déja vu. Not surprisingly, four years later, the inevitable letter arrived at the Department.

1907: Currying Favour

The letter alleged that Currie did not live in the new house provided by the government at the

Big Tub lighthouse, 1910, beautiful post-Asia hexagonal tower. The lighthouse many coveted but no one kept.
– National Archives of Canada PA172518

light. Instead he was said to have kept the local post office, worked his farm and slept at the farm after having lit the light. A township official defended him, writing:

> its no mariner that has reported him. He has a plot of land a mile from the Harbour that he grows a little stuff on to help to keep soul and body together as his salary is not sufficient to keep his family they would starve on $250 per annum in this country . . . If he can't get away in daytime he will have to give it up and if so we will have a hard time to get another good man for the position at the same salary. Hoping . . . you will do what is right for the interest of the [Liberal] party.

Currie wrote four pages denying he had absented himself, except a few times when his wife could not handle the mail because of a sore hand. He did concede however that, "I have to plant my potatoes and vegetables as I could not afford to buy them all at the salary I receive." The inevitable rumour mill started to grind, suggesting the keeper might be in trouble and almost immediately the Department was inundated with creative letters from prospective candidates, including this one from a local police constable:

> To mister of marrin, Otway.
> Dear Sir,
> I was over too the lighthouse to see what damage was dun to the bildens and onley one windo broken and a hole shot thru the dore, not as bad as the report gone around, sir pleas find my letter of recomend and sir if you think fit to put me thare I and my wife will moove eney time you say.
> Michael Belrose

Currie wrote the Department accusing Belrose of lying and characterized him as "a conservative of the meanest type." In keeping with long established departmental procedures, no action was taken.

In July 1910, Superintendent Harty visited Big Tub to deliver supplies. For some curious reason Currie was absent and Harty had to obtain a key to the lighthouse in town. When Currie was subsequently dismissed, he blamed it all on political partisanship. In his mind apparently, absenteeism was not reasonable grounds for dismissal. Currie's replacement was a Baptist fisherman from St. Catharines, John H. Smith. Uniquely, in July 1914, Smith was reported to be "... present upon inspection" and that September the station was actually found to be "in first class order".

Despite the fact that Smith carried out his duties faithfully, a recommendation was made in 1925, that the light be converted to an unwatched light, and that use of the hand horn be discontinued. Superintendent J.N. Arthurs later conceded under pressure, that "... the public seems to resent in many cases the replacement of keepership lights by unwatched lights" and he revised his recommendation. A year later, the 80-year old Smith asked to be replaced as he was too ill to look after the light. His tenure had been a welcome change for the Department after years of unpredictable keepers.

T.A. Hopkins, a veteran of the Great War, was appointed part-time keeper in 1926 and remained on duty until the light was automated in 1952. His application had received strong support from the Great War Veterans Association of Canada who urged his appointment on the ground that " . . . Comrade Hopkins risked his life in France and we think he should come before a man who never saw military service . . . ."

Tobermory's unusual hexagonal light still stands, warning of the numerous small islands, rock outcroppings and shoals, and welcoming mariners into the shelter of Big Tub. Friends of Fathom Five and the Township of St. Edmunds have made the site accessible by clearing a pathway. (Considering how many times Davis, Butchart, and Currie beat a path from the light, it is surprising that it was not already well worn!)

Michael Belrose (left); Hector Currie (Flowerpot 1904-12); John MacLeod (right). Belrose was one of several trouble-makers in Tobermory who vied for the Big Tub position.
– Hewers of the Forest, Fishers of the Lakes

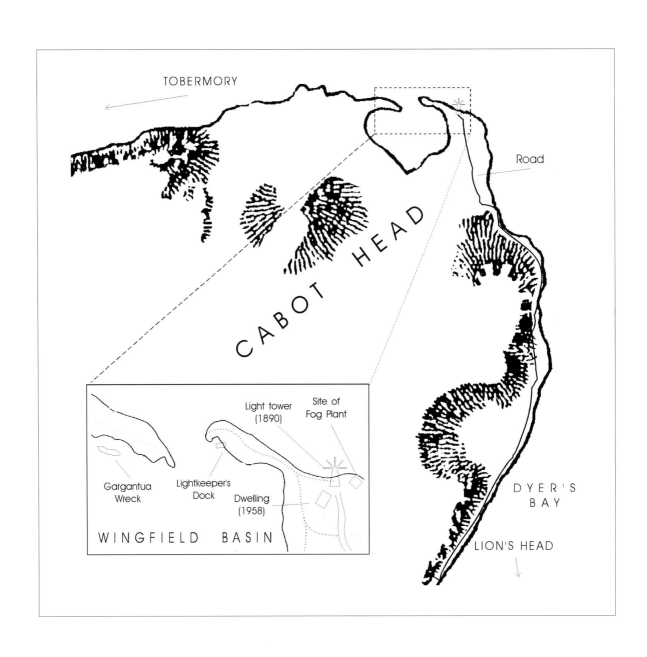

TOBERMORY

Road

CABOT HEAD

DYER'S BAY

LION'S HEAD

Light tower (1890)

Site of Fog Plant

Gargantua Wreck

Lightkeeper's Dock

Dwelling (1958)

WINGFIELD BASIN

CABOT HEAD

---✦---

It took years of shipping disasters before the authorities acknowledged that this treacherous stretch of the Bruce Peninsula warranted a lighthouse. Ships entering Georgian Bay headed for ports south of Parry Sound, did so at their peril. Cabot Head, the promontory around which they had to sail, was chosen for a lighthouse and a steam fog alarm. Because of their importance, the Department made a major investment of about $7,500 in the buildings and equipment, even duplicating the fog alarm boilers and machinery in case of breakdown. On May 18, 1896, the lighthouse went into operation. The light also marked Wingfield Basin, the entrance of which was dredged a few years later to provide a safe harbour on this cliff-lined coast.

After the fog plant was destroyed by fire in August 1907, a new fog alarm building was erected containing diaphone fog horns activated by compressed air. They were extremely effective according to Kim Hopkins who remembers fishing on foggy days just off the point and being deafened by the blast. Like other fog plants, the building had two large doors facing the water facilitating movement of equipment and supplies. The supply ship would anchor a half mile off-shore, and men would ferry the coal or other supplies on a work barge. At the back of the building was a bed-sitting room and verandah for the comfort of the watch on a foggy night.

Early Keepers: Parties and Patronage

Before the former reeve, William Campbell, was appointed Cabot Head's first keeper in 1896, there was much political controversy over who should gain the coveted position. One thing was certain, it had to be given to a Conservative. Campbell fit the bill and he made his first visit to the light in April. Unfortunately he could not start working until July and so he placed his son temporarily in

Cabot Head, 1917. Note the newly cleared grounds.
– National Archives of Canada PA172462

Storm signal tower. Lightkeepers would raise a black conical wicker basket to warn mariners of an impending storm.
– Friends of Cabot Head

charge. In June, the Liberals won the federal election and Campbell found himself out of a job before he even began! A Grit, S.J. Parks was duly appointed but resigned after only a season and a half. Charles Webster Sr., a Scottish farmer from Lion's Head, had a little more staying power, lasting eight shipping seasons before the government changed again. In 1906, Leslie Martindale took over and remained until his death in 1925.

Except for the Meneray family fishery and the sawmill at nearby Wingfield Basin, the lighthouse was initially very isolated. Until a wagon trail was cut through the woods north of Gillies Lake, the only way in was by boat. The first voice contact came in 1915 when a temperamental phone line was strung from tree to tree between Gillies Lake and Cabot Head.

Howard Boyle

After World War I, lightkeeping positions were reserved for war veterans, and Howard Boyle was the lucky applicant. He held the position for an impressive twenty-five years, carrying out his official duties in exemplary fashion. Boyle and his wife had a vegetable garden (which they fertilised with scrap fish from the Meneray fishery), and kept pigs, chickens and a cow. But his greatest pleasure was in beautifying the grounds with lilac trees, stone walls and flowers — a legacy that survives today.

Clara and Howard Boyle (1926-51) — Friends of Cabot Head

The Hopkins Years

In 1951 Boyle was succeeded by Harry Hopkins who held the post even longer: thirty-one years! When interviewed in 1993, his wife Ruby's first two thoughts were of biting flies and rattlesnakes. A happier memory was of freighters passing late in the season, all lit up with Christmas lights. She enjoyed her years at Cabot Head, but had little free time. In the beginning, she had a wood cook stove but no running water. A wire angled down from the top of the cliff into the water along which she slid a pail and then pulled it back up with a rope. With Harry working the usual six hours on, six off routine of a lightkeeper, much of the work of raising their nine children (Ken, Karen, Carl, Klyde, Kelly, Kim, Keith, Kris, and Candace Marie) was hers. But when Ruby stayed in Tobermory with the school-age children during the winter, Harry took over responsibility for the younger ones, in addition to tending the light and fog horn and finding time to bake homemade bread.

Occasionally an event occurred to break the routine. One foggy night about three in the

Harry Hopkins (1951-82) keeper at Cabot Head for thirty-one years. — Friends of Cabot Head

morning, the Hopkins' were awakened by someone hollering. A man in a small outboard wanted to know where he was. Harry went down, guided him into shore and then pointed him toward the shelter of Wingfield Basin. It turned out the boater had only a road map and a couple of chocolate bars on board. Ruby remembers Harry was so mad he almost regretted helping the stranger. Only idiots went on the water without survival rations. For Harry that meant at least a basket with pork and beans, sardines and an onion.

The Hopkins era oversaw many changes. A new bungalow was built in 1958 so that the Hopkins and their assistant could have their

The remains of the Gargantua *that was towed into Wingfield Basin become a favourite playground for the Hopkins' children. A family friend, Mr. Schutt, would play Captain and order commands through the vents. It is now home to a family of beavers.*
— Friends of Cabot Head

own homes. The oil house, blacksmith's shed and fog alarm building were torn down, and Hurricane Hazel made short work of the boathouse and dock, tossing huge boulders up onto the marine railway. In the mid-1960s a road was built, linking the light to Dyer's Bay, and in 1971, electricity arrived. However welcome it might have been, electricity was responsible for hastening the end of lightkeeping. An automated skeleton tower was built and the original tower removed from the house. The last keeper, Brent Skippen, stayed until 1988 to maintain the equipment and care for the site. When he left, the station was abandoned.

Friends of Cabot Head: A Study in Action

The stage was set for Cabot Head to join a long list of extinct lighthouses. Fortunately, a local group stepped in and made sure this did not happen. They formed the Friends of Cabot Head

to save the building from destruction. In 1993 they received a two-year lease during which they hoped to conduct a feasibility study, and an environmental assessment and impact study. By the end of the two years, they had not only completed the environmental studies but they had also restored the building to its former glory, reopened the lighthouse, established a visitor interpretation centre, rebuilt the tower, replaced the dome, and built new trails. Along the way, they incorporated and registered the Friends as a charitable organization. In the summer of 1995, the lighthouse celebrated its one hundredth anniversary and was able to welcome hundreds of people to the site to learn of its marine and natural history. For information on how to get involved, contact the Friends of Cabot Head, RR#1, Miller Lake, Ontario N0H 1Z0.

After touring several decrepit sites, it was encouraging to see a part of our Canadian heritage so carefully maintained. The building, with its replica tower and lantern (slightly squat so as not to obstruct the beam from the skeleton tower) is reshingled and freshly painted white with red trim. Inside, displays interpret the local history and nature.

Cabot Head, 1897. Old fog alarm building in foreground burned in 1907.
— National Archives of Canada PA182877

LION'S HEAD

✦

With a potentially excellent harbour at their doorstep, why were the inhabitants of Lion's Head having to rely on the flat rock at Whip-poor-will Bay as their supply depot? It was an impossible situation for a developing community and so pressure was put upon the government to dredge a channel. In 1883, the sandbar which had effectively blocked the harbour for years was cleared away and a thirteen-foot deep channel allowed ships to make their way into the dock.

In 1903 a light was established on the outer end of the breakwater at the north entrance to the harbour. It consisted of a square lantern with a red catoptric light hoisted on a pole fifteen feet high. The light, which could be seen from six miles out, cost $197.16 to complete. Charles Knapp, a former shoemaker, was appointed the first keeper. By 1909, Lion's Head had grown into a feisty lumber village, with sawmills lining the north and west shores of the harbour. The dock was extended, and in 1911 a square tapered lighttower was added at the end of the pier. In less than a year it was knocked down by high winds and pounding waves.

Great Storm of 1913

No sooner was the lighthouse restored than the infamous Great Storm of November 9, 1913 struck. That Sunday would be remembered as the blackest day in Great Lakes marine history. For days the gales had raged but a lull on the 9th lured many ships back into open waters. The ships could not afford to sit in port for long as the end of the navigating season was fast approaching. Then, without warning, it hit. Hurricane-force winds grew up to ninety miles an hour, and thunderous waves exceeded 35 feet. To make matters worse, the winds changed direction with frightening rapidity, often blowing a different direction from the waves. This combination of forces twisted and strained the hulls of even the most massive steel vessels.

Early pole light on end of pier at right of photo. The end of Lion's Head Point ravaged by fire. The tug Meaford *is at the dock.*
– *With permission from* Between You and Me and the Gatepost; *contributed by Oliver Tackaberry family*

Within a few days, the devastation became clear. Eight ships had gone down on Lake Huron and two on Lake Superior. Bodies washed up on Lake Huron's east shore, three and four at a time. The final count was an appalling 248 lives lost. No one remains to tell of the ships' fates, yet the storm left many questions unanswered. Why, for example, did the chief engineer of the *Charles S. Price* wash ashore wearing a life jacket marked the *Regina*, when the two ships were eventually found in different parts of Lake Huron? And why was the *Price*, a newly built steel freighter, found turned turtle in southern Lake Huron? The ship was supposed to be unsinkable.

An even more bizarre story centred around a John Thompson who was reported lost on the *James Carruthers*. He read of his own death in the newspapers and on returning home found a coffin sitting in his parents' living room. According to accounts, John's father had identified "the body" immediately, citing a particular scar and the initials J.T. tatooed on his arm. One can imagine the mixture of shock and joy John's appearance must have occasioned. Evidently, he

LION'S HEAD

Location: Outer breakwater at north entrance to Lion's Head harbour
Date: Pole light erected in 1903; tower in 1911
Description: Short square white tower with tapered sides
Light: Fixed red catoptric (changed to green in 1944 to avoid confusion with street lights). Electrified 1951.
Visibility: 6 miles/9.6 kms
Demolished: 1969. Replaced with red navigational light at end of pier

KEEPERS:

1903-c.1912	Charles Knapp
1912-1924	P. Webster Brady
1924-1956	Ivan Butchart
1956-1969	Ed Rouse

had left the *Carruthers* for another ship before the storm.

In Lion's Head, the vicious storm had destroyed part of the dock and driven the lighthouse onto the harbour's south beach. It was recovered and restored to its mountings. In 1919, the structure was prudently moved back from the end of the wharf. Sometime in the 30s, a concrete deck was poured over the timber crib

Victims of the storm washed up on beach near Goderich after the Great Storm.
— *Institute for Great Lakes Research, Bowling Green State University*

Lighthouse wreck on the south beach of the harbour after the Great Storm of November 9, 1913.
— *Courtesy of Margarett Bogers, Lion's Head*

and the lighthouse securely anchored, but that could not protect the tower from a fire that ravaged it in 1933. Repaired yet again, the tenacious lighthouse stood proudly on the pier for years — a community landmark second in popularity only to the great cliff face with its profile of a recumbent lion.

William Corson Mystery

The beacon provided a comforting promise of security to those townspeople who ventured out into the Bay. Why, then, on September 24, 1923

had fisherman William Corson and his young assistant Robert Parker not returned from setting their pound nets? The night had been clear. It made no sense. Men searched the shoreline and dragged the bay but found only the fishermen's launch, not the men or their punt.

Two weeks went by without locating any bodies, and so when a travelling clairvoyant named "Mem-o-rea" said he could locate the bodies through a technique mentioned in the Grecian Bible, the townspeople urged him to try. Mem-o-rea's powers were purported to be derived from his being the "seventh son of a seventh son". His detection devices were loaves of bread hollowed out and replaced with lime which he then set afloat in the presumed location of the bodies. Supposedly, the place where the loaves submerged marked the spot. The Wiarton *Echo* elucidated:

> It is stated by the unsophisticated that when a loaf of bread passes over the body, an electrical current is formed, which is evidenced by the bread vibrating, thus giving the location of the body. Another explanation is that certain gases are emitted from a dead body and constantly bubbling to the top of the water, and when the gas comes in contact with the lime, the bread will demonstrate it.

Whatever the process, within half an hour of dragging bread, Mem-o-rea discovered the body of Robert Parker. His clothing had been caught by a grappling hook. Mem-o-rea claimed he had also found the body of William Corson, but lost it. Many soggy loaves later, he was still unsuccessful.

Rumours began to circulate when equipment thought to be used for distilling liquor was found along the shore near the fishing site. Perhaps William Corson had survived and just disappeared for some reason. But the town's reeve, Walter Warder, dismissed these speculations saying Mem-o-rea was nothing but "the seventh son of a son of a gun." Probably, both men had drowned when their boat, loaded with rocks needed for the pound netting operation, had swamped. The disappearance occasioned the exciting arrival of the first airplane in Lion's Head. After searching the bay, the pilot had to admit defeat. No trace was ever found of either William Corson or the punt the men had used. If only the lighthouse could speak.

Photograph taken by Lottie Chapman three days before the lighthouse's demise in May 1969. With it she wrote "for generations it stood four-square to the changing winds of time." Anchor ends embedded in the concrete pier still mark the spot where the lighthouse once stood.
– Courtesy of Lottie Chapman, Little Current

First airplane to visit Lion's Head. Left to right: Reeve Walter Warder; a pilot; Canon James; a pilot; and Mrs. James Parker, mother of Bobby Parker.
– Warder Reunion Display, Frank Stuart House, Lion's Head

1969

For the next forty years the lighthouse served the marine community faithfully. Then one May morning in 1969, before the residents knew what was happening, Coast Guard personnel arrived and dismantled the tower. The building debris was taken to the local landfill site and burned. The townspeople were outraged. If they had been made aware of the light's impending fate, they would have taken over its maintenance in order to preserve their historical landmark.

When pressed for an explanation, the Coast Guard responded in a letter that the lighthouse had been "rotten beyond repair". This assessment was vehemently denied by the harbourmaster. While the lighthouse had become a tempting canvas for graffiti artists, even the men who were involved now admit that graffiti is not a legitimate reason to destroy a lighthouse. That autumn, the beautiful old Flowerpot Island light was also demolished. Only a public outcry prevented others said to be on the list from meeting a similar fate.

Autumn gale. Former Lion's Head resident Lottie Chapman observed that "during stormy nor-easters, many a practised eye measured the velocity of the wind by how high the waves broke against the lighthouse."
– Photo by Gladys Blake, Lion's Head

The citizens of Lion's Head continued to mourn their loss. Their story sparked the imaginations of design students at the Bruce Peninsula District School who, in 1980, decided to build a replica. Despite reams of red tape, the students persisted and, in 1983, their lighthouse was completed and erected on the beach where it stands today.

Lighthouse with row of fish tugs at pier.
– National Archives of Canada RD90

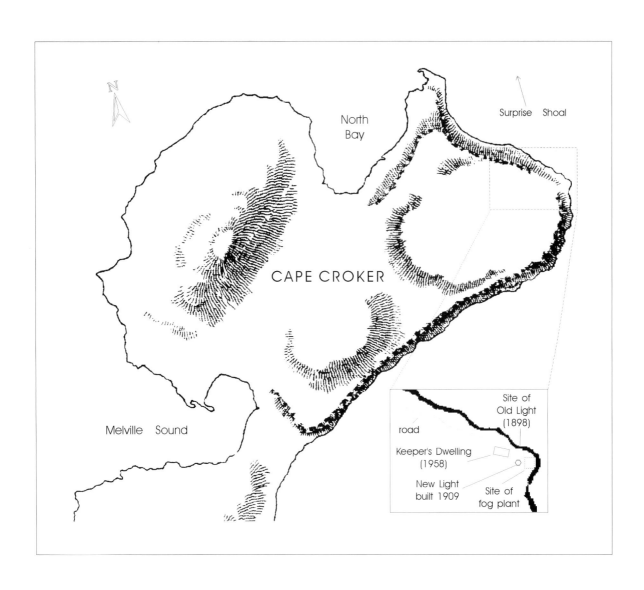

North
Bay

Surprise   Shoal

CAPE CROKER

Melville   Sound

Site of
Old Light
(1898)

road

Keeper's Dwelling
(1958)

New Light
built 1909

Site of
fog plant

CAPE CROKER

---+---

The first lighthouse, a small wooden structure with a tower on the roof, was built in 1898 to protect boats navigating the Bruce Peninsula. At that time, the closest safe harbour was Wiarton, 39 miles away. One of the worst dangers on this perilous stretch of shore is Surprise Shoal. Over a mile long, it lies almost directly in the path of the route taken from Cabot Head to Cape Croker, Wiarton, Owen Sound, and Collingwood.

In 1903, plans were drawn up which would put Cape Croker on the Canadian architectural engineering map. A new tower was to be built; one of the first reinforced concrete lighttowers in the country, and one of the country's earliest experiments with this new technology. Completed in 1909, it proudly displayed a large diamond-like Fresnel lens. Cape Croker also led the way by being the first station in the country to have both the fog plant (1902) and lighthouse (1909) powered by electricity.

The Golden Road In

The road in to the Cape Croker lighthouse is famous among those who worked at the light. Juanita (Rourke) Keefe fondly remembers it as "the golden path in the fall" while John Adams (1969-77) recalls visitors constantly complaining about its rough condition. "We called it 'Trudeau's Trail,'" he laughed, "because there was never any money to maintain it."

The road in passes the thriving Chippewas of Nawash First Nation community, one that began in 1857 after the band surrendered Nawash and Sarawak around Owen Sound and moved here. The end of the road is the site of Cape Croker's old fog plant. An unattractive chain-link fence surrounds the reinforced concrete tower. Once a meticulously maintained area, it is now frequented by porcupines, not known for their spit and polish.

Norman Whetton and his grand-daughter.
– Courtesy of Nancy Armstrong

CAPE CROKER

Location: On point 1⅓ miles
    southeast of Cape Croker
    community

1898
Description: Tower on top of
    frame keeper's house
Discontinued: 1909, lighthouse became guest
    house

1909
Description: New reinforced concrete octag-
    onal tower with red circular metal lantern
Light: Group flashing, 3rd order Fresnel
    dioptric
Visibility: 13 miles/20.8 kms
Fog Horn: Diaphone with compressed air;
    1 blast every 60 secs.
Additional: First reinforced concrete tower on
    Georgian Bay; first lightstation in Canada
    with both lighthouse and fog plant electri-
    cally operated. Four-bedroom house built
    c.1909; bungalow built 1958
Present: Tower and bungalow remain; white
    light, group of two flashes every five seconds

KEEPERS:

1902-1910	Richard Chapman
1910-1916➤	W. Chapman
◄1949-1965	Norman Whetton
1965-1968	Frank Rourke
1969-1979	John Adams
1980-1986	Frederic Jerome Proulx

The road is a memorial to one lightkeeper's sweat and toil. After tending the light each day, Norman Whetton would take his motorboat up the wooded coast to the place he had last cleared, and then determinedly clear the next short stretch. His daughter Nancy recalls her mother Doris having to help her father into the house one day after he had arrived at the dock overcome with severe sun stroke. He was bedridden for three days. It was fortunate Doris was a nurse because assistance was ten miles away by boat at the Cape Croker Reserve. With her dislike of the water, it is unlikely she would have taken her husband and children in the motor boat on her own. She was so frightened of capsizing that she would watch over the side of the boat, insisting that the rocks on the bottom always be visible. While agreeing that an open boat on this rugged, exposed shore could be dangerous, her husband could not help teasing, "Doris, if there's a boat with wheels I'll be the first to buy it!" The road was finally completed and Norman's daughter Nancy clearly recalls their first bumpy ride when the car was shaking and rattling so much they feared it would break apart at any moment.

Later, the road became a selling point for potential lightkeepers. John Adams called his former post on Lonely Island a treacherous place;

"it was 25 miles to the mainland and I don't know many trips where I didn't get caught between Tobermory and Lonely. Sometimes you'd get stuck in Tobermory two weeks before you could get back out." When the opportunity came for a transfer to Cape Croker, Johnny's wife argued that the peace of mind would be worth any loss in wages.

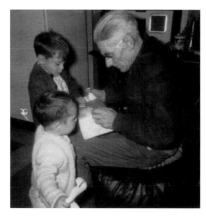

Frank Rourke with grandchildren.
— *Courtesy of Juanita Keefe*

Building tower using new technology of reinforced concrete, 1909.
— *National Archives of Canada PA182859*

Inside forms, new concrete tower, 1909.
— *National Archives of Canada PA182859*

The Rourkes, who spent years on two of the most isolated lighthouses, the Western Islands and the Great Ducks, agreed. An incident at the Ducks helped convince them. When a commercial fisherman capsized in front of the lighthouse, Frank and his son Gillard had to rescue the floundering man by rowboat. Juanita believes the strain and worry of rescuing the man and towing his overturned boat brought on Frank's heart attack the following day. They radioed for help but the fog rolled in and it was twenty-four hours before Frank could be taken off the island. The time had come to be at a lighthouse accessible by car. As Juanita flipped through pictures of Cape Croker, she laughed at the size of the light, "Imagine coming from the Ducks to this peanut!"

Cape Croker Storms

The intense storms at Cape Croker left as strong an impression on the keepers as they did on the battered shoreline. John Adams recalled that previous keepers had made a harbour enclosed by a wall of stones hauled from the water:

> One gale, a nor'easter, the one that took down the *Edmund Fitzgerald*, tore that whole harbour clean out of there, nothing left, flattened it right out. The wind was so strong that night that instead of walking to the lighthouse it seemed you were out the door and you were at the lighthouse!

New lighttower, erected 1909.
— *Courtesy of Nancy Armstrong*

Old lighthouse with tower removed. Used as guest house when new tower was constructed.
– Edward Mole Collection

"Oh could it blow out there, Holy Jesus," he continued,

> you'd go to bed at night and the wind would get up, and those big slabs of rock sliding back and forth, back and forth on the bottom; they would squeal. You couldn't sleep because of the noise. You'd go down there in the morning and see slabs of rocks that weighed tons. You wondered how the hell they could've moved but it was the force of that water!

Nancy Whetton also remembers,

> the fog, the storms. The wind I remember. We live on Lake Huron now. I am petrified of wind – it reminds me of the lighthouse. There were a couple of times boats were in trouble and my Dad heard them yelling for help. The wind brings back those things.

Foresight Saved the Fog Plant

The location of the Cape Croker light, butted up against a steep cliff, made John Adams nervous. If a fire blocked the road, the only choice was to take to the lake, and more often than not the lake was too dangerous. One afternoon while walking to the tower during an elec-

trical storm, he glanced at the lake just as a bolt of lightning hit the spar of a sailboat. The electricity shot back into the sky and arced over to the Cape Croker fog plant. As he watched, the bolt rolled down the metal roof and shot underneath. He charged into the building and grabbed the fire pump which he had kept hooked up for just such an emergency. By the time he had climbed the ladder, the attic was already smoking. But because of his quick actions, the fire was already extinguished when the Wiarton fire crew arrived.

The Wild Life

Porcupines and bears were considered part of the scenery at Cape Croker. Removing quills from the family hound was just one of many daily tasks. Bears were almost as common. Juanita (Rourke) Keefe recalls playing cards with her visiting American cousins and their friends when the group noticed the distinctive smell of a bear. Suddenly, the house began to shake so hard the dishes in the cupboards rattled. Juanita laughed,

> the bear hit the side of the house. Everyone went out the back door except this man and me. I said 'come on we'll go out the front.' He refused and so here is this panic-stricken American pacing up and down the kitchen saying 'Why? Why? Why?!' The poor man was convinced I was purposely leading him right into the bear.

Today only the tower and bungalow of the Cape Croker complex remain. The other buildings were destroyed by the Coast Guard including the fog plant which years earlier they had commended John Adams for saving. Although Cape Croker is one of only three lighthouses on Georgian Bay that can still boast a Fresnel lens, it is in imminent danger of losing it.

Cape Croker fog plant, 1917.
— National Archives of Canada PA182857

Fog plant, 1934. Note old tower on far right, and new tower on extreme left.
— National Archives of Canada PA182879

GRIFFITH ISLAND

---·✦·---

It was a hot, sunny September day, still and moody. We anchored and took our zodiac into the beach — at first sight a sun-bleached, rather drab, rocky strip. However, while pulling the zodiac up, it was impossible not to notice the soft colours of the rocks patterned with dozens of small fossils.

The site is beautiful, with a panoramic view of the blue expanse of Georgian Bay stretching to the horizon. A sense of passing time imbues the place. Up a small incline, the whitewashed Imperial light and stone house stand defiant yet serene against the ravages of time. The house's slate roof and thick stone walls struggle to hold together against the pressure of a young tree pushing out the window. Surrounding the house are thistles in bloom, myrtle, raspberries, and birch trees. Peering in through an open window we see a devastating sight of neglect. The interior has been completely demolished. The stairs to the second story have collapsed and lie flat on the broken floor amid piles of fallen plaster. Yet one wall still shows patches of wainscotting, lovingly painted in soft green with a salmon border.

The Imperial light tower gleams white in the sun and casts an impressive shadow, but inside, it too is fly-ridden and filthy. The interior walls are covered with a thin layer of moss — an aesthetically pleasing contrast to the red metal stairs perhaps, but not what would have been acceptable to a keeper whose daily chores included lighting, polishing, cleaning, and regular painting sessions.

The Griffith light was one of six Imperial towers built by the Department of Works, Canada West in the late 1850s. It was positioned to guide vessels up and down the Bruce Peninsula, and into the safety of Colpoy's Bay. The dolomite limestone is believed to have been brought from cliffs on the west shore of Owen Sound. Sixteen acres of land were bought for the site from the Nawash Band at five dollars an acre, but the formal surrender did not go through until thirty years after construction of the light had begun.

It was a lonely spot for the early keepers, about whom little is known. The first settlers, Mr. and Mrs. Frederick Thornley, did not build their house and sawmill operation on the south side of the island until 1904. On one issue the keepers can be heard clearly — the inferior quality of the sperm whale oil with which they were provisioned. It was "too old and too thick to make a good light", they wrote. The quality of the light improved when coal oil was developed, but they still had to haul the five-gallon oil cans from the beach up the hill and up the lighthouse's six staircases; and they still had to polish the glass. In 1924, the government installed an acetylene gas plant to power the light. While this meant less maintenance, mariners complained that the light given off was dull and unreliable. It went out for a few days in August of that year, making people wish for the return of the old oil lamps and their attendant keeper.

The *Nellie Sherwood*

During these early years, the lighthouse stood witness to many sad events which may account for the brooding atmosphere that permeates the site. On September 15, 1882, the keeper, Garrett Patterson, woke to a clear, calm day, a relief after the terrible intensity of the storm that had threatened to knock down his house the night before. He had also feared it would smash the glass of the lantern room while he refilled the lamp and he remembered the feeling of foreboding as he

GRIFFITH ISLAND

Location: North east side of
    Griffith Island, just outside
    Colpoy's Bay
Date: 1858
Description: Circular limestone
    Imperial tower. Red circular
    iron lantern.
Height: 16.7 m
Light: Fixed white dioptric light of third order.
    Acetylene light installed 1924.
Visibility: 17 miles/27.2 kms
Fog horn: Hand horn in 1913
Additional: Dock and lifeboat house (now
    gone)
Present: Tower remains, keeper's house in ruins.
    Solar-powered white light flashes every 4
    seconds

KEEPERS:

1858	John Frame
1859-1882	Vesey C. Hill
1882-1884➤	Garrett W. Patterson
1889-1916➤	William S. Boyd
◄1921-1922	George Bennett
1922-1924➤	Frederick W. Thornley

Although the passenger-freight steamer the Manasoo *sank near Griffith Island on Sept. 14, 1928, those on the island did not hear the terrible news for a few days. During a vicious storm, the cargo, 116 head of cattle, all moved to one side causing the ship to turn over. After a harrowing sixty hours on a raft, five passengers from the* Manasoo *were picked up by a lifeboat from the steamer* Manitoba. *Sixteen others were not so lucky.*
– Rose MacLeod, The Story of White Cloud, Hay, and Griffith Islands

Griffith Island Imperial tower completed 1858.
– Author's collection

Twins Frances and Susan Thornley about 14 years of age. It was a common sight to see Frances standing on the railing of the tower while cleaning the panes of lantern room glass.
– Lillian Thornley Williams, Memoirs of Griffith Island

looked out at the seething waters of the Bay. There wasn't much shelter along this shoreline and any boat caught on the open water would be in grave danger. The morning's calm only

increased his feeling of unease, and then down on the beach, he saw it – the body of a young boy lashed to a timber. It was later identified as William Blanchard, son of Captain Blanchard of the *Nellie Sherwood*. Had the father lashed his son to the timber to save him or at the very least ensure he had a Christian burial? The boy was the only one of the *Nellie Sherwood*'s crew ever found. According to eyewitnesses, the schooner had been overloaded with timber and had been spotted wallowing in the waves. As it turned out this was not the only tragedy that night. It was the same storm that brought down the *Asia* with such tremendous loss of life.

George Bennett

Not long before Christmas of 1922, George Bennett went in to Big Bay for supplies. Upon his return, a big storm blew up. He stopped at the dock on the south end of the island but ignored warnings to wait out the blow rather than continue around the exposed side of the island to the light. If he was determined to go, the men on the dock advised him to cross the island by horseback, entreating that "the winds and currents out there wreak havoc!" They graciously refrained from mentioning that he was a war veteran with only one leg and in most people's opinion not much of a seaman. Bennett waved them off, and the men watched helplessly from the pier as the boat rounded the island. The light was not lit that night and nothing was seen or heard of Bennett again.

The Joyful Times

Lillian Thornley Williams, granddaughter of keeper Frederick Thornley, has quite different recollections of the island. Hers are romantic

Picnic Day at the lighthouse beach. Artemesia Boyd is the elderly woman centre-right. Fred Thornley is second from left in back row and wife Annie is third from left. Stan Boyd, the Boyd's son, is holding Lillian Thornley. Children loved hiking up to lighthouse to visit the Boyds.
— Lillian Thornley Williams, Memoirs of Griffith Island

house, Lillian's favourite room was the board-and-batten summer kitchen from which emanated the smell of freshly baked pies cooling in the tall glass-fronted cupboard. Lillian recalls the strong love everyone had for the lighthouse and the feeling in 1924 when an acetylene plant made her grandfather's job as keeper redundant, "When it didn't need us anymore, it was a sad time. It lost a lot of its romance."

Derelict interior of the lighthouse dwelling.
— Author's collection

childhood memories of Sunday afternoon boat trips or hikes up the two miles from the south shore to visit the Boyds at the lighthouse. Lillian recalls always knowing when they were getting close because through the woods would waft the distinct smell of fresh paint. The Boyds were a warm and generous couple. Artemesia Boyd would always have cookies, lemonade, or hot cocoa for the intrepid hikers and William loved taking people in his steamboat to different islands for picnics. Inside the brightly painted

Griffith Island, pre-1953.
— County of Grey – Owen Sound Museum

In an old quarry near Owen Sound, the quantity of rock removed matches what might have been needed to build Griffith. To find the quarry, take 7th St. West from Owen Sound out to the escarpment. From the end of the road a path leads to the old quarry.

PRESQU'ILE

---+---

It was 1864 when John Mackenzie moved to his farm at Presqu'ile. Before long he had built a combination home and store close to the water, and with government assistance, a huge dock stretching 400 feet into the water. This was a smart move. It was the age of the steamer, and Presqu'ile lay on the regular route between Collingwood and Duluth, Minnesota at the far end of the Great Lakes. The dock attracted hundreds of vessels carrying goods and supplies, lumber and produce, and immigrants heading west. Ships needed cord wood to feed the insatiable stoves that fired their boilers and the local farmers were more than happy to oblige. Stacks of wood reportedly stretched a half mile along the harbour in piles thirty to forty feet deep and almost as high.

Because of the trade, Presqu'ile grew into a thriving port village of nearly 400 inhabitants. The historian Andrew Armitage wrote that in 1870, the first full year of operation, 136 ships made port in Prequ'ile, and exports valued $3,000. Four years later, 343 steamers visited, and exports had climbed to $35,000. Baled hay, grain, and meat were other lucrative commodities. It is said that in one night, three butchers dressed 115 lambs and sewed the meat into cotton bags, ready to put on a morning boat. To meet the increased demand for services, the village opened a wagon shop, blacksmith shop, sawmill, cooperage, tinsmithy, bake shop and in, 1873, a lighthouse.

The Department of Marine and Fisheries built the light on lot number six of Centre Street which they had bought from Mackenzie in 1876 for the sum of $1.00. Mackenzie was named the first keeper (in addition to his roles as postmaster, general store proprietor and harness shop owner) and was paid $50 per annum. The light was strategically placed to guide ships into the dock, and to warn them both of the rocky reef extending from the tip of the peninsula, and the sand bar at the approach to nearby Owen Sound harbour. In 1879, an oil house was also built because Mackenzie complained about the danger of storing oil in the tower.

John Mackenzie, lightkeeper and founder of Presqu'ile.
— Sarawak Saga/County of Grey – Owen Sound Museum.

Mackenzie had two assistants: his youngest daughter Margaret, who often lit, extinguished, and cleaned the lamp; and his famous collie Buller, who always knew when his master should light the lamp. If Mackenzie was sleeping, Buller would waken him at the appropriate hour, lighthouse key at the ready. (The key is now on display at the County of Grey–Owen Sound Museum.) One night during a dense fog the steamer *Manitoba* was delayed, not arriving off Presqu'ile until three in the morning. Buller, cannily differentiating between the steamer's whistle and that of the many friendly salutes ships made as they passed by, woke Mackenzie, who returned the signal. However there was one ship that neither Mackenzie nor his wonder dog could help. When the *Asia* entered port on Sept 14, 1882, Mackenzie vainly attempted to convince the captain not to continue in the storm. The subsequent shipwreck was the worst ever marine disaster on Georgian Bay.

While Mackenzie could not protect the village from the infamous Bay storms (storms capable of hurling the big flat shore rocks so high they hit the lighthouse), he did make sure the village was protected from one thing: the bawdiness of Owen Sound and its 35 watering holes. From the beginning, Mackenzie had insisted Presqu'ile must be a teetotalling community. A proviso was attached to the sale of every lot

Buller (right) carried the key for lighthouse.
— County of Grey – Owen Sound Museum

stating that no intoxicants could be consumed anywhere in the community. These principles did not seem to apply to trade however. One old-timer claimed a major source of Owen Sound's firewater was none other than "untainted" Presqu'ile! Supposedly, liquor was off-loaded from the large cargo ships into smaller boats or onto wagons for delivery to the free-wheeling town next door.

The 1870s marked the village's heyday, but when range lights were built at Owen Sound, and its harbour approaches dredged in the 1880s, marine traffic shifted to the larger centre. Presqu'ile's economy also suffered when coal replaced wood as the fuel of choice. Yet Mackenzie was a survivor and in 1897, he turned to the tourist trade. He developed a resort complete with an aerial railway that drew pleasure seekers from Owen Sound and neighbouring centres. Nevertheless, despite his efforts, the forces of decline continued to gather strength.

A Ghost Town

Mackenzie's son Hugh took over the light until 1910 when the Department discontinued its operation. The light inspector who arrived in June 1911, had this to say:

Inspected Presqu'ile Station today. The whole place has gone to seed. The wharf is in ruins, dangerous to walk on, several houses have fallen, and the two inhabited houses yet left are the worse for wear. [The lighthouse] looks in fair order but the only article of value about it would be the plate glass. There is an old oil store with some boxes and an old stove in it, also a boat house by the wharf.

PRESQU'ILE

Location: 9 miles north of Owen
    Sound
Built: 1873
Description: White square wooden
    tower, octagonal lantern
Height: 27 ft./8.1 m
Light: Fixed white catoptric light, three
    mammoth flat-wick lamps, 16-inch reflectors
Visibility: 8 miles/12.8 kms
Additional: Storm signal station nearby on water;
    frame oil shed near light
Discontinued: 1910
Torn down: 1985

KEEPERS:
1873-c.1907   John Mackenzie
c.1907-1910   Hugh H. Mackenzie

Presqu'ile light, discontinued 1910.
– National Archives of Canada PA172526

The next month, the *Simcoe* was requested to call at Presqu'ile and remove all supplies from the dismantled station. But the light's story does not end there. In 1918, a farmer asked permission to use the lumber from the light to repair his house. He argued that the dock had washed away, and Presqu'ile had been abandoned. The Department was willing to accept the offer of $40 but he never submitted a formal proposal.

In 1922, serious about divesting themselves of the site, the Department placed tenders in the local papers for the property and light. The only response came from the Canadian Wrecking Company in Toronto! When asked their price, they said they were too busy to examine the property. The next year a J.R. Brown offered ten dollars on the grounds that the property was worthless and the lighthouse should have been burned long ago. Worn down, the Department granted him both the lot and the light for ten dollars, and a deed was made out to his wife, Margaret Ann Brown. If the Department thought this was the end of their involvement,

they were wrong. For two years later, Brown wrote complaining that "the Estate of the late John McKenzie original owner of the land, claims that I have no rights to enter upon the water front for any purpose even to take a pail of water. They claim they bought the water front 500 feet out into the lake and some 500 or 600 feet of shore line."

At some point, a cottage was built adjacent to the light and around 1952 the two buildings were bought by Cecil Corfe. One condition of the sale was that vessels should be allowed to sail over the lighthouse property if the level of the Bay rose to accommodate them. This was not as unlikely a scenario as it seemed. For according to Cecil's son John, seiches (quickly rising or lowering water levels) have been known to occur on Georgian Bay when a strong west wind forces water into the stretch between Manitoulin Island and the top of the Bruce Peninsula and that water becomes "caught" in the Bay. "You might go out one day and find a lot of rocky beach and go out the next day and find it practically up to the door."

When the Corfes acquired the light, it had been so neglected, the wood looked like weathered barn board. Restoring it was no easy job but worth every penny, according to John, after he spent almost a year in this quiet getaway. "What a great feeling", he said, "to stand on the deck surrounding the big windows of the light and watch the freighters and steamers go by. Some of them even got to tooting their whistles as they passed down the sound. I felt like I was part of something vast." As perfect as it was for John, the light was also ideal for a persistent colony of cockroaches. After innumerable attempts to eradicate them he finally admitted defeat and even befriended one who waved his antennae each morning as he watched John shave. Since the previous owner had not felt it necessary to inform the Corfes of their co-habitants, John did not think it necessary to impart that information to the subsequent owners, "repugnance would turn to affection in time on their part."

Eventually, the cottage was sold to the Rotary Club who turned it into a youth camp. Mackenzie's old store became the camp's dining hall, and the lighthouse was torn down. Rumour has it that the disassembled lighthouse is presently lying up against a barn in a nearby farmyard. Maybe its story is not over yet.

Presqu'ile light, discontinued 1910.
– Sun-Times/County of Grey – Owen Sound Museum

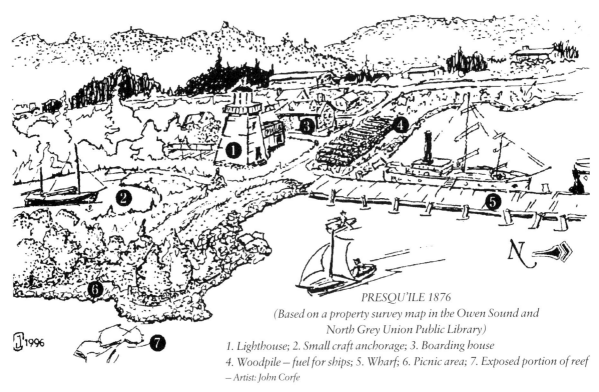

PRESQU'ILE 1876
(Based on a property survey map in the Owen Sound and
North Grey Union Public Library)
1. Lighthouse; 2. Small craft anchorage; 3. Boarding house
4. Woodpile – fuel for ships; 5. Wharf; 6. Picnic area; 7. Exposed portion of reef
– Artist: John Corfe

OWEN SOUND

---✦---

Dredging, Progress (and Confusion!)

In 1860, the enterprising Captain William Henry Smith, ship owner and pioneer of regular boat service on the Lakes, had a dilemma. How could he refute the government's belief that the river mouth at Owen Sound was unsuitable for a harbour? How could he convince them that the sandbar blocking the entrance was merely inconvenient, and could with their assistance, be removed?

His was an audacious plan. He ordered everything off-loaded from his steamer, the *Clifton*. Even the boilers were pumped dry. He had the anchors lowered into rowboats and had his men row until the line drew taut. The anchors were fixed hard into the clay, and then the crew winched the ship forward with the capstan. In this laborious manner, they eventually succeeded in dragging the vessel up and over the offending sandbar and towing it up the river to a small dock and celebratory crowd at what is now 11th street (formerly Peel St.) There the pleased Captain Smith had the *Clifton* photographed by a man he had hired from Toronto for the event. But this was only stage one of the enterprise. He and his photograph then rode horse-back all the way to Quebec City, the seat of government, and refused to leave until the first $12,000 towards dredging the sandbar had been approved.

As early as 1851, there was reference to a lighthouse in Owen Sound. Apparently, ships using the harbour paid a fee to maintain the lighthouse, a common practice in the United States, but uncommon in Canada. A customs declaration from the Port of Owen Sound, May 17, 1851 reads, "this is to certify that Mr. John Miller one of the owners of the schooner *Eliza White* of this port . . . has paid me one pound ten shilling being one shilling per ton for Lighthouse duties on the above schooner for the current year." However, little is known about these early lights as an 1874 fire burned most of the harbour records.

Although the harbour was taking shape, the dredging was going too slowly for some citizens. They were rankled that boat traffic bypassed their town, stopping

OWEN SOUND RANGE LIGHTS

Location: Mouth of Sydenham
 River
Type: Range lights
Earliest known date: 1851

Date: 1884
Description Front Light: Square white
 wooden tower
Height: 21 ft./6.3 m
Location: Right side of dredged channel
Light: Red dioptric light
Visibility: 6 miles/9.6 kms
Description Back Light: White wooden tower
Location: Western pier at mouth of river
Light: White dioptric
Visibility: 11 miles/17.6 kms

Date: 1895-6
Description Front Light: (old back range tower) –
 square wooden building, square iron lantern.
 White with vertical red stripe
Location: East side of Sydenham River mouth
Height: 34 ft./10.2 m
Light: Fixed red catoptric

Visibility: 7 miles/11.2kms
Description Back Light: New square wooden
 building, square wooden lantern. White with
 vertical red stripe
Location: SW of front tower
Height: 46 ft./13.8 m
Light: Fixed red catoptric
Visibility: 8 miles/12.8 kms

Date: 1909
Description Front Light: Square skeleton tower
 with sloping sides, surmounted by enclosed
 wooden watchroom and octagonal iron lantern
Height: 50 ft./15 m
Description Back Light: Same as front light
Height: 82 ft./24.6 m
Additional: Fog bell, east side of harbour in front
 of first range light

KEEPERS:
1880➤	George Scott Miller
1897-1903	Arch McLean
1903-1929	Alex Robertson
◄1949➤	E.C. Holmes

instead at the nearby hamlet of Presqu'ile. It was humiliating for a substantial community such as Owen Sound! In 1883 it was announced that the Canadian Pacific Railway Company's boats would come to Owen Sound if the harbour was dredged deeply enough. That was all confectionery merchant James McLauchlan and other enterprising local men needed to hear. Why not buy their own equipment to speed the process? In early April, they heard about a sale of dredges, scows and tugs to be held in Collingwood. Immediately, McLauchlan took off through mud, rain and melting snow and arrived in time to buy a No. 9 dredge, two scows and a tug. Then he had a horrible thought. What if rivals in Collingwood bought their own machinery and

dredged their harbour first? Without hesitating, he bought the other dredge and the remaining two scows. Then, much to his embarrassment,

*Volunteers returning from second Riel Rebellion debarking
from the CPR steamers in Owen Sound, 1885
– Archives of Ontario ACC9814-515961*

*Range tower in pre-1912
Owen Sound*
– National Archives of Canada
PA172536

he realized he did not have enough cash on hand. Undaunted, he scrounged the money somehow and was on his way.

As soon as the ice went out, the group set to work and by the time the CPR boats arrived the harbour was ready. The community of Owen Sound never looked back. A second set of range lights was built in '83 and '84 to guide mariners to the dredged channel at the mouth of the river. Within only twelve years, the burgeoning port of Owen Sound outgrew even these. It had become an important harbour — the eastern terminus of the CPR's steamer line. Better lights and a deeper channel were needed. This time, both the CPR and the government chipped in to improve the harbour. The approach was widened and deepened, and in 1896, the range lights were heightened, improved, and moved — again! A dredge remained a common sight in the harbour, and as piers and ranges moved and were added (one tower was formerly used at Pointe au Baril), the chart-seller in Owen Sound prospered!

But feverish harbour activity wound down quite abruptly when the CPR moved its headquarters from Owen Sound to Port McNicoll in 1912. It was a sad morning when, beginning at 8 a.m., at five minute intervals, each of the fleet's ships steamed away. Nevertheless, Owen Sound recovered, growing from its boisterous port town roots into a prosperous small manufacturing centre. Today, the only remnant of the days when freighters and steamers filled the harbour are the occasional cement barges, and grain freighters still coming in to Owen Sound's elevators.

Far left: Short wooden back range tower in front of warehouse (it apparently required height enhancement).
— National Archives of Canada PA195264

Left: Steel back range tower built on the exact spot of the shorter wooden one.
— National Archives of Canada PA195263

CPR Steamer Alberta at the dock, Owen Sound Harbour. Note the lighthouse on pier in distance.

— Bruce County Museum and Archives

MEAFORD

✛

Early steamers and schooners could not land at Meaford even though a wharf had existed since 1856. A sandbar blocked the mouth of the Bighead River, a predicament Meaford shared with its larger neighbour, Owen Sound. Eventually the harbour was dredged and by 1869 the residents could enjoy the spectacle of the steel-hulled *Chicora* or the *Francis Smith* racing into the harbour on their regular runs between Collingwood and Owen Sound. There was an on-going battle with the ever-encroaching sand resulting, in 1874, in an extension of the dock into deeper water and more dredging to improve the harbour. By 1882, Meaford had become quite busy as a port from which supplies were shipped to extend the ribbon of C.P.R. tracks in Western Canada. Farmers brought barrels of apples down to the dock to be picked up twice weekly for delivery to Parry Sound, Little Current, Killarney, and beyond; and when they were not off at fishing grounds as far away as the Bustard Islands, fish tugs filled the harbour.

At the turn of the century a new grain elevator was completed and the Grand Trunk Railway moved its terminus to the water, turning Meaford into another Great Lakes grain-shipping port. Regrettably for the town, this status lasted only twelve years, as the terminal was destroyed by fire in 1913. The harbour continued to need regular dredging to accommodate the ships that were still coming in, like those carrying hardwoods for the town's hardwood flooring industry.

The acetylene light, installed in 1906, no longer needed daily tending. Instead, the light was serviced by the *St. Heliers* out of Midland. Former resident John Hillis recalls standing on the old iron bridge one stormy November morning, watching the waves sweep the old breakwater. Before his eyes, one giant wave completely obscured the acetylene light, and when it pulled away, the light was gone. Presto.

MEAFORD

c.1875
Description: Light hoisted up wooden frame
Light: Fixed white
Visibility: 5 miles/8 kms

1878-1880
Location: End of wooden breakwater
Description: Short square tapered tower, polygonal lantern
Removed: 1906

1906
Location: West end of breakwater extension built c.1901 (removed 1987/88)
Description: Black, cylindrical, steel gas holder surmounted by lantern
Height: 20 ft./6 m above water
Light: Originally white occulting, acetylene gas; by 1955, flashing green

Visibility: 8 miles/12.8 kms
Fog Horn: Hand fog horn on west pier until c.1930s. Afterwards, fire siren, or "wildcat" served as answering fog horn when needed
Light Removed: 1987/88

Date unknown (pre-1955)
Location: Southwest of western breakwater
Type: Back range light placed on roof of Waterworks building (now the Meaford Museum)
Height: 32 ft./9.6 m
Light: Fixed red
Discontinued: 1987/88
Present: Lights on east pier and new yacht basin pier

KEEPER:
1877-1916 ➤   Samuel Dutcher

Acetylene gas light being installed on east concrete wall, 1906.
– Courtesy of Knight's Pictorial Meaford

John Hillis standing on newer acetylene light, c. 1940s.
– Courtesy of John Hillis

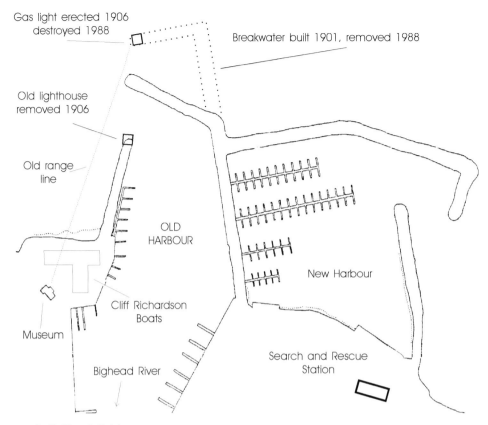

Gas light erected 1906
destroyed 1988

Breakwater built 1901, removed 1988

Old lighthouse
removed 1906

Old range
line

OLD
HARBOUR

New Harbour

Museum

Cliff Richardson
Boats

Search and Rescue
Station

Bighead River

— from map supplied by Victor L. Knight

Old lighthouse on wooden pier, 1897, with Mr. Sing's
Olivet *and Jas. Pillgrem's* Mascot *in foreground. The*
Mascot *was one of the fish tugs that ran out of the*
harbour. The lighthouse was on a pier that jutted out
from the east side of the harbour.
— Courtesy of Knight's Pictorial Meaford

Early Meaford Harbour. Note Meaford Waterworks Plant (now the
Museum) with adjacent tall chimney in background left of centre.
A range light was later shown from its roof.
— Courtesy of Knight's Pictorial Meaford

THORNBURY

Front range light on outer end of west break-water pier stands on spot where the first light was hung on a mast in 1887 to mark the harbour entrance. When the back range tower was added in 1901, the two lights led through the centre of the dredged channel. The colour of the back range light was changed from white to red in 1903 to distinguish it from town lights.
— National Archives of Canada PA172520

THORNBURY

Date: 1887
Location: Outer end
   of west breakwater
   pier
Description: Originally
   on mast; c.1902
   white square wooden tower
Light: Fixed white dioptric
Visibility: 10 miles/16 kms
Upgraded: 1911

Date: 1901
Location: West side of Beaver River
Description: Back range, mast with
   daymark and shed
Light: Fixed white; then fixed red
   dioptric, 1903
Fog signal: Hand fog horn

KEEPERS:
1887-1916➤   Robert Lowe
◄1949➤   H. Pether

Nottawasaga lighthouse. In 1885, a red sector of glass was added to the light to warn vessels of the lethal shoal that extended between the light and Collingwoood Harbour. Vessels making Collingwood were safe if they kept north westward of the red sector. Note the old dwelling in ruins beside the tower.
— Courtesy of David Baird

NOTTAWASAGA
ISLAND

———— ✛ ————

Captain George Collins was disgruntled when, in May 1858, he was "banished" to the hinterland of the Isle of Coves on the tip of the Bruce Peninsula to look after the temporary lantern pole. Nottawasaga, the new light just two miles from his Collingwood home, was the position he had coveted and for which he had applied. His discontent might partially explain why he was described by the head engineer during construction at Cove, as obnoxious, selfish, demanding and of unkindly spirit.

Within the year, David McBeath, Nottawasaga's lightkeeper, received a letter from Collins expressing a strong desire to exchange positions. Collins may have made it look more attractive by saying that, at present, Cove had no assistant and suggesting that McBeath could save money by having his own son do the job. McBeath agreed and their transfers received official approval from the Department of Public Works in Quebec City soon after. In April 1860, Collins began the first of his thirty-one seasons on Nottawasaga. (See *Cove Island* for McBeath's harrowing first season on Cove.)

The Hero of Nottawasaga

Collins' bumpy start might also be put down to a drastic change in lifestyle. Since the age of thirteen he had been at sea, first as crewman and then as captain. After marrying his beloved Sophia in Newport, England in 1831, two and half years passed before she next heard from him. When he finally turned up, thin and heavily

Captain George Collins (keeper 1860-1890).
— *Courtesy of Jamie McMaster*

Sophia Collins died in Nottawasaga house after a bout of influenza. Photo taken 1880s.
— *Courtesy of Jamie McMaster*

NOTTAWASAGA ISLAND

Location: North point of
    Nottawasaga Island 2 miles
    from Collingwood Harbour
Built: 1858
Description: Limestone Imperial
    Tower, separate limestone
    dwelling
Height: 85 ft./28.7 m
Light: Fixed white second order dioptric,
    switched to revolving prior to 1879; one red
    section of glass warned of shoals southeast-
    ward of tower
Visibility: 17 miles/27.2 kms
Automated: 1959
Present: Tower, ruins of house. Light flashes
    white every 10 seconds.

KEEPERS:

1858-1859	David McBeath
1860-1890	George Collins
1891-1902	A.G. Clark
1903-1911	Fred Burmister
1912- 1913	Jim McNabb
1914-1915	Mrs. McNabb
1915-1924	Thomas Bowie
1924-1932	Thomas Foley
1933-1942	Samuel Hillen
1943-1952	William Hogg
1953-1956	James Keith
1957-1959	James Dineen
1960-1961	Ross White
1962-1963	Harry Ward
1964-1983	Wilfred Johnston

bearded, she did not recognize the stranger standing before her. After they emigrated to Canada, their son Charles was born and it may have been a desire to spend more time with his family that prompted Collins to turn to light-keeping.

Collins was a man with an impeccable reputation. He took his job seriously and the light-house was always immaculate and in excellent working order. He so beautified the grounds that they became a favoured picnic location for the townspeople, and as a devout Methodist, he offered Sunday prayer services. At one point he even sued a Collingwood citizen who jeopardized the light by starting a brush fire.

A Fenian Scare

For a brief period during the 1860s, the Nottawasaga light took on military importance. The Fenian Brotherhood, a group of Irish patriots and exiles in the United States, organized terrorist attacks against Britain to further their fight for Irish independence. Their strategists hit upon the idea of hurting the British by attacking Canada. When reports reached the province that armed Fenians were assembling in Chicago for a planned assault on Toronto via Collingwood, the Georgian Bay community

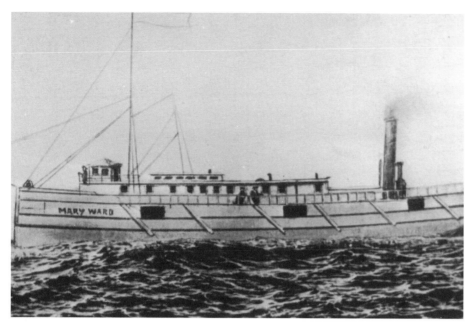

George Collins saved 24 passengers from the steamer Mary Ward.
– National Archives of Canada C2679

mobilized. While the Collingwood Rifles patrolled the shore day and night, out on Nottawasaga, lightkeeper George Collins and his assistant were ordered to keep a vigil for enemy ships. If he sighted any at night, Collins was to signal the town by extinguishing the light. Women and children would be evacuated, and the men would prepare for battle. One night, the light did go out. Immediately Collingwood's evacuation plan went into action. A group of men charged up and down the streets rousing women and children, while others made sure the trains were ready. The excited townspeople were quite stunned when twenty minutes later the light reappeared. A local fog had wreaked havoc on their carefully laid plans. This was as close as Collingwood ever came to a Fenian raid.

SAVING LIVES

The *Mary Ward*

During his illustrious career, Collins was tested on many desperate occasions. One calm Sunday night in November 1872, a farmer saw the *Mary Ward* stranded on Milligan's Reef, her whistle blowing frantically, her lights glowing. As she was not taking on water, no one was aware of any immediate danger. A passenger described the situation for the Collingwood *Enterprise-Bulletin*:

There was no confusion and all seemed to take the matter lightly since they were near land and it was so calm. I can remember standing out on the stern after she had struck looking up at the stars and feeling on my face the gentle warm south-west breeze. . . I could hear them singing in the cabin . . . Frank Moberly and Mr. Corbett, part owner of the steamer, embarked in a small boat leaving the *Mary Ward* around 10 p.m. for the shore of Craigleith, then to walk into Collingwood and obtain assistance.

That calm did not last long. Another passenger later told the newspaper:

Shortly after midnight the wind suddenly shifted, and heavy, black, swiftly moving clouds arose over the mountain and the stars soon disappeared. There was an ominous moaning in the rigging, the import of which I knew too well. There was an uncanny stillness . . . After a little time I did suggest to the watchman that he call the Captain. This he did and the Captain realized the danger at once and began blowing the *Mary Ward*'s whistle again frantically and calling all hands on deck.

Too late. The storm hit, pushing huge breakers over the stern. On deck, passengers braced themselves against the railings. Drenched and numb, they wondered which blow would tear the ship to pieces. Eight panicked passengers launched a lifeboat, but only yards from the steamer the yawl flipped and was sucked under.

The tug *Mary Ann* which had been dispatched by Moberly and Corbett, tried to reach the ship but was turned back by the ferocious seas. In desperation another six passengers launched the last lifeboat. Among them was Charles Campbell who had his eyes glued to a light glowing from his house where his pregnant wife awaited his return. The lifeboat was flung into the waves that seethed over the smooth limestone shelves and within moments all six were drowned.

Late that afternoon, when the storm abated, George Collins and his twenty-one-year-old son Charles launched a lifeboat and headed for

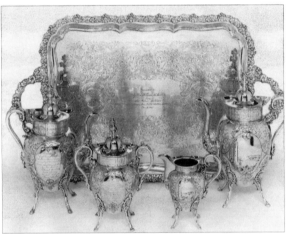

Silver tea service awarded to lightkeeper George Collins in gratitude for saving four Masonic Lodge members from Boston in 1879.
– Courtesy of Jamie McMaster

Collingwood. By the time they reached harbour, only one oar remained. Three brave fishermen volunteered to join the Collins' rescue attempt. The group of five rowed out to the *Mary Ward* and saved the remaining passengers (either nine or twenty-four depending on the account) just before the battered steamer split apart and slid down onto the ledges that still bear her name.

Captain Johnston of the *Mary Ward* later claimed the ship struck Milligan's Reef because he had confused the light from a Craigleith tavern with Collingwood harbour. (But how could he confuse the two with the Nottawasaga lighthouse off his port bow? Serious allegations were levelled against him: alcohol was involved; an unproven logging device he had designed was being used; the compass was malfunctioning . . . . But at the funeral for the fourteen people of the *Mary Ward*, the question in most minds was why the Captain had allowed passengers and crew to settle down for the night when the barometer reading was so low?

For their heroic rescue, George and Charles Collins and the fishermen were each awarded fifteen dollars. Collins was no stranger to such honours. Previously, he had been the recipient of a gold watch commemorating four other life-saving acts. And in 1879, seven years after the *Mary Ward* rescue, George Collins was presented with a silver tea service from the Masonic Lodge in Boston after a spectacular rescue of four of their members in which the 68-year-old Collins had capsized four times before reaching the imperiled men. It is estimated that Collins saved a staggering 52 lives in his 31 years of service.

In 1880, the cruel, fickle sea dealt Captain George Collins a devastating blow. His only son Charles, now married with four children, was fishing the ledges that took down the *Mary Ward* when a surprise wind shift caught his sail. The jib knocked Charles into the water where he became entangled in the nets and drowned. George Collins was devastated. His relatives remember him pacing the shores of Nottawasaga the entire night, anguishing over the one life he had been unable to save. Some comfort came from his grandchildren who lived at the light until Charles' wife remarried. After his death in 1897, his grandchildren imagined the blink of the Nottawasaga light was George waving to them.

Captain Arthur Clark (keeper 1891-1902) surrounded by his children.
— Courtesy of Arthur Clark

The Captains

As Collingwood gained the reputation of being the "Chicago of the North", the Nottawasaga light became one of the most important on the upper Lakes. The lightkeeping position continued to be reserved for other highly-

Captain Jim McNabb (keeper 1912-1913)
— Courtesy of Jamie McMaster

respected and accomplished captains like the formidable Collins.

Nottawasaga's third lightkeeper (1890-1902), Arthur Clark left his Michigan school to become a sailor at the age of thirteen, upon the death of his parents. His first journey was down the Mississippi River. He later was promoted to captain and ran the Buffalo-Chicago route before settling in Collingwood in 1853. His schooner, the *Sonora*, was the first to carry mail between Collingwood and Manitoulin Island. His memory lives on in the local name for Nottawasaga Island – Clark's Island.

Captain Jim McNabb (1912-13), Nottawasaga's fifth keeper, has gone down in the annals of Canadian history as one of the two captains who piloted Colonel Garnet Wolseley and his troops up Lake Superior to the Lakehead, on their way to quell the Red River Rebellion in 1870.

Nottawasaga Today

Tropical blue-green waters stretch out over the limestone shelves surrounding Nottawasaga Island. The grounds once carefully groomed by George Collins have been overtaken by bushes and poison ivy. Instead of picnickers and church-goers, the island is home to double-crested Cormorants, Great Blue Herons, a Green Heron, Black-crowned Night-Herons, Herring Gulls, Mallards, Gadwalls, and Red-breasted Mergansers. The day we visited with former lightkeeper Jim Keith, the tall, whitewashed tower gleamed against the clear blue sky.

Foley children picnic at Nottawasaga.
— Courtesy of Archer family

William Grenville Foley, son of keeper Thomas Foley, was named after the lighthouse tender the Grenville.
— Archer Collection/ Huronia Museum L995.0002.0005

Standing high up in the light, we had an excellent view of the grounds and two crumbling walls, all that is left of the original limestone house. He explained how the old house was ravaged by a fire started by a spark from the stove pipe, and how, as a final blow, vandals broke into the tower and tossed large stones through the dwelling roof. The elements have done the rest.

After the 1959 house fire, Nottawasaga's light was converted to acetylene gas and the weights that worked the old Fresnel lens were removed. Wilfred Johnston (1964-83) recalled having to lift the 400 lb. acetylene cylinders into the tower with a rope. A few nicks in the stairs remain. Another big scar stands as a reminder of the night the cable that supported the weights snapped, sending the weights crashing to the bottom of the tower. The Fresnel lens is gone, and now the lighthouse beam emanates from a battery-powered light bulb charged by solar panel.

Nottawasaga Island, 1934.
— National Archives of Canada PA182873

COLLINGWOOD

———————— ✛ ————————

Collingwood could hardly contain its pride the day the Ontario, Simcoe, and Huron Railway (later the Northern Railway of Canada) first rolled into town in 1855. Located at the southernmost point of Georgian Bay, the town was the key link in the "northern" shipping route for goods coming from the Great West to lucrative eastern markets. This route proved to be faster than the traditional one through southern Lake Huron and Lake Erie and soon won most of the traffic. Collingwood took to its new role as a major shipping terminus with gusto and in its heyday, ships were crammed along the docks like sardines in a tin. An 1855 map described Collingwood in glowing terms, concluding "it may well be doubted that any City in Canada or the United States was ever founded with fairer prospects of a rapid and substantial Growth than the embryo City of Collingwood."

Collingwood Life Saving Station

As traffic on the Great Lakes increased, the need for lifesaving stations to assist sailors in distress became obvious. The first Canadian station was established at Cobourg on Lake Ontario, in 1882. More were desperately needed, but nothing was done until Dr. John Platt directed scathing criticism in the House of Commons the following year at the government's seeming indifference to public safety. The speech spurred a twenty-four year construction effort during which thirteen lifesaving stations were built, including Collingwood's in 1885, the only one on Georgian Bay.

The Parliamentary Sessional Papers report that in September 1885, Patrick Doherty was Collingwood's first federally appointed coxswain. He was a respected boat builder and brother of Robert Doherty, the keeper of the harbour lights from 1878. The Collingwood crew consisted of six men hand-picked by Doherty. Crews were mainly fishermen who could be alerted easily by a flag or gun

Above: Map showing the position of Collingwood in reference to course of trade.
— *National Archives of Canada NMC23888*

Right: Collingwood breakwater light *as proposed, 1872.*
— *National Archives of Canada NMC22942*

Below: Detail from "Chart of Collingwood Harbour and It's Connections," by William Gibbard.
— *National Archives of Canada NMC24034*

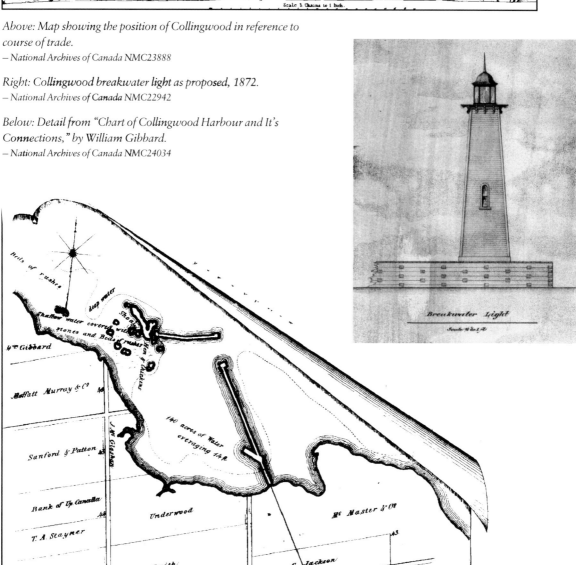

Hauling a Dobbins lifeboat.
— Freshwater, *Summer 1988*

signal, as most of the fishermen and boat builders lived on the first block of Maple Street, close to the water and their operations. Each was paid $1.50 per bi-monthly drill which meant launching the boat, practicing artificial respiration, and maintaining the station and boat according to a set of specific departmental rules. Doherty was paid $75 a year for his services and for writing monthly reports to the Department of Marine and Fisheries in Ottawa. The Collingwood vessel, valued at $575, was a 25-foot Dobbins self-righting lifeboat. These boats were heavy, so while relatively easy to pull in good weather, they were difficult in headwinds and big seas. For this reason, many stations sacrificed their self-righting advantages in favour of lighter, more manoeuvrable boats.

Records about the Collingwood crew and station are scarce, but in general each station consisted of a wooden building which housed the rescue boat and temporary crew quarters. (Collingwood had many buildings along the water that could have served this purpose.) Boats were launched using a marine railway and winch or tackle. By the end of World War I, the importance of lifesaving stations began to decline. Wireless was being regularly used on board ship; the number of sailing schooners was

COLLINGWOOD

1858
Location: Outer end of west
    breakwater pier
Description: White wooden tower
    and lantern
Light: Fixed red catoptric, then
    white dioptric
Visibility: 6 miles/9.6 kms
Fog Horn: Hand crank

1884
Location: On cribwork pier
Description: Mast with shed; then square white
    wooden tower, red wooden lantern
Light: Fixed red dioptric

1902
Location: On shore
Description: Back tower of outer range for 1884
    light. Galvanized square steel skeleton tower,
    surmounted by enclosed white wooden
    watch-room. Range leads into curve in
    dredged channel
Light: Fixed red catoptric

1906
Location: On cribwork pier
Description: Back tower of inner range for 1884
    light leads from curve in dredged channel to
    Grand Trunk Railway freight shed wharves.
    Square tapered white wood.
Light: Fixed white catoptric

Present
Shore range: front — white circular daymark;
    back — white square skeleton tower, both
    fixed red.

KEEPERS:
1878-1882	Robert Doherty
1882-1883	William Bishop
1883-1903	Andrew Lockerbie
1904-1912	J.W. Lunan
1912-1916➤	J. Wilde
◄1922-1932	Isaac VanKoughnet
1932-1952	Barton VanKoughnet
1959➤	Ross White

declining; navigational equipment and weather reporting was improving; and shipping traffic in general was decreasing. By 1938, Point Pelee on Lake Erie was the only remaining lifesaving station on the Canadian Great Lakes.

Collingwood tower struck by lightning, 1940.
— *National Archives of Canada PA172470*

Georgian Bay Captains, 1891. Standing left to right: Captain Foote and Captain Bassett; seated left to right: Captain McNabb, Captain Collins, and Captain (Black Pete) Campbell. The captains were notorious for racing each other.
— *Courtesy of Jamie McMaster*

Collingwood lifesaving crew looking dapper, oars poised.
— *Collingwood Museum*

CHRISTIAN ISLAND

✝

For the Naval Establishment at Penetanguishene to receive its staples of molasses, flour, spices, and rum, ships had to sail up the Nottawasaga River to Georgian Bay then transfer their cargo into schooners to sail around the Tiny Township peninsula. This meant they had to pass through the difficult mile-wide Christian Island passage. In fact, all traffic between the three white settlements on Georgian Bay — Penetanguishene, Collingwood, and Owen Sound — had to use this route and the trip was normally taken during daylight hours because of the absence of navigational aids. The problem was a broad sand bar stretching from Bar Point to the mainland at Gidley Point. A lighthouse was imperative.

In 1850, Indian chiefs had surrendered the 30,000 islands on the Bay to the British Government which immediately established a reserve for them on Christian Island. Following the decision to build a lighthouse, in 1856 the Indians surrendered over 35 acres of the most southeasterly part of the island for this purpose. Christian Island light was the first of Georgian Bay's Imperial towers to be completed, thereby gaining the honour of being the first official lighthouse built on the Bay. However, for some reason, it was the last of these towers to be lit. The shortest structure of the group, it was built to enable schooners and the wooden paddle steamers to navigate the passage safely at night.

Christian Island's first keeper was the resplendent William Hoar. He kept the light for ten years, and upon retirement was replaced by his equally colourful son, John. Taking over at age 22, John later claimed he had been the youngest light-keeper in the Dominion at the time. Apparently John Hoar was not highly regarded by the Department. When in 1888 he wrote requesting a new fence, the report was

Christian Island, 1921.
– National Archives of Canada PA182861

CHRISTIAN ISLAND

Location: Bar Point on southeast
      spit of Christian Island
Date: 1857 but first permanently
      lit in 1859
Description: White circular stone
      Imperial tower with adjacent
      stone dwelling
Height: 60 ft./15.5 m
Light: Fixed white fourth order dioptric
Fog horn: Hand crank
Present: House in ruins. Dock and other build-
      ings long gone. Windows boarded up on tower
      and original stairs removed. Lantern room
      cut up for scrap during World War II. Fixed
      white light now sits atop lanternless tower.
Discontinued: 1922

KEEPERS:
1857-1868   Captain William Hoar, R.N.
1868-1891   John H. Hoar
1891-1914   Allan Collins
1914-1922   Thomas Marchildon

annotated by the inspector, "I cannot help feeling to a certain extent the repairs are required through carelessness and shiftlessness on the part of the keeper." However the request was granted and Hoar had a workman erect the fence. When he later submitted a bill for $2.50 to cover the man's wages, it was refused with the terse annotation, "if a man cannot put up a board fence without assistance, he is not worth much."

During his long tenure on Christian Island, John Hoar witnessed his share of marine disasters. On a stormy October day in 1873, the schooner *Elizabeth* stranded herself on the island, and on Nov. 22, 1879, John Hoar was

William Hoar,
Christian Island's first
lightkeeper, sporting
his regalia as a Royal
Arch Mason, Manitou
Chapter, Collingwood.
– William Northcott
Collection

perhaps the last person to see the doomed *Waubuno*. It was 6 a.m. when she passed, and all he could make out in the darkness were the steamer's cabin lights bobbing up and down in the turbulent waters. Then she disappeared into the thick, blinding snow. Apart from two lumbermen hearing the *Waubuno*'s whistle at noon, she was never seen nor heard from again.

Hoar became dissatisfied with Christian's accommodations and in 1891 he agreed to switch positions with Allan Collins, the Hope Island keeper, who wanted his children to attend school on Christian Island. Relations quickly soured when Hoar was denied a request to take with him some stables and a shed for which he had paid. A quarrel broke out between the two keepers. Hoar accused Collins of not paying fully for a sailboat; Collins accused Hoar

c. 1880. Note the old fence before John Hoar had it replaced. When he billed the Department for the labourer's wages, they responded, "if a man cannot put up a board fence without assistance, he is not worth much."
— *National Archives of Canada PA143582*

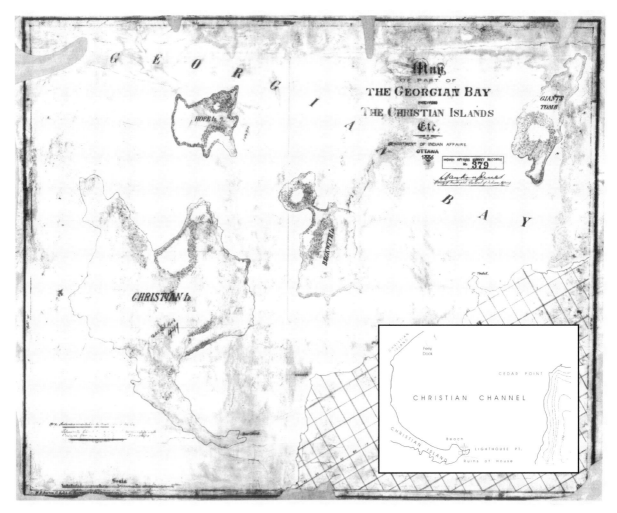

Christian Island lighthouse, at the bottom tip of Bar Point, looked over the busy ship passage between Bar Point and the Township of Tiny peninsula.
— National Archives of Canada NMC222307

Christian Island wharf under construction. Lightkeeper Marchildon (bearded) with the saw.
— William Northcott Collection

of taking his stove. The final straw came when the Superintendent sided with Collins, and Collins was awarded seventy dollars to make

repairs on the island. At that point, Hoar's nose bent permanently out of joint. These antics later proved to be only a preamble to his short but eventful tenure on Hope Island.

The Christian Island light was abandoned in 1922 after over sixty years of service. At that point the tower and house were already being affected by frost. Today, the light is in the most pitiful state of all the Imperial towers. The wharf is gone and the keeper's residence is in ruins. During the war her iron lantern was taken for scrap metal and no trace is left of the shed or the infamous fence.

HOPE ISLAND

———— ✦ ————

Saving the Old Lighthouse

D r. Bob Stubbins, a cottager at Silver Birch Beach, could not believe the rumour – the lighthouse at Hope Island was to be destroyed. It was a landmark that had served mariners for nearly a century. After confirmation from the Coast Guard, Stubbins offered to buy it. The Coast Guard wrote that because others had also shown an interest in owning the light, Stubbins would have to place a formal bid. This letter arrived just two days before the deadline. As it turned out Stubbins was the only bidder and soon the proud owner of a lighthouse – provided he could move it within a year.

The lowest bid for its removal and restoration totalled $100,000. In addition, Stubbins would be liable for damages if the structure fell into the shipping lanes during the move. Stubbins admitted defeat. But because of his efforts, removal of the lighthouse was delayed several years, time enough for the old building to celebrate its 100th birthday, thereby requiring it to be reviewed by the Federal Heritage Building Review Office. The Review Office's perspective is national, and while other lighthouses of similar design were recommended for protection, Hope was not. The onus fell back on the local community. Over the years, Hope has been vandalized and neglected. Now boarded up, she silently awaits a decision about her future while contemplating her eventful past . . .

A Legend of Murder

"Watch out or the boys might get you."

Today the dank cellar with its crumbling limestone walls is barely illuminated by the dull light filtering through one dirty window. When Dorthea Herron was

HOPE ISLAND

Location: NE point of Hope
    Island
Built: 1884
Description: Square white
    wooden tower, dwelling
    attached
Height: 57 ft./17.1 m
Light: Revolving white catoptric; fixed white
    c.1918
Visibility: 12 miles/21 kms
Fog signal: Diaphone 1908
Additional: Diesel generating plant for elec-
    tricity c.1940; Radio beacon synchronized
    with fog alarm for distance finding; Radio-
    telephone
Present: Skeleton tower next to dilapidated old
    tower, flashing white light every 5 secs. Wharf
    and boathouse, earlier fog plant, generator
    room, radio room, two bungalows, heli-pad.

KEEPERS:

1884-1885	Charles Tizard
1885-1886	Mrs. Tizard
1887-1890	Allan Collins
1891-1893	John Hoar
1893-1898	Thomas Marchildon
1899-1910	Charles Vallee
1911-1911	Thomas Marchildon
1911-1912	P. Leblanc
1912-1914	Thomas Marchildon
1915-1916	J. Stewart
1917-1940	William Ross Wallace
1941-1963	Arthur Alexander Herron
1964-1965	Dalton Crawford
1966-1966	C.D. Graeme Webb
1967-1972	Marvin Graham
1973-1984	Ray Dawson
1985-1985	Elwood Richardson
1986-1987	Ernie McCombe

little, the assistant, Lou Brandon liked to frighten her as she descended the rickety steps; "watch out or the 'boys' might get you." The "boys" were two fishermen allegedly murdered by Hope Island's third lightkeeper, John Hoar. To put it mildly, Hoar was an ill-tempered man. One account states he tried to commit suicide and when he was stopped by François Marchildon and William Lacourse, he reacted violently. On his death bed, Hoar is said to have confessed to murdering the men and tossing them into a well he had built himself. (The well is no longer visible on the lighthouse grounds.) Dorthea recalls the story of the RCMP investigation as told by her parents, "they went through the lighthouse with a fine-tooth comb. They went to the old ice house, dug under it, dug every-where . . . ."

Thomas Marchildon Receives a Shotgun Welcome

As Achille Marchildon (age 97), son of light-keeper Thomas Marchildon (1893-8, 1911, 1912-13) tells it, Hoar was a "crazy bugger". This is his version of the legendary story of his father's near murder.

Thomas Marchildon was in the interior of the

This wooden cabin, nicknamed the "Royal York" by William Wallace, was where John Hoar was living at the time he shot at Thomas Marchildon.
– Courtesy of Jim Wallace

Men in front of Hope Island light, 1909, the year after the fog plant was erected.
— Archives of Ontario

Thomas Marchildon (bearded) and family in front of Hope light, 1911.
– Courtesy of Marchildon family

island when a bullet whizzed past his head. He ran for his life. It didn't take much imagination to surmise the perpetrator was John Hoar. The former keeper was still living on the Island and still sore about his demotion. Marchildon charged to the lighthouse and grabbed his gun, then ran to Hoar's cabin and waited. Not long after, Hoar entered, put down his rifle, and peered through the cracks in the wall at the lighthouse. "You look'n for me?" Marchildon snapped, grabbing Hoar's gun. Hoar spun around to find himself facing straight down the gun barrel. Marchildon headed back to the lighthouse and told Charles Vallee to get the police. (The dutiful Marchildon would not leave the lighthouse himself.) Vallee set out in a sailboat, taking nearly a day before landing at Thunder Bay Beach, then walked into

Lafontaine to contact the police. Shortly thereafter, Hoar was arrested and jailed. Achille Marchildon still marvels at Hoar's audacity. He is convinced he tried to kill his father in order to get the lightkeeping position back.

Former Lighthouse Children Return

Keeper William Wallace arrived at Hope in 1917 and stayed until 1940 when his assistant Alexander Herron took over for the next 23 seasons. In the early years, Hope was equipped with a diaphone fog horn operated by two steam engines that ran the compressors. The large 65-foot chimney behind the power house belched smoke continuously as the fires were kept banked in order to bring the boilers to full steam at the first sign of fog. In an interview with Juanita Keefe, William Wallace's wife Pearl described arriving for the first time, "they burnt soft coal and everything was thick with black coal dust." Eventually the soft coal was replaced with coal oil and sometime later the steam engines were replaced with diesel engines. Mrs. Wallace remarked, "I don't know where they got 'em but it's a wonder Bill and Alex weren't suffocated with the way those things smoked.

> When the inspector came one day I said to him, 'I don't know how it is that you bring all the junk to Hope Island.'"

By the 1930s, the shipping lanes were almost empty as the number of freighters had dropped and pleasure boats were few. The only regular visitors were some sport fishermen who had a shanty on the island. For women, the light could be particularly lonely. Pearl Wallace remembered, "you didn't see many women

Hope Island lighthouse.
– Courtesy of Jim Wallace

Pearl and William Wallace. On her 89th birthday she told reporters she did not care if she ever saw Hope Island again; "as I always say, if there's an island in heaven, my husband will have me parked on it."
—Wallace Collection/ Huronia Museum L995.0007.0006

to discover its weather was completely clear. The fog held for three days at which time they decided to attempt a return to the Westerns. Pearl Wallace said she would not bid them goodbye because they would be back, and sure enough they were. She also predicted that the government boat would soon come out to investigate and shortly they saw the smoke of the *Murray Stewart*. A passing C.P.R. boat had reported that the Westerns' light was out.

at Hope Island in those days. One fall I went into the telegraph office in Midland to send a telegram to my sister. I looked at the girl in the office and said 'you are the first woman I have seen in months.'" Even contact with neighbouring lighthouses such as Giants Tomb and the Westerns was rare unless precipitated by chance. One night the Wallaces awakened to find the lightkeepers from the Westerns on their dock. They had taken advantage of a sunny afternoon to go for a boat ride when fog suddenly rolled in obscuring the island. They travelled helplessly around and around, wondering why the Hope fog horn wasn't sounding. When they finally happened upon Hope they were amazed

For the children of these two keepers, Jim Wallace and Dorthea Herron, returning to Hope brought back many memories, especially those centred around the kitchen. Jim fondly recalls his mother quilting in the corner by a coal oil light but shudders at the thought of all the salted food he ate. With no refrigeration, everything from fish to eggs had to be preserved in salt. On hot afternoons the family would eat dinner in the summer kitchen at the back of the house but only after his father had fumigated the room with Fly-Tox, shut the doors, then returned to sweep up several dustpans of dead flies. For Dorthea, spying the unpainted spot on the kitchen wall where a clock once hung evoked a picture of her mother,

Alex Herron (1941-63) polishing the lens.
—The Globe and Mail

Visitors were rare at Hope. Wallaces (at left of group) on punt.
—Wallace Collection

she was just like the books: laundry on Monday, ironing on Tuesday . . . . Mother had a whistle and dinner was at twelve noon. She would never say 'I'm too tired, or too tied up doing this – I'll just put out sandwiches.' It had to be a hot meal at 12:00.

Merle Herron setting the clock in the spring for another season's regimentation.
– Star Weekly, April 28, 1945

Death Of A Pilot

Howard Warner recalls Alex Herron's story about a Harvard training plane that crashed northwest of the lighthouse on April 13, 1942. A Royal Canadian Air Force search plane located the wreckage and the tug *Bayport* was sent out to raise it. Something was peculiar – the pilot's parachute and uniform were folded neatly on the seat but there was no body. Alex found the dead airman along Hope's shore five days later. The pilot had survived the crash and made his way to shore, but had died of injuries or hypothermia. Alex signaled the search planes which then dropped a parachute with instructions to take the body to a passing freighter. When the *Emperor* was sighted, Alex loaded the body into a boat and headed for the ship. But the captain forgot to shut down his engines soon enough. The ship drifted past Hope and down the Bay, Alex chasing it through the ice floes, the

corpse propped in the bow. Alex was in a rage by the time he finally caught the *Emperor*, halfway to Giants Tomb. He cursed every one of the crew within earshot for being so inconsiderate and for putting him at such risk.

Radio Days – Tragedy on Hope

In 1944 Hope entered the communications age. The Department of Transport erected a one-hundred-foot radio beacon, added a transmitter room to the fog horn building, and built living quarters for a wireless operator. Norman Lancaster became the first licensed operator. He suffered from diabetes and so when he caught a cold and showed no signs of getting better, Alex Herron became concerned. He inquired whether Norman was taking his insulin and was assured he was. Nevertheless Alex remained uneasy. He pleaded with Norm to call the VBC (the Midland coast station) to ask the *St. Heliers* to get him ashore. Soon after, Alex noticed Norm was talking irrationally. At that point Alex wrote a telegram, dragged Norm to the transmitter and ordered him to send it. The VBC operator later

Assistant and radio-beacon operator, Howard Warner and dog Pat in front of the transmitter tower c. 1945.
"My first reaction was sheer horror that I had dedicated myself to this isolated, God-forsaken spot."
His opinion soon changed.
– Courtesy of Howard Warner

told Alex that he knew something was seriously wrong because he could barely decipher the message.

The *St. Heliers* was pulling up buoys near Thunder Bay on Lake Superior. She set sail immediately but did not arrive until six the following morning, two hours too late. Norman was dead. The radio beacon station was shut down for the remaining season. Howard Warner, the man hired the following year as radio-beacon operator and Alex's assistant wonders why the Department of Transport allowed a diabetic to take such an isolated job. When Howard arrived on March 15, 1945, "my first reaction was sheer horror that I had dedicated myself to this isolated, God-forsaken spot" and the first thing he did was to teach Alex enough Morse Code so that he could use the transmitter in an emergency.

Old coal chimney and new radio beacon tower show Hope in transition.
– Courtesy of Howard Warner

Dorthea Herron as a young girl, c. 1947
– Arthur Collection/ Huronia Museum L995.0009.0063

A Close Call: The Birth of Dorthea Herron

The radio proved to be a God-send when Merle Herron became pregnant. At the age of 45, and with two grown sons at war, she was understandably concerned at first. But after being assured by the doctor that she was healthy, she began to relax. As September neared, Merle's

presence became a constant worry to Howard. These were the days before helicopters and no one could predict where the *St. Heliers* would be at the required time. Six-foot waves weren't uncommon, so how could they ever take Merle to shore in a boat? Obviously, Alex Herron and Howard Warner would be attending the birth! When a pleasure boat pulled into the dock Labour Day weekend, one of the passengers was an obstetrician and the sight of Merle alarmed him. He cautioned her to get ashore immediately but she said she would know when to go. Around 8 a.m. on September 27, Alex shouted that Merle was in labour and Howard must alert VBC that an extreme emergency existed. VBC then had to contact the *St. Heliers*, get Doctor Johnson aboard and set sail immediately. The hours of waiting seemed endless, but around 11 a.m. the *St. Heliers* came steaming in. Merle was soon on her way to the hospital, fretting as she boarded, "I didn't even have time to fix my hair." Around 9 p.m. that evening Alex radioed Howard that Dorthea had arrived and all was well. That trauma over, Howard began his 36 straight hours of watching the light until Alex returned.

Another new experience for Howard came later in the fall when he watched a group of fishermen engaged in a wild melee of raucous

Fishermen visit the lighthouse, c. 1930.
— Courtesy of Jim Wallace

While lightening the grain cargo from a foundered ship, the Riverton, *in November 1943, the* Michigan *was driven sideways into the shallows by strong winds. The* Riverton *managed to escape along with the* Michigan's *crew, but the barge was not so lucky. Assistant lightkeeper Lou Brandon attempted a get-rich-quick scheme of salvaging, without success.*
— Courtesy of Howard Warner

laughter, French ditties and dancing. Alex explained it was their annual thanksgiving for a successful season. "They brought out a big jug of LCBO alcohol and concocted a brew called 'Wild Moose' from molasses, pine cones and I don't dare to guess what else — all brewed on a stove." Alex warned him that the fishermen would soon be at the light and he must accept the proffered drink as it was their way of thanking him for his weather reports. One taste and Howard's stomach turned over. For the rest of the night he quietly dumped their offerings down the kitchen sink.

From a distance, long grasses and beech trees give the area around the Hope Island lighthouse an almost tropical appearance. It beckons. Upon closer examination, the cement paths are crumbling, the boat house is showing years of neglect and the tower is riddled with gaping holes. In its present state, the tower can last only a few more seasons. The paint is cracking and peeling off walls, and in the summer kitchen, vines cover the windows and spread gracefully along a bench onto the floor. As the waves crash over the boulders lining the point, and the apple trees blow in the wind, there is a sense that, despite the desolation, this complex may yet have a hopeful future.

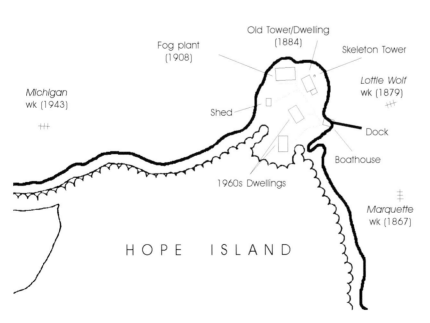

Giants Tomb

A Child's Memory

I can recall the first time I went up (to the island).
It was a sailboat and my father hadn't built the cabin. I was only three
years old and I can recall how frightened I was. I buried my face in
my grandmother's lap — overwhelmed by all this water.

— Rita Martin

Rita's father, Joseph Martin, would have been on the light since April and with the coming of warmer weather, looking forward to his family's arrival. He knew he was one of the lucky ones. After the First World War, jobs were tight. The reason he got this one was because he was the first Penetang veteran to return home. Out of his pay, $100 per month, he supported his family of five and paid an assistant. At least finding eager assistants was no trouble, as many considered Giants Tomb a vacation resort.

Rita recalls, "everyone was poor in those days. We were very fortunate our father had a job. All my friends were on relief, they bought all their food through stamps. We never considered ourselves poor. If you had food and clothes you were happy." The Martins kept a garden, an apple orchard, and chickens, and the boys fished. Rita's mother baked bread, and sold it to Indians from Christian Island. Every two weeks the family went into town for supplies. Meat was kept fresh by putting it on the ice Mr. Martin had cut during the winter. All the children's clothes were sewn by Rita's mother.

The house was simple — grey plank floors, wooden chairs, and some furniture left by the previous keeper, Mr. Griffith. There was a winter kitchen with a wood stove for warmth, and a cooler summer kitchen with a coal oil stove. Looking out over the water, without electricity and with no cottages on the mainland, evenings

Giants Tomb at the turn of the century.
— *National Archives of Canada PA172480*

Bernice Gendron pretends to smoke while little Rita Martin looks on.
— *Martin family/ Huronia Museum L995.0008.0016*

GIANTS TOMB

Location: Southern tip of
   Giants Tomb Island
Built: 1892
Description: White square
   wooden tower with dwelling
   attached
Height: 40 ft./12 m above water line
Light: Originally fixed white then rotating,
   dioptric, 7th order lens, then flashing
Visibility: 11 miles/17.6 kms
Automated: c.1939; blown up sometime after
   1967
Fog horn: Hand crank
Additional: Built under contract with Alphonse
   Tessier of Penetang for $1,595.
Present: Square skeleton tower that flashes
   white every 4 seconds

KEEPERS:

1893-1898	Rowland B. Little
1898-1924	Alfred H. Griffith
1924-1939	Joseph Martin

were dark and quiet. They made their own fun, singing around the organ, and applauding the children's concerts (the same ones repeated over and over!) And everyone looked forward to the nights when they could gather around the radio straining for every word of *The Little Theatre off Times Square*, and *Fibber McGee and Molly*.

Without much activity on the water, when a boat did approach, the children raced down to the dock in anticipation. Often it was Mr. Wallace or Mr. Vassair from the neighbouring Hope and Western lights. If mainland friends wanted to visit, they would signal with two fires and Rita's father would go over to pick them up. During the school year the children and Mrs. Martin spent Monday to Friday in town, and were brought out to the island only on weekends. But once school was over, their days were filled with fishing, picking berries, boating, and swimming. Sundays were special. The whole family went on a picnic. If it became too foggy, they would pull into a bay and sleep in the boat overnight. This was wonderful for the children; the Bay was part of them and they feared nothing.

When it was stormy I felt the power of the Bay. I used to stand at the point and let these big waves pour all over me. I remember thinking, "now this is heaven!"

— Rita Martin

The dock extending beyond the canopy is submerged due to a seiche. This is the same dock on which the girls (pictured above) are standing.
— *Martin family/Huronia Museum L995.0008.0009*

Vern Lalonde and Raymond Martin with hounds.
— Courtesy of Rita Martin

It was a different matter for their mother, Exina. The water — among other things — terrified her. Once when she was in the boathouse scrubbing clothes, she felt her foot become entwined in a rope. She kicked at it but what she thought was a rope was really a snake. She became hysterical and stormed up to her perplexed husband crying, "I'm not staying here another night, I am not staying here!" A couple of days later, all was forgotten.

Rita also remembers the dismal days when the Bay rolled and the buoys rang dolefully all day long — dong, dong, dong! "By the end of the day it was enough to pull your hair out!" When

The people of Midland petitioned the Governor General in February 1886 to erect lighthouses on Giants Tomb and Snake Islands.
— Martin Collection/Huronia Museum 1995.0008.0001

the fog closed in, they had to keep a close ear for the signal of passing ships so that they could crank the fog horn. It was an important job. Giants Tomb lay on the main route to Penetang, Midland, Victoria Harbour, Waubaushene, Muskoka Mills, Port McNicoll and the Severn River. The CPR passenger boats passed regularly en route to the Lakehead, as did grain freighters on their way down from Port Arthur and Fort William (Thunder Bay) to the elevators at Midland.

> One foggy night when I was about six (c.1929) I remember waking up to this incredible noise, and there was this ship, a grain boat all lit up and beached on the island — this massive figure looming out of the fog like a glistening city.
>
> — Rita Martin

At the end of the season, late November or early December, the ice-breaker, the *Murray Stewart*, would pick up the keepers and their families as well as the buoys along the way. Rita recalls one trip back to shore when she was very young. The ship became lodged in the ice. They were stuck all night with engines churning, the boat struggling to break free. After waiting patiently, Rita, whose first language was French, could resist no longer. She stood up and asked the captain, "is the boat, she's walking yet?!" which served to break the tension on board.

Around 1939 the Giants Tomb light was replaced by an automatic beacon; then sometime after 1967 it was blown up. Today at sites like Giants Tomb, the only hints of their once colourful past are sterile skeleton towers.

Grandfather Martin's tug Geraldine. *"He would go to the bush and tow the booms to the lumber companies. Log booms are very slow. When we saw him approaching we would take the boat out and have lunch with my uncles and him. It usually took two or three hours to go by when they were right in front of the lighthouse."*
— Martin family/Huronia Museum L995.0008.0038

The Martins with visitors. Standing left to right: Vanier Gendron, Archie Picotte, Bernice Gendron, Joseph Martin (keeper), Victoire Marchildon, Jeannette Martin, Laurier Gendron. Seated: Raymond (Pitou) Martin, and Rita Martin.
— Courtesy of Rita Martin

Normally it was the children's chore, but on this day Joseph Martin went to collect the eggs from the chicken coop. He lit a match as it was dark inside and was dumbstruck when he saw a huge fox snake, over six feet long, curled up in the nest. It had polished off every egg in the coop. But that wasn't all. A big bulge in the snake suggested it had also downed the white doorknob that was left in the coop to encourage the chickens to lay!

Exina Beauchamp Martin standing on rock with daughters Jeannette on left and Rita on right. Rita: "Dad would come with a pail of water and it would be just like having a pop."
— Martin Collection/Huronia Museum

Joanne Paradis in front of lighthouse, 1937.
— Paradis Collection/Huronia Museum L995.0005.0003

Back Range tower, built 1915 and "shed"
— National Archives of Canada PA195249

Joanne Paradis and one of her father's finely crafted birdhouses.
— Paradis Collection/Huronia Museum L995.0005.0001

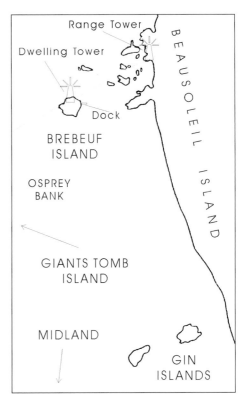

BREBEUF ISLAND

✢

Brebeuf Island is quintessential Georgian Bay, a smooth expansive flat rock with erratic boulders and a clump of windswept trees. Its lighthouse, moved from Gin Rock in 1900, now stands guard over the entrance to the 30,000 Islands cottage country. Brebeuf is next after Giants Tomb in a string of lights that lead to Penetang, Midland, Victoria Harbour and Port Severn.

Life on this island was not easy. Yet Mary Paradis, now in her nineties, has fond memories of her thirty years at the station. It was the Depression and Mary remembers her relief when her husband Clifford burst in with the news he had found a job. She had dreaded his return to the grain freighters. A few years earlier they had met at the Minnicognashene Hotel — Mary, an Irish immigrant working in the dining room, and Clifford, the young man hired to tend the horses.

Keeping the light meant hard physical labour. Before they had the luxury of a propane refrigerator, each February, Clifford would cut blocks from the frozen lake to fill the ice house. To feed the cook stove, they had to depend on picking up driftwood. After a storm, if they were lucky, they found stray logs along the shores of Beausoleil Island and towed them back to Brebeuf. Because of the storms which sometimes pushed waves within three feet of the lighthouse, replacing their dock became a seemingly endless task. Mary could not count the number of docks that washed away — many times with the boat still tied alongside. Without comment the Department would either deliver wood to construct a new one, or the Paradis' would once again beachcomb. Their second season at the light, Mary tried her hand at gardening. "It was coming along real nice" she grinned, "then with the first storm — good-bye." She can still picture the fresh green onions bobbing along the shore.

It is often said, keeping a light is like having a newborn child. One ear is always cocked for any variation in sound. For Mary and Clifford, the hiss of the coal-oil vapour light was quite distinctive. It changed if the vapour tube was plugged, bringing an instant reaction. Even the range light shining through their bedroom window became so routine that on occasion Mary still wakens, surprised that

Location: Gin Rock
Built: by 1878
Light: Fixed white catoptric

KEEPERS:
1878-1884   Israel Mundy
1885-1899   William Baxter

Location: North end of Brebeuf Island
Date: 1900 – Gin Rock lighthouse moved to
    Brebeuf
Description: Front Range – square white tower,
    attached dwelling, red polygonal iron lantern
Light: Fixed white dioptric
Height: 40 ft./12 m above high water
Visibility: 10 miles/16 kms
Present: Leased for a cottage
Location: West shore of Beausoleil Island
Date: 1900
Description: Back Range – square white
    wooden tower; then red square steel
    skeleton tower
Light: Fixed white

KEEPERS:
1900-1931   William Baxter
1931-1962   Clifford Paradis

Dock destroyed in a fall storm. Mary says, "When they were losing a dock from across the bay, we were gaining one."
– Courtesy of Mary Paradis

Clifford Paradis and his unofficial assistant, Mary.
– Courtesy of Mary Paradis

the light isn't glaring in her face.

For their daughter Joanne, the light was a very lonely, alienating place. Unlike other lighthouse children, she was confined to a small island with no companions her own age. Mary recalls being concerned when Joanne suffered a persistent fever. It was Sam Baxter, the brother of Brebeuf's first lightkeeper, who diagnosed her ailment – acute loneliness. Sure enough when Mary took the two-year-old to Midland to see her favorite aunts and uncles, the fever vanished. One profoundly frightening experience for Joanne was staring through the kitchen window at dusk as her father battled the sea to light the range light on Beausoleil Island. The sight of him disappearing in the troughs of the waves terrified her. But it was even more difficult when Joanne reached school age because she had to leave her parents to stay with guardians in town. To this day, both she and her mother have feelings of anxiety as Labour Day approaches.

The Long Journey Home

In common with many keepers, spring and fall marked nearly all Mary Paradis' worst memories. After one of Clifford's trips back in the fall, she recalls having to take a hammer to remove the ice from his jacket. Another year the conditions were even worse. The passage to the

Clifford Paradis with fish, c. 1944.
— Paradis Collection/ Huronia Museum L995.0005.0004

range light had frozen particularly early and Mary and Clifford had to drag the row boat with them each evening in case they broke through the fresh ice. It was the end of the season and they were waiting to be picked up. Everything was packed, and while they waited they ate their meals out of boxes. Supplies were carefully rationed in case the tender was delayed.

"They're not going to pick us up!" Mary and Clifford watched in disbelief as the *St. Heliers* steamed right past Brebeuf Island. Not one to sit back, Mary packed a sled with eggs and a few cans of peas and corn and headed out over the newly frozen lake. Unsure of which direction to go as no trails had been blazed, she cut across to Beausoleil, the ice groaning and creaking beneath her feet. As she trudged over the Bay the supplies continually slid off the sled until, completely aggravated, she pushed them onto the ice and marched on. Arriving

William Baxter, keeper 1900–31.
— Courtesy of Rita Martin

in town, Mary confronted the Captain of the *St. Heliers* on the dock. "Why didn't you pick Clifford up?" she demanded. "Too damned much ice," he scowled back. Mary immediately complained to the Parry Sound agency who ordered the Captain to return for him. She still chuckles at the memory, "That captain never liked me much after that." Surprised to see her in town, a local man enquired how she got there. The man paled at her response, "those were your tracks I seen on Beausoleil . . . ?" Only then did Mary learn she had walked over a particularly hazardous stretch of ice and seriously risked falling through. Later when she confessed to Clifford about abandoning their food, he was so upset he went back to retrieve it.

During their lighthouse years, 1931 to 1962, Clifford and Mary Paradis witnessed many changes in the boating and shipping traffic around Brebeuf. They saw the steamers such as the *Midland City* and the *City of Dover* that had serviced island hotels and delivered cottagers up the shore, vanish. And, when the highway to Honey Harbour was opened and a new channel marked, they saw the disappearance of the flotillas of "one-lunger" run-abouts filled with cottagers embarking from Midland.

Mary Paradis dressed up for a rare trip into town.
— Courtesy of Mary Paradis

WHISKEY ISLAND

✦

WHISKEY ISLAND

Location: Entrance to
    Penetanguishene
    Harbour
Built: 1882
Description: White
    square tapered tower
    on small timber crib
Height: 36 ft./10.8 m
Light: Fixed white, sixth order dioptric
Visibility: 11 miles/17.6 kms
Additional: Replaced by an iron pole
    with flashing white light to guide
    vessels through the cut into
    Penetanguishene Harbour.

KEEPERS:

1882	Joseph Dions
1882-1886➤	W.A. Thompson
1893-1916➤	Christopher Columbus

Whiskey Island, c.1880s. In 1882, the year the town of Penetanguishene was incorporated, a light was constructed on Whiskey Island to point out the low island and adjacent shoals to vessels using the harbour. It was part of a string of lights between Hope Island and Midland Harbour. The tower was struck by lightning and repaired in 1894.

PENETANGUISHENE

✛

In Penetanguishene, the lighthouse was a relative newcomer. During the final stages of the War of 1812, the British Royal Navy had established a naval garrison at this spot as a precaution against possible American military incursions. While it was never needed for that purpose, the post did kickstart a lively community of British pensioned officers, and British, French, Indian, and Métis farmers, fur traders, and fishermen. The property on which the light stands was first acquired by the province for a penal settlement. This was short-lived and in 1859 it became a reformatory for boys. By this time, the community had developed into a lumbering, fishing, ship-building and shipping centre. Schooners and steamers filled the harbour, and over the years, the obvious need for navigational beacons grew. Finally, in 1877, a small lighthouse was built at the end of the reformatory pier.

Today, several of the Naval Establishment buildings have been reconstructed and the replica schooners the *Bee*, the *Perseverence*, and the *Tecumseh* are docked at the wharf.

PENETANGUISHENE

Location: On pier at Provincial Reformatory
Built: 1877
Description: Small square white wooden tower
Height: 18 ft./5.4 m
Light: Fixed white catoptric light
Visibility: 6 miles/9.6 kms

KEEPERS:

1877-1878	Peter Kilgraine
1879	P. Gordon
1882➤	W.A. Thompson
1893-1916➤	Christopher Columbus

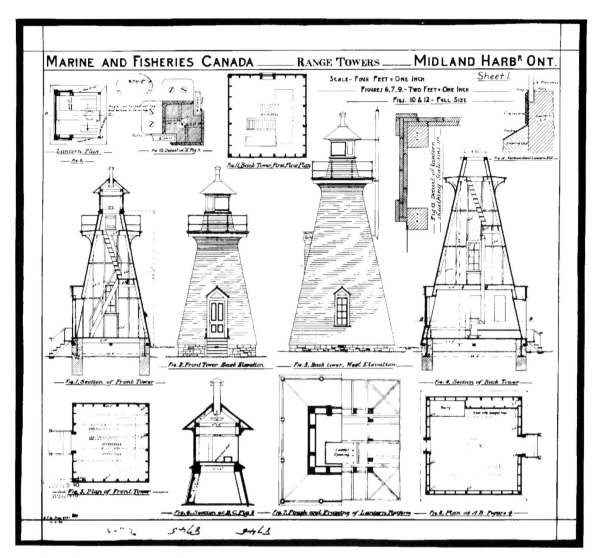

1899 plans, elevations, sections, and lantern details for front and rear range lights, Midland Point
— *National Archives of Canada NMC162340*

Midland Point back range tower. Replaced by daymarks in 1912, the front tower was subsequently moved to Turning Rock c. 1915.
— *National Archives of Canada PA148109*

MIDLAND POINT
AND MIDLAND

—————— ✛ ——————

MIDLAND POINT

Location: Northward of
    Midland Point
Built: 1900; daymarks in 1912
Description: Square white
    wooden tapered range lights;
    replaced in 1912 by white
    diamond-shaped
    daymarks on masts
Light: Fixed white catoptric
Visibility: 7 miles/11.2 kms
Additional: Lights lead to an intersection with
    the Victoria Harbour range

KEEPERS:
1900-1906➤ Napoleon Sommers
1911-1911   F. Sommers
1912-1916➤ T. Williams
◄1949➤   Edwin Walker

MIDLAND

Built: 1901
Location: In town
Description: Range lights on
    masts
Light: Fixed red dioptric,
    incandescent electric
Visibility: 4 miles/6.4 kms
Additional: Lights lead in from Midland Point
    to wharves in harbour. Wireless telegraph
    station in town which had contact with the
    area lighthouses

TURNING ROCK

—✛—

TURNING ROCK

Location: Turning
    Rock, just west of
    Canary Island
Erected: c.1915, moved
    from Midland Point
    front range
Description: Square white wooden
    tapered tower, red lantern, cedar
    shake siding
Light: Flashing white
Visibility: 7 miles/ 11.2 kms

KEEPERS:
Unwatched

*Turning Rock, 1915. Moved from Midland
Point.*
— National Archives of Canada PA195268

VICTORIA
HARBOUR

+

Range lights were built at Victoria Harbour in 1910 to guide ships to the entrance of the channel to Port McNicoll and Victoria Harbour. Pictured here is keeper Raymond Belcher.
— Courtesy of Ted Belcher/Huronia Museum

WESTERN
ISLANDS

——— ✢ ———

One of a group of outer islands known as the Westerns, Double Top stands exposed to the full power of Georgian Bay. The day of our visit, with the white tower standing on a carpet of brilliant orange lichen and sharply delineated against a backdrop of cobalt blue sky and water, the island gave off an aura of great tranquility. Yet we knew from our fellow visitors, former keepers the Wings and the Keiths, that this was only one face of this small rocky island. The other could be totally inhospitable; even hostile. As they stood atop the concrete helicopter pad, gazing out over the shipping channel that once was filled with grain freighters heading to Midland, they searched for signs of the former boathouse and fog plant, finding only the odd pipe, strewn wires, and a thin patch of coal. Although the large black spiders were not in evidence (much to Lillian Wing's relief), the hated biting flies were out in full force. They reminded her of the inspector who would tape the eyelets of his shoes in a vain attempt to keep the flies away from his feet. But what most disoriented the visitors was the fact that they were standing on the site of their former dwelling, the legendary Westerns house that stood so near the edge of the island that waves would break against it in severe weather.

The Tough Little House

Arnold and Lillian Wing, with their daughters Beth and Lois and one assistant, shared this rock for nine years between 1938 and 1946. During one particularly

Western house as seen from tower, 1962.
– Couling Collection/Huronia Museum
L995.0053.0006

fierce storm, Lillian was in the process of giving Arnold a haircut in the kitchen when a wave broke through the wooden shutter that protected the pantry window, smashing the glass. Water crashed into the room sweeping everything in its path. As Lillian scooped up the children and ran into the adjoining room, Arnold frantically tried to block the window before the next wall of water hit them. Needless to say, mopping up took precedence over the haircut about which Arn quipped, "the only difference between a good haircut and a bad one is three days."

For visitors, this proximity to the power of the elements could be quite unnerving. James Keith (1950-52) recalled his sister and her husband standing in the upstairs bedroom enquiring about some marks on the floor. They

Arnold Wing washing baby's hair in the Westerns' only "bath tub".
– Courtesy of Wing family

THE WESTERNS

Location: Double Top Island, the south group of the Western Islands, 27 miles/43 kms southwest of Parry Sound
Built: 1895
Description: Hexagonal wooden tower
Height: 60 ft./18 m
Light: Fixed dioptric, then flashing white
Visibility: 14 miles/22 kms
Fog horn: Diaphone
Additional: House, fog plant, boathouse, A-frame to winch boats up into boathouse
Automated: 1966
Present: Tower, cement walkways, one auxiliary building, fixed light

KEEPERS:

1895-1900	Richard Smith
1901-1906➤	Thomas Richardson
1912-1913	H. Hewitt
1913-1918	E. Smith
1919-1925	Joseph Dixon
1925-1931	Charles Vassair
1931-1938	Lawrence Tyler
1938-1946	Arnold Wing
1947-1950	P.A. Campbell
1950-1952	James Keith
1953-1955	Lloyd McAuliffe
1956-1958	Frank Rourke
1959-1966	Harry Couling
1965-1966	Gordon Champion
1966-1966	Vladimir Kruglov
1966-1967	George Bishton
1967➤	William Maguire

Arriving at the Westerns in the spring. Taken from the lighthouse tender.
— *Courtesy of Wing family*

were told they would find out soon enough. That night strong waves pummeled the house, and in the morning they awoke to find their bed on the other side of the room!

In their exposed position, lightning storms could be very frightening and on occasion the family would sit in the house wearing their outer jackets in case the house caught fire and they had to evacuate. Arnold remembers returning to the house after starting the fog alarm during an electrical storm when suddenly there was a deafening bang. The air was filled with the pungent odour of gun powder, and after the smoke cleared, Arn was shocked to see a deep gouge in the wall just steps away. His assistant, who had been standing in the door of the fog plant, was thrown backwards by the power of the bolt's shock wave.

The Stark Seasons
Surviving Fall And Spring

Bad weather could strike at any season but the Spring and Fall were most dreaded. In the Spring, all the lightkeepers of Hope, Giants Tomb, Brebeuf and the Westerns met in Midland to board the *St. Heliers* for their trip out to the islands. One exceptionally cold spring the ice was so thick it took three days for the *St. Heliers* to punch her way from Midland to Giants Tomb. The *St. Heliers* was not an ice breaker, nor did she have the bulky weight of the grain boats, which were also anxious to break out of their winter quarters into the open channel. The freighters would shove ahead six feet, back up and then push ahead again. The *St. Heliers* tried but snapped a propeller blade in the process. All the boat's water had to be pumped from her stern to her bow to raise the propeller far enough out of the water so that crewmen lying on boards on the frozen lake could replace the blades.

Lake boats in spring, cutting their way out to the open water (taken from the St. Heliers*).*
— *Wing Collection/Huronia Museum L995.0022.0006*

Isolation — A Way of Life

Each Spring the Wings would arrive with 100 lb. bags of flour and sugar, a 50 lb. drum of powdered milk and several months' supply of eggs preserved in brine. Fruits and vegetables were canned, and their principal meat, six or seven sides of bacon, was hung in the shed.

Lillian and Arnold Wing and their daughters, Beth and Lois being lowered from the St. Heliers to start a new season at the Westerns.
— Star Weekly, *April 28, 1945*

Wings carrying their belongings. St. Heliers *anchored in the distance.*
— Star Weekly, *April 28, 1945*

The Wings posing in front of the tower.
— Star Weekly, *April 28, 1945*

Before eating it, they had to wash off the green mould with vinegar. One year Arnold brought a chicken to the island thinking it would be a welcome alternative to bacon, but when the time came, the children wouldn't hear of "their pet" being slaughtered. Fish was abundant, and occasionally they would collect gull eggs to be used in baking. After months of this nutritional but rather repetitive diet, they looked forward to some variety. But on returning to town, their well-meaning friends usually welcomed them back with fresh loaves of bread. Since they made their own all season "that's the last thing we wanted!"

The little contact the Wings had with the outside world was through Meaford and Parry Sound fishermen like Bill Edmonston, who kept a fishing camp on the North Group of the Westerns. Little remains of the camp today except dock cribs and a lone apple tree. Friends and relatives would mail letters and packages to the fishermen in Meaford who in turn would deliver them to the Wings. When the seas were too rough for a landing, they would attach the deliveries to the cable that was used to crank the boat up into the boat house. The Wings now

1. Hauling the boat up into the boathouse.
– *Couling Collection/Huronia Museum L995.0053.0001*
2. One of the Rourke boys winches the boat into the boat house.
– *Keefe Collection/Huronia Museum L995.0006.0003*
3. Left to right: Beth and Lois Wing, and Jerry Emery standing at spot where the cable was anchored. This cairn can still be seen.
– *Courtesy of Wing family*
4. Job done.
– *Keefe Collection/Huronia Museum L995.0053.0004*

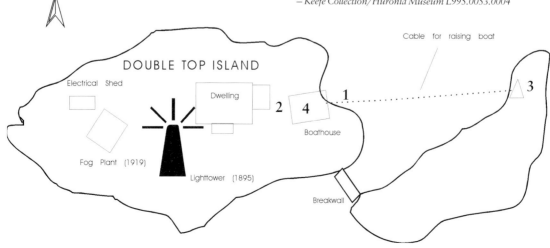

laugh at the degree of their isolation which at times was so complete they did not hear of major developments in the Second World War until months afterward.

In later years the radio brought welcome contact with the outside. Beth remembers racing through her school work on Monday nights so that she could listen to her favourite program, *Lux Radio Theater*. On blowy nights she would sit on the floor with her back pressed against the wall and feel the rhythmic pounding of the waves against the house. Her correspondence courses went far beyond the traditional "three R's" and even dealt with such subjects as etiquette, "[My mother] would have to leave and knock on the door, and I would answer it and say, 'how do you do. Won't you come in? Won't you sit down?'" Beth spent hours reading books and magazines, which held her in good stead when she returned to town for the winter. But having been alone so much, Beth sometimes felt like a square peg in a round hole at school.

In spite of the isolation, privation and heavy work load, the Wings have fond memories of their years at the Westerns. Although when Lill was asked the question, "if before you married you had known you would be coming out here for eight years, what would you have done?, she

Bags packed, Bill Couling is thrilled to be leaving "Little Alcatraz."
– *Couling Collection/ Huronia Museum L995.0053.0007*

teasingly responded, "Well I suppose I would have found myself another man!" In a more serious tone, she confessed the job was considered a very good one at the time, and they were happy to take it.

There was an ongoing joke on the Westerns about the lightkeeper who went stir crazy on the 40 by 200-yard rock and requisitioned the Coast Guard for thirty gallons of green paint and a lawn mower. To a degree, most Westerns' lightkeepers felt some empathy with him. Harry Couling (1959-65) renamed the island "Little Alcatraz". Perhaps this was after the experience he had with his son Bill. While playing in the tower, Bill was struck by an agonizing pain in his abdomen. As time passed and the pain continued, Harry attempted to launch a boat into the rough sea. Bill recalls, "they finally radioed Midland. It was getting on to night, and the pain was getting worse. They got Dr. Swan to the C.B. but the weather wasn't getting any better —it was like something out of a movie."

Midland contacted a sea plane company who at first refused to help because of the weather. Harry and Dr. Swan conferred about Bill's condition. "I was eleven so I wasn't really paying attention, but I guess they figured if it got any

Lightkeeper Harry Couling (1959-66) approaches the Westerns Lightstation.
– *Couling Collection/Huronia Museum L995.0053.0004*

worse my Dad was going to have to do emergency surgery to take out my appendix. He would have done it too — it wouldn't have bothered him." After considerable discussion one pilot agreed the situation warranted an attempt in the morning. He would take one run and one run only, as there was a good chance he could land but not be able to take off again. The following morning, Harry put his partially conscious son into the boat and they bobbed out in the heavy rollers. The plane managed to land; Bill was lifted inside, and within no time he was in Midland having his appendix removed.

Bill recalls one visit to the Westerns that nearly pushed him over the edge. Although the waves were too much for his twelve-foot molded plywood boat, being young, stubborn, and determined, he pressed on:

> There was nothing I could do. I couldn't turn around so I just kept going. I knew how to get out there — you go off the mount at Hope, and go straight and you'll hit the island. As I got closer and closer I could see my Dad standing down by the front shaking his fist. I went up for one day and I got stuck there for three weeks. It was too rough to get off. The first two weeks was the weather — the last week it was that my Dad was still mad at me! I had had it! Enough of rock! Fog! Seagulls! Distant boats you could hear, but couldn't see.

If the spring weather was bad, the fall was worse. Both Arnold Wing and Jim Keith agreed it was also profoundly lonely. After their wives and children left for the mainland, each man had only his assistant for company. With frequent storms, the windows remained shuttered making the residence dark, day in and day out. By December, the weather was so cold and intense that the island turned into a scene from a nightmarish fairy tale. Spray leapt so high over the house and even the tower's lantern room, 74 feet above water level, that the entire island was transformed into a gleaming frozen mass. To get around without being swept away, the men had to hang on to a steel safety line installed along the icy paths. Keith recalled, "that cable would get a foot thick with ice. It would get so that all you could do was hook your arm around it, walk and pull yourself along. You'd take a hammer and smash it off when you got a chance."

In a strange way, the ice-encased house gave comfort to Arn Wing:

> You could look right down Lake Huron, she was looking right back at us — a sixty-mile sweep. It would be below zero and the waves would hit that house pretty heavy but with that much ice covering the place you'd think 'let her go, she's not going to hurt us.'

Arnold Wing at the Westerns in late fall. Jack Kennedy, Superintendent of Lights (1950-88) recalls "from the ice the island formed into a steep mound. We had to buy the keepers cleats. They had even run out of water! They would throw the bucket down and by the time they pulled it up the sloped ice there'd be nothing left in it."
— Wing Collection/Huronia Museum

Westerns house being dynamited — note fire ladder.
— Courtesy of Jack Kennedy

The Demolition

Once the Westerns house was slated for demolition by the Parry Sound Coast Guard, she did not accept her fate gracefully. Starting with the boat house, the crew ripped down the walls with axes and crow bars. Moving on to the house, they pounded away with little result. Pat Johnston who was working at the Parry Sound base at the time recalls their difficulty, "they worked three or four days on that house and then finally called the base. There was no way they could make a dent in her — she was too well built." If the tower hadn't been so close they would have torched the house. In utter frustration, one of the men suggested dynamite as being the only option if they hoped to get off the Westerns before December. The dynamite was suspended from nails driven into the ceiling of each room, then strung together with the detonating wire leading out to a concrete building. It took an entire case of dynamite. Pat Johnson helicoptered out to watch, "the walls blew out so fast that the chimney fell down straight through the roof." As the air cleared, the men saw that the chimney still stood as if to say 'look it's not over yet.'

SPRUCE SHOAL

—✛—

1909 Report by Chief Engineer

A reinforced concrete beacon is in course of construction on the southern extremity of Spruce Shoal. It consists of an octagonal cribwork foundation 13½ feet high, which was sunk in 17 feet of water, on August 31, 1907. The superstructure will be of reinforced concrete and will be built to a height of 21 feet above the level of water, and upon this will be erected a gas light with the necessary reservoirs. The work is being done by contract by Mr. Thos. A. White of Parry Sound, the contract price being $12,875 [an enormous sum for the time.]

SPRUCE SHOAL

Location: On shoal near southern extremity
Description: Octagonal reinforced concrete tower on octagonal reinforced concrete pier
Light: Fixed white dioptric, acetylene
Visibility: 11 miles/17.6 kms
Abandoned: Pre-1955

KEEPERS:
Unwatched

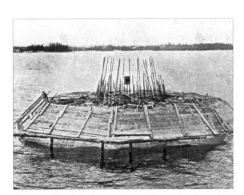

Spruce Shoal Crib near Parry Sound, where it was first sunk August 12, 1907.
— Canadian Parliamentary Sessional Papers

Spruce Shoal concrete gas beacon.
— Canadian Parliamentary Sessional Papers, 1909

PARRY SOUND
LIGHTHOUSE DEPOT

✛

Repair shop, Parry Sound Base, c. 1905. Note the acetylene testing station at far right with overhead vents and the gas light fixture hanging from ceiling.
— *Canadian Coast Guard*

Lighthouse depot was established in 1905 in an old bobbin factory.
— *National Archives of Canada PA172534*

PARRY SOUND RANGES

✤

Jones Island and Snug Harbour

Jones Island, Snug Harbour, Walton Island, Gordon Rock, and Hugh Rock were the chosen locations for five lights leading into Parry Sound. During his Georgian Bay Survey (1883-94), Staff Commander J.G. Boulton left survey marks to aid in positioning these future lighthouses. Through weather or mischief, these were lost. In 1893 when the Deputy Minister of Marine and Fisheries received a telegraph announcing the marks had been rediscovered, he cautiously advised, "... if you think there is any reason to doubt the accuracy of the locations as now marked, I have to instruct you to take whatever steps you think necessary in order to secure the proper locations of the towers before their construction is too far advanced to permit change without entailing very great expense."

In the spring of 1894, only Walton Island, Gordon Rock and Hugh Rock lit the approaches. Jones Island lighthouse and Snug Harbour lighthouse remained dark. An 1895 Parliamentary Sessional Papers Report reveals why: while the contractor claimed the buildings were in good condition, during an inspection,

> it was found that the winter had made many defects, and the work was still far from being in accordance with the specifications. The work was therefore taken out of the contractor's hands, and Mr. W.H. Noble, a foreman of works for the department, completed the buildings. It was found necessary to remove the whole of the siding and roof shingles and reshingle both walls and roofs and renew the cornices before the buildings were weatherproof. This and other extra work which cost $647.40 is charged against the contract price.

JONES ISLAND

Location: Southwest point of Jones Island
Built: 1894
Description: Tower rising from rectangular dwelling, red stripe facing open channel; originally, wooden lantern
Height: 50 ft./15 m
Light: Fixed white catoptric; then 4th order dioptric and acetylene
Visibility: 8 miles/13 kms
Range tower: Square white wooden tower on summit of northernmost Gordon Rock, fixed red dioptric, acetylene.

KEEPERS:
1901-1907 ➤ Edward Taylor

SNUG HARBOUR

Location: S. extremity of island on N. side of Snug Harbour entrance
Built: 1894
Description: Tower rising from rectangular dwelling; originally, wooden lantern
Height: 50 ft./15 m
Light: Fixed white catoptric. Oil then acetylene.
Additional: Boathouse, radio beacon, search and rescue station
Range tower: Square white wooden tower on westernmost Walton Island. Fixed red catoptric. Oil then acetylene.

KEEPERS:
1894-1903 ➤	Charles White
1909-1914	Adam Brown
◄1930s➤	Dan Boterell
◄1965-c.1977	E. Scott, Gus Olson, Tom Flynn

(Charles Mickler, the original contractor, is reputed to have successfully sued the government for the "hold-back" money, as he had previously done at Pointe au Baril.)

In the heavily trafficked and shoal infested channel leading into Parry Sound and Depot Harbour, these five lights were vital. For the ship captains however, both Snug and Jones were considered major headaches. Either they vanished in the sun's glare, or they faded into the backdrop.

In addition to the lighthouse, Jones Island boasted of an apiary housing exotic Italian and Middle Eastern bees owned by "Honey Bee Jones". Over the years, the lighthouse was home to squatters and a hiding place for stolen goods.
– National Archives of Canada PA148102

The first solution was to paint them white with a three-foot red stripe facing the shipping channel. That didn't work, and so in 1902 they were painted entirely white including their roofs and lantern rooms. Later experiments included garish

Snug Harbour lighthouse, 1910.
– National Archives of Canada PA148154

Department of Marine and Fisheries, Canada.—Lighthouse Service.

Diary of Lightkeeper at _Jones Island_ for the month of _November_ 1905

WEATHER.	WIND. A.M.	WIND. P.M.	Day of Month	TIME OF LIGHTING.	TIME OF EXTINGUISHING.	TIME OF BURNING.	OIL USED. Galls	OIL USED. Pts.	Chimneys	Wicks	REMARKS.
Stormy & Snowing	SW	SW to	1								NW. a Proper Son of a B
Calm			2								
Stormy & Snowing	SE	SW	3								a Sun of a Gun
Light Breezy	W	W	4								went to Red Rock today
Light Breezy	SW	SW	5								
Light Breeze	N	N	6								Snowing. Telegram on the Rocks at Black Rock
Cloudy & Rain	SE	SE	7								
Stormy & Snowing	NW	NW	8								
Light Breeze	N	N	9								
Light Breeze	SW	SW	10								
Light Breeze	NW	NW	11								
Light Breeze	NW	NW	12								
Stormy & Cold	N	N	13								
Fine & Clear	N	N	14								Herbey went to the Grand today
Stormy & Snowing	SE by	S to	15								SW. Sun of a Gun
Light Breeze	N	N	16								
Snowing	SE	SE	17								
Fine			18								
Lovely Day Calm			19								and Clear the Best for 60 days
Lovely Day Calm			20								Capt Clark Lifted Lone Rock Buoy today
Lovely Day Calm			21								
Light Breeze	SW	SW	22								
Lovely Day			23								set the net on the Snake Shole today.
Light Breeze	SE	SE	24								Cloudy & Rain a Sun of a Gun
Fine & Cloudy	NE & S		25								
Fine some Showers	SW	SW	26								
Fine & Clear	N	N	27								
Stormy & Snowing	SE	SE	28								a Sun of a Gun
Stormy & Snow	SW & SW		29								NW fell
Clear & Cold Ice			30								Formed on the Shore first this Season
			31								

In exhibition of light ....

In house lamps ....

At fog alarm station ....

Destroyed, spilt, &c. ....

Page dated November 1905 from log book of Jones Island keeper, Edward Taylor.

— West Parry Sound Museum

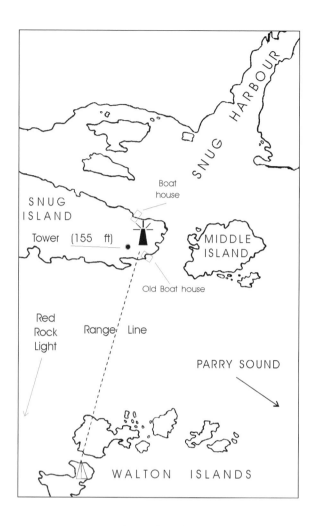

Bon Aire Island cottage with siding of flattened calcium carbide cans retrieved from Snug lighthouse.
— West Carling Historical Society

neon orange roofs or day-glo rocket-red paint, none of which proved wholly satisfactory.

All five lights were automated with volatile acetylene gas before 1913. Predictably, an acci-

dent occurred in the mid-1930s at Walton Rock, when the light malfunctioned and exploded. The damaged lighthouse had to be rebuilt with a false front. The use of acetylene was not without benefit however, at least for one enterprising Snug Harbour cottager. Known for his salvaging prowess (his kitchen floor was made from the deck of a wrecked ship), he eyed the lighthouse's accumulation of square-shaped calcium carbide cans. Painstakingly, he cut off the bottoms, opened the seams, flattened them and then used these sheets to shingle his cottage. He finished it all off with a brilliant red-lead paint job. His inventive siding would surely have survived many Georgian Bay seasons, but it did not survive the more conservative tastes of the cottage's new owners.

In more recent years, the threat came not from a volatile fuel used in the lights but from the number of oil tankers which supplied the 22 storage tanks in Parry Sound. Groundings were frequent, including the *Glen Eagles, Eastern Shell, Lake Shell,* and *Imperial St. Clair.* The *Lake Shell* ran aground on a shoal, after ice

Snug Harbour lighthouse before auxilliary buildings added.
— West Carling Historical Society

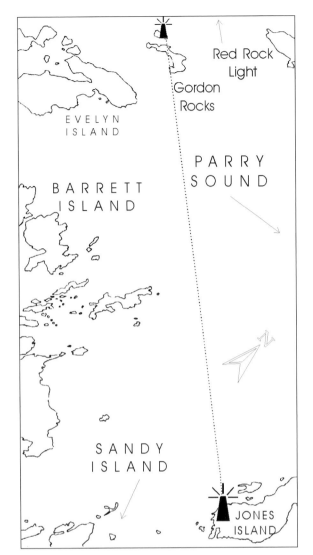

pushed buoys out of position. The captain of the *Eastern Shell* claimed he had turned at the wrong buoy because the sun had distorted his vision. Whatever the reason, diesel and gasoline spewed out and the Coast Guard had to deploy booms (plastic fabric curtains) around the ship and along the coast of Franklin Island. The Parry Sound storage tanks have been removed and the tankers no longer come in.

During the 1930s, Snug Harbour keeper Dan Boterell devised some clever schemes to minimize his workload: a mirror in the tower reflected the light down into his living space; and snuffers rigged with a long string would put the flame out in the morning. In addition to lightkeeping, he performed fire patrol along the shores by canoe — one day travelling up to Pointe au Baril, the next down to Sans Souci.
— West Carling Historical Society

FIVE RANGE LIGHT TOWERS

In the approaches to Parry Sound, both in the Georgian Bay, Ontario.

Plans and Specifications can be seen, and forms of tender procured, at this Department, Ottawa, and at the Post Offices, French River, Parry Sound and Collingwood.

Tenders for the two localities must be kept separate.

Each Tender must be accompanied by an accepted Cheque of a Canadian Bank equal to five per cent. of the whole amount of the Tender, which will be forfeited if the party declines to enter into a contract. If the Tender be not accepted the cheque will be returned.

WM. SMITH,

Deputy Minister of Marine and Fisheries.

DEPARTMENT OF MARINE AND FISHERIES,
OTTAWA, CANADA, 17th May, 1893.

Tender announcement.
— Department of Fisheries and Oceans

RED ROCK

---✦---

*L*anding at a steep-sided rock face studded with steel rods can be tricky at any time, but at Red Rock it is often worse, as waves build up and storms appear out of nowhere. Buried from view under the azure Bay is a sinister world of granite shelves, rocks and shoals littered with the skeletons of ships including the Jane McLeod, Seattle, *and the* Midland.

The need for vessels entering Parry Sound to have some navigational assistance was so critical that sawmill owners contributed half the cost to the first lighthouse built on Old Tower Island in November 1870. When this succumbed to the punishing sea, a second was built on Red Rock Island in 1881. Staff Commander J.G. Boulton pointed out that this structure would be no better in withstanding a heavy blow, nor was it large enough to accommodate a needed steam fog whistle, and

a fire occurring in this wooden building in a south-westerly gale and consequent sea might entail destruction to the keeper's family as the only small boat which can be hauled up on this rock would be difficult to launch under such circumstances.

A report in the 1895 *Canadian Parliamentary Sessional Papers* added:

This is one of the most exposed stations on our inland water, and consists of a wooden lighthouse standing on a crib-work pier on a bare, rounded granite rock, exposed to the full force of all westerly storms, and to the full sweep of the Georgian Bay. In bad weather the sea breaks completely over the whole building.

Fourteen years later the cribwork foundation had to be replaced by a steel cylinder 45 feet in diameter, 12½ feet high, filled with masonry and concrete. Even this wasn't the answer. So, in 1911, a Mr. White was contracted to replace the wooden lighthouse with the reinforced concrete structure that is seen today.

After the lighttower on Old Tower Island was destroyed by waves, this odd structure was raised on Red Rock, 1881. Note boat storage, second floor entrance and support wires.
— West Carling Historical Society

The Third Lighthouse

The lighthouse's long entranceway emphasizes the massive girth of the steel and cement foundation that roots the superstructure to this tiny island. Encased by the steel shell, the main floor is dark, oily, and dank. Stairs hug the wall leading up to the fog plant and workroom, with its curved wooden work bench, drawers still brimming with hardware. A kitchen and three other rooms can be reached by a spiral staircase. According to old-timers, it was quite cozy despite the Spartan appearance. In keeper Adam Brown's time, two rocking chairs sat near the coal stove and during fall storms the steel shutters were closed to prevent the waves from exploding through the glass. From the kitchen, a ladder climbs to the lantern room. This room is dwarfed by the large flat roof on which it stands. It is also overshadowed by a helicopter pad installed in the early 1970s, after numerous near disasters. It wasn't easy to land on a postage

RED ROCK

Built: 1870
Location: Old Tower Island
Description: Square wooden tower on top of dwelling, wooden lantern
Height: 40 ft./12 m
Light: Fixed white catoptric light, 4 mammoth flat-wick lamps, 15" reflectors
Visibility: 10 miles/16 kms
Destroyed: In storm

Built: 1881
Location: Red Rock Island, Parry Sound
Description: Wooden octagonal tower on wooden pier, then on steel and concrete base
Light: Fixed white catoptric
Height: 44 ft./13.2 m
Replaced: Wood unsuitable for exposed location

Built: 1911
Location: Red Rock Island
Description: Reinforced concrete, nearly elliptical. Standing on 12 ft. high red steel-sheathed cylindrical stone foundation. Red polygonal iron lantern
Light: Oscillating white, acetylene
Height: 60 ft./18 m
Fog Horn: Compressed air diaphone

KEEPERS:
1870-1881	William McGowan
1881-1885	Adam Alexander Lawson
1898-1937	Adam Brown
1938-1965	Lawrence Tyler
1966-c.1977	Gus Olson, E. Scott, Tom Flynn Jr. (beginning in 1962 keepers alternated between Red Rock and Snug Harbour)

stamp-sized patch of slanting rock without catching the blades on the lighthouse walls, and there was always a risk of having the powerful waves pull the helicopter off the rock.

Red Rock lighthouse, completed 1911.
— Parry Sound Public Library

Adam Brown

Although the Red Rock light might look like a steel and concrete prison to some, to Adam Brown it was home for almost forty years. Brown was known as a fine man, a masterful story-teller and a jack of all trades. In addition to a stint as a lumber salesman, he sold fish to the Mink Island operators, offered his carpentry skills to cottagers around Snug Harbour, and piloted ships into Parry Sound and Depot Harbour. Freighters and passenger ships like the *South America* would signal from the shipping

Keeper Adam Brown at right, piloted boats into Parry Sound to supplement his keeper's income. Note curtains covering lantern room windows.
— Parry Sound Public Library

channel for Adam to come out to lead them safely through the treacherous passages. But with all this extra-curricular work, when did he find time to tend the lighthouse? The fact is, he often did not. He didn't need to.

Alex Parker, the hermit of Red Rock, assisted Adam Brown for 21 years. When stormy weather kept Brown off the light for a week, he apologized to Parker, who shrugged and said, "I don't care if you never come back."
— Toronto Daily Star, December 8, 1937

The Hermit of Red Rock

Alex Parker assisted Adam Brown for twenty-one years, and was more than happy to devote all his time to the light. On one occasion when a storm kept Brown away from the island for a week, Alex shrugged and said, "I don't care – I don't care if you never come back." He was so content on Red Rock he once asked permission to stay all winter. Charlie Parr, a former Minks fisherman recalled:

the most you'd get out of him when he was at the light was 'the weather is going to be west tomorrow.' He never left the light either. In town, in the winter, he'd ask 'How long is the ice gonna be around? God I wish I was out on the light, nothing to do around here.' He sure looked after it. He would always be down there waving at us, no matter what time of night we would go by or what snow was flying.

They knew they could depend on Alex. Because their tugs drew seven feet of water, and the depth off the lighthouse was ten feet, the fishermen would hug Red Rock on their way into the Minks. On foggy nights, Alex would invariably be on the shore, coal-oil lantern in hand, to ensure their safe passage.

Fishing tug Dolphin *at the Minks' net shed. Building in foreground is one of the last remnants of the Minks' fishing station that died around the second world war.*
– Courtesy of Verna Parr

Putting in the dock at Red Rock. Adam Brown is next to the boat.
– Courtesy of Verna Parr

A Jolly Location

Before coming to Red Rock as keeper, Brown had been a fisherman on the Minks, a nearby cluster of red granite islands where nearly 100 men, women and children spent each summer. This fishing station was one of the liveliest places on Georgian Bay. The weekend dances were renowned, even drawing people from Parry Sound to join the festivities.

Cleveland Hamilton, a travel writer, remembers his introduction to these islands:

We came to the Red Rock lighthouse, where we hailed a fishing smack and asked for the course

to Parry Sound. 'If you will haul up a bit I'll go with you,' answered a young fisherman. Glad of his company, we soon had Adam Brown on board and in charge of the tiller . . . every rock in the bay and each short cut, through the mazes of islands was familiar to him . . . . We got to the Minks around 9 p.m. The fishermen welcomed us heartily and gave us the use of a shanty, where supper was soon spread. We were invited to the gaieties going on near by . . . . A visiting fiddler made music, and shoes, not the lightest, beat the floor, not the smoothest, and happy couples performed as they called, cotillions, quadrilles and Sir Roger.

Fishing families at the Minks.
– Parry Sound Public Library

As well as being known for parties, the Minks was known for its colourful characters, some of whom devised imaginative schemes to circumvent the authorities. One such character was Bill Sergeant, who decided to bring ship-to-shore radio to the islands. He wasn't the least deterred by the fact that at that time the Marconi family owned the franchise to carry communications across water. Bill thought he had found a loophole. He installed a car radio-phone in an old abandoned truck on the Minks. He was surprised when an inspector came to check if the equipment was truly in a vehicle. The conversation went well, until the inspector demanded Bill start the engine. The old thing hadn't worked in ages. With the threat of losing his radio-phone, Bill paid a mechanic a hefty sum to get the clapbox running. By law, each time he used the phone he had to start the truck. Unfortunately it sputtered and clunked so loudly, no one could hear what he was saying.

In 1903, Adam Brown, while keeper at Red Rock, was part of another scheme, to "mislay" a quantity of lumber that had washed onto the Minks, after the wreck of the steamer *Seattle* on the ledges of Green Island. With the help of two men from Parry Sound, Adam salvaged the

Leaving your mark on Red Rock was a popular pastime.
— *Parry Sound Public Library*

wood and hid it until the heat from the owners, insurance agent and police subsided. One wonders if suspicions were piqued when the Adanac Hotel acquired a new floor and when locals and cottagers initiated a frenzy of renovations.

Shared Duties

After the Minks station wound down during the Second World War, Red Rock was not considered so amenable by later keepers. By 1962, a system had been implemented whereby four men shared the duties of Red Rock and Snug Harbour. Two men were always at Red Rock, one at Snug, and one on rotational leave. This was to "allow for complete safety at each site, and give the men a chance to escape the

Late fall storms transformed Red Rock into a prison for its keepers.
— *Courtesy of Pat Johnston*

utter boredom andbachelor status of Red Rock, which . . . is a small rock barely large enough to stand on."

Rescuing the Light

After a somewhat circuitous journey, the original 1870s light from Old Tower Island is now in the West Parry Sound Museum. For several years, it was in Adam Brown's possession. Then he heard of a man who had taken to moulding his own metal trout baits. Ever the fisherman, Brown brought the light to Don Christie, a long-time Snug Harbour resident, and asked him to use the copper to make baits. Don in turn took it to his father-in-law, Sarnie Crawford's repair station. As Crawford's mother had spent many happy summers on Old Tower Light with her uncle, keeper William McGowan, he couldn't bring himself to destroy the light. And so for many years the old lamp, with its large German silver-coated reflector (German silver is a compound of

On his retirement, December 7, 1937, Adam Brown looks back at Red Rock for the last time after 40 years of tending the light. He retired at the age of 75, but had another 31 years to enjoy Georgian Bay before his death in 1968 at the age of 106.
— Parry Sound North Star, December 13, 1979

nickel, copper and zinc), was a prized curiosity to all his customers. Eventually, it was given to Parry Sound's ex-mayor, C.C. Johnson. After he died, the light disappeared until someone found it in the basement of the Library and donated it to the Museum.

The lighthouse before the helicopter pad was added. The helicopter pad was built in Parry Sound and towed to the light by a scow with a crane. During construction, a surprise storm snapped a cable, tossing the crane into the lake. It was later salvaged.
— Parry Sound Public Library

Adam Brown (left) leaving Red Rock, c. 1920.
— Courtesy of Verna Parr

POINTE
AU BARIL

✦

At night, it was tricky for fishermen to find the entrance to the channel while returning to McIntosh Island. The problem was solved when someone came up with the idea of upgrading the old voyageur keg that was being used as a marker on the branch of a dead tree. A side of the barrel was removed and a lantern placed inside, giving the fishermen something to guide them safely into the channel. If they were off course, too far to one side or the other, the light was obscured. Although it was make-shift, the barrel worked and in time gave name to the area – Pointe au Baril.

When lumber boats began to ply the waters, companies paid local fishermen, Gilbert and John McIntosh, to keep lanterns lit at night. However, by 1887, something more permanent was needed, and the companies petitioned the Minister of Marine and Fisheries to erect two range lights. One company even offered to pay much of the cost. The Department must have agreed, for in the spring of 1889, it contracted with Charles Mickler of Collingwood to build a substantial lighthouse at the front range site and a simple frame structure at the back site. Mickler's costs were well over budget and the dispute over payment ended in a lawsuit which he won.

The first keeper, Samuel Edward Oldfield, immigrated from England and settled in nearby McKellar. Hearing a lighthouse was to be built at Pointe au Baril, he applied for the job. Although he arrived in July of 1889, he was not able to put both lights into operation until October, as the back range lantern was late in arriving from the foundry in Montreal. A bustling community soon grew up around the light and the McIntosh store, with Oldfield becoming its first postmaster in addition to keeping the light.

At the turn of the century, fishing Mackinaws and tugs were a common sight, as were lumber boats, whose captains often chose to tow the log booms through the

POINTE AU BARIL

Front Range:
Location: Southern extremity of
    peninsula known as Pointe au
    Baril
Built: 1889
Description: Square wooden
    tower with kitchen attached (other additions
    added later)
Height: 33 ft./10 m
Light: Fixed white dioptric
Visibility: 10 miles/16 kms
Fog horn: Hand cranked until 1980s
Automated: 1978
Present: Tower and boat shed remain in good
    condition. Fixed red light.

Back range:
Location: Summit of Macklin Island
Built: 1889; upgraded to steel and
    heightened 1908-10
Description: Square open frame tower
    surmounted by enclosed lantern.
Light: Fixed red catoptric
Height: 1889: 44 ft./13.2 m; 1910: 81 ft./
    24 m
Visibility: 10 miles/16 kms

KEEPERS:

1889-1907	Samuel Edward Oldfield
1907-1929	Ole Hansen
1930-1940	James A. Vail
1941-1949	Kenneth Malcolm Evans
1949-1977	Carl Madigan
1978-1983	Emmaline Madigan

Ole Hansen in his sailboat with young Ted Eberhard
c. 1913-15
– Ruth McCuaig Collection/Eberhard Album

neur. He managed a small fishing operation, repaired and built boats, and hired himself and his Mackinaw sailboat out to tourists.

In 1908, the CPR's Parry Sound to Sudbury line was routed through Pointe au Baril, spurring development around the Station, but the community near the light continued to be the hub for fishermen and early cottagers. By 1922, word of this island paradise spread, and a building boom began. The early cottagers were mainly clergymen, university professors, and their families.

Samuel Edward Oldfield (first keeper 1887-1907) and wife Elizabeth taken on upper veranda of original Bellevue Hotel.
– Courtesy of J. W. Dickinson/Gail and Robbie Oldfield

inside steamboat channel, rather than risk the open water. Steamers from Parry Sound and Midland brought so many summer visitors, the enterprising Oldfield built the Bellevue Hotel on Lookout Island across from the lighthouse. When Oldfield retired in 1907, the lightkeeping job passed to a Norwegian fisherman, Ole Hansen. Like Oldfield, Hansen was an entrepre-

Pointe au Baril lighthouse. Note new kitchen has not been added. Photo taken by J. D. Gould.
– Ruth McCuaig Collection

Carl and Emmaline Madigan

The last keeper was Emmaline Madigan who moved into the Pointe au Baril lighthouse in 1949 when she was seventeen, and who took over her husband Carl's duties after his death in 1977. The day she returned to her former home, one of the fisherman at the dock enquired, "where's the laundry?" It was over a decade since she had run the light and her laundry business, but she had not been forgotten. These are some of her memories.

With a salary of only three dollars a day, Carl was forced to supplement his income in order to support a wife and six children. He did this by building cottages on contract and other jobs. Emmaline did her part by taking in laundry. When an elderly woman asked Emmaline if she could wash and iron a number of blouses, a light went on. Here was a job she could do at home while earning some pocket money. Out of a Javex bottle, Emmaline cut a sign shaped like a small blanket and hung it on a miniature clothes line. In

no time, she required five lines to handle her growing business. The children were put on storm watch to alert their mother of any black clouds on the horizon. Occasionally, they were too late in gathering the washing and would find themselves having to fish missing articles out of the lake, or retrieve a pillowcase from the top of a pine tree.

Emmaline was also known for her giant marigolds. Envious gardeners would ask about her brand of miracle food. She still laughs, "how could I afford plant food with all these children

Taken from Pointe au Baril Lighthouse. Log boom on the protected inside channel route.
– Ruth McCuaig Collection

Detail from Bellevue Hotel letterhead used in 1905 by Elizabeth Oldfield. Note spelling of 'Point aux Baril,' first seen on revised Bayfield chart.
— Ruth McCuaig Collection

to feed? The only thing those Marigolds got was soapy laundry water!" Emmaline remembers those days fondly, "everyone around judged if it was going to be a nice day by if the laundry was out at the lighthouse."

Besides bringing up six children and doing laundry for area residents, Emmaline used to practice the violin in the tower while watching to make sure the light did not flare. Neighbours used to joke, "heard you skinning the cat last

Carl and Emmaline Madigan, 1955.
— Madigan Collection/ Huronia Museum L995.0015.0005

night Emmaline!" She also baked pies for the two elderly women who ran the Bellevue Hotel, and helped them with sweeping and table setting. They had definite ideas about how to run a hotel — no drinking and lights out at 10, despite their American fishermen clientele. Even modern conveniences were spurned. Instead, they preferred to wash all the hotel laundry with a scrub board in the lake.

Modernization was a long time in coming to the lighthouse as well. Emmaline used a gas washing machine and gas iron. Not until the late 1960s did they acquire a diesel plant, enabling Carl to string a hydro line into the lighthouse. The children were glad to have television, but with so many other things to do, they didn't spend much time watching. They could fish, play baseball on a large flat rock, or build rafts. Sometimes they helped record the weather or list the species of birds killed flying into the light. For the younger children there was an imaginary line beyond which they dared not cross without their lifejackets. The jackets became a second skin; Barry, the youngest, would even nap in his.

Stanley and Bobby Madigan with anchor. Bellevue Hotel in distance—at night its windows now glow an eerie red, reflecting the lighthouse's beam.
— Courtesy of Madigan family

Major Evans (keeper 1941-46) was a railway surveyor who fell in love with the Pointe au Baril area.
— Courtesy of Wayne Maxwell

Major Evans

One year, while searching for a bass hole, two of the children, Gwen and Kelly, discovered an enormous anchor at Black Bales. A few years later, a friend, Lorne Goodwin, winched it under his boat, and towed it to a spot near the pump house. With help from the Coast Guard it was lifted out of the water and now rests in front of the lighthouse. The Madigans liked to imagine the anchor was from the fated *Asia*, but Emmaline believes it came from one of the many lumber barges that once plied these waters.

Pointe au Baril lighthouse, 1898.
— National Archives of Canada PA195265

Many lighthouses are thought to harbour a ghost. Pointe au Baril was no different. Emmaline and Carl swore they often heard the distinct sound of creaking footsteps on the tower stairs. The children's friends used to guffaw at the notion, until they too saw a door knob turn or a door swing open. Emmaline was convinced their "visitor" was benevolent and nicknamed him "Major Evans" after a former keeper. As potential ghosts go, he was quite an interesting one. During WWI, after being told he would not be going overseas, he went AWOL from the Canadian Army and hopped a freighter to England, where he joined the British forces. He was wounded at Paschendale, in Belgium and later saw action at Gallipoli on the Dardanelles. Evans was a railway surveyor, and during one of his surveys fell in love with the Pointe au Baril area. In 1922, he bought property, built a cottage and quickly became a part of the community. Between 1941 and 1949 he tended the light and was the first keeper to also service the channel lights. He died in 1959. Emmaline comments, "I never met the Major but I heard he liked the light very much. It makes sense — if I died this is where I would want to come back to. I loved it here."

GEREAUX ISLAND

In 1870, an open gallows lighttower funded in part by the Magnetawan Lumber Company, was built on Gereaux Island at the entrance to Byng Inlet. Only eight years later the Department of Marine and Fisheries found it to be in "very poor condition, not worth the extensive repairs which it now requires." A new lighthouse was constructed by the Department and put into operation in 1880.

Lighthouse Central

Gereaux Island lighthouse has been a magnet for visitors for over one hundred years. One of the earliest recorded visits, of an 1898 group of Americans, appears in James Barry's *The Sixth Great Lake:*

> At the house, we were directed to inquire at a boathouse near at hand, by a stout, barefooted Frenchwoman. Upon opening the door we found the keeper, a most picturesque old child of the seas, reclining in a wonderful home-made hammock, smoking a short-stemmed pipe, and recounting early adventures to a black-eyed grandson. He acknowledged our arrival with easy unconcern, and in a few words of broken English made us feel quite at home.

It must have seemed a place out of time, literally. Apparently when the Americans arrived at 8:30 a.m. the keeper had already eaten lunch — his only clock was running four hours fast! He graciously toured the group around the grounds, showed them his dog team, and answered their many questions. It was a routine that would be followed by all the lightkeepers who came after him.

In 1946, Joseph Barron won the competition for the job at the Gereaux light. It took some time for his wife Viola to grow accustomed to the extremes of life on the lighthouse. During the summer, she and Joseph felt more like tour guides than lightkeepers. Everyone wanted to climb the tower, but unfortunately there was always one person too frightened to come down the steep stairs alone. At other times of the year, they might not see a soul — except of course, for their eight children and two goats.

GEREAUX ISLAND

Location: Gereaux Island, south
   side of entrance to Byng Inlet
Built: 1870; 1880
Description: 1870 – Open
   gallows tower; 1880 – square
   wooden tower, attached
   dwelling
Height: 48 ft./14.4 m
Light: Fixed white catoptric then 4th order diop-
   tric; later rotating
Visibility: 12 miles/19 kms
Fog horn: Hand cranked
Additional: Bungalow built 1966,
   helicopter pad
Destaffed: 1989
Present: Original tower with flashing white light
   every five seconds. Boathouse and 1960s
   bungalow remain.

KEEPERS:

1877➤	Joseph Lamondin
1883➤	James Milne
	(Magnetawan Lumber Co.)
1885➤	Joseph Lamondin
1901-1918	Louis Lamondin
1918-1925	Charles Lamondin
1925-1946	Louis Lamondin
1946-1966	Joseph Barron
1966-c.1970	John Joiner, Dalton Crawford
1967	George Rozel
1968-1968	Herbert Christenson
1971-1972	D.N. Sullivan
1973-1977	Bert Hopkins
1978-1989	Art Niederhumer

But despite living on an island, Viola never worried about their safety. They played freely and at a
young age, learned to swim and navigate the
waters. The biggest problem was getting them to
school at Byng Inlet. This was solved when the
eldest was about nine or ten and was given a small
motorboat to do the job.

Gereaux, 1937.
– National Archives of Canada PA148781

The light continued to attract visitors well into
the '80s. For Bert Hopkins (1973-77), Gereaux
was the most active of the five lighthouses he
served. Art Niederhumer (1978-89) agrees,
pointing to over 200 names per year in his
Gereaux Island guest book, some from as far away
as New Zealand and Kenya. "The way I looked at
it, it was a government job on government property and the people paid taxes and had the right
to look at the island."

The Barrons brought up eight children at the light.
– Barron Collection/Huronia Museum L995.0019.0002

Lightkeeper Bert Hopkins (1973-77) (right)on the helicopter pad he painted.
— Hopkins Collection/Huronia Museum L995.0016.0018

Gereaux lighthouse, the place to visit.
— National Archives of Canada PA182839

Over the years, the big ships entering Byng Inlet changed from coal freighters to fuel tankers, among them the *Texaco Warrior*. When her Captain, Anil Soni, reached the bell buoy, he would radio Art to check that the channel was clear. In return for holding back the cruisers, Art would receive two or three 45-gallon drums of fuel. He also fondly remembers the ship's cook, "Herman the German" who would call from Byng Inlet to say, "come over for lunch Artie — what would you like? Wienerschnitzle? Whatever you like."

The Ghost Of Gereaux Island

The Gereaux Island lighthouse was haunted. At least that is what many people believed, especially Art Niederhumer's assistant. Art would receive panicky calls on the intercom entreating him to come over because the assistant was hearing footsteps and voices. As often as not, it was nothing more than a watering-can knocking against the wall in the wind. When reporters asked about the ghost, Niederhumer would reply, "gee, I haven't seen anything yet . . . it probably saw me, got scared and moved out."

We arrived at Gereaux Island just as the setting sun cast an orange glow over the lighthouse. The boathouse and dock, house and lighttower are still in use and the light still shines from atop the shuttered tower. A maze of cement paths lead in every direction to the ruins of former buildings which were destroyed by the Coast Guard in 1989 (except for the above buildings now serving as a seasonal rescue station, and an oil shed which Steve Wohleber of Britt, had moved into town.) As we sat on the rocks the sun was slowly swallowed by the waves and a string of tiny flashing lights, marking the channel into Byng Inlet and Britt, winked on, one by one.

Art Niederhumer, last lightkeeper at Gereaux.
— Courtesy of Stephen Wohleber

BYNG INLET RANGE

---‑✢‑---

A quick lunch before erecting the new Byng Inlet back range tower, 1936.
— *Courtesy of Jack Kennedy*

BYNG INLET RANGE

Front:
Location: Close to south side of channel
Built: 1890
Description: Square white wooden tower
Height: 34 ft./10 m
Light: Fixed red catoptric
Visibility: 8 miles/13 kms

Back:
Built: 1890; replaced 1936
Description: Square white wooden open-framed tower, lantern and top enclosed, slats below
Height: 49 ft./14.7 m
Light: Fixed red catoptric
Additional: Alignment leads into mouth of Byng Inlet, clear of Magnetawan Ledges and Burton Bank.

KEEPERS:
Kept by Gereaux Island keepers

Construction of the new Byng Inlet back range light.
— Courtesy of Jack Kennedy

FRENCH RIVER INNER RANGE LIGHTS

———— ✛ ————

In 1875, trellis range lights were constructed on the Bustard Islands to lead lumber vessels to the mouth of the French River. Inner range lights were also built at the mouth of the river to guide vessels into the river and up to the wharf. The four lights were collectively referred to as the French River Ranges. French River grew into a bustling lumber village. Huge piles of lumber from the sawmill lined the docks, waiting for schooners to carry it away. The traffic was so considerable that Staff Commander J.G. Boulton, head of the Georgian Bay Survey, recommended permanent structures be built, and a third range light added to the Bustards in 1893.

Edward Borron Jr. was appointed keeper of both sets of lights with a generous salary of five hundred dollars per year, reflecting the difficulty of this post. The two sets of range lights were five kilometres apart by water – a long row in stormy weather. Edward was the son of Edward Barnes Borron Sr., who was Stipendiary Magistrate, responsible for the growth of much of the territory north of Georgian Bay. In 1883, Edward Jr. married Emma La Hays of Killarney. They stayed at the Bustard Islands during the summer and at their year-round residence on Lefroy Island beside the French River front range, for the other months. For eighteen years they followed a simple routine: during the day, their children attended school in the village; at night Edward tended the lights and afterwards relaxed by playing the piano.

In 1902, when Edward died quite suddenly, life for his family changed dramati-

FRENCH RIVER INNER RANGE LIGHTS

Front Range:

Location: Lefroy Island, west side of river mouth

Date: 1875

Description: White tapered wood, open framework

Light: Fixed red 7th order dioptric (in 1913)

Visibility: 6 miles/9.6 kms

Present: Fixed white light, white daymark with orange vertical stripe on pole

Back Range:

Location: East side of river

Description: 1875 (open gallows frame work; 1893 (square white wooden tower surmounted by red square wooden lantern

Height: 33 ft./10 m

Light: Fixed red

Visibility: 6 miles/9.6 kms

Present: Range light still standing, fixed white light

KEEPERS:

1875-1902	Edward Borron
1902-1920	Emma Borron
1920-1921	Dean Udy
1921-1935	Robert Young
1935	Destaffed

cally. Left with few resources, Mrs. Borron pleaded to be allowed to take over the post, but dozens of men from the area also applied for the job. After much deliberation, the Department relented and appointed Emma Borron keeper of the Bustards and French River lights with the proviso that "she had a good man who would stay on the Bustards and that her able sons would always help." It was a demanding job, for there were five lights, three at the Bustards and two at French River.

Troubled Waters

At midnight, September 10, 1909, the steamer *Soo City* ran aground just north of the Bustard Islands. A letter to the Superintendent of Lights from the Captain a few days later, read, "I must inform you that on the night of September 10th we were entering French River when we ran

Front range light and Borron home on Lefroy Island.
— National Archives of Canada PA195252

aground, the reason being that the light at the Bustards was dark. This is unfortunate and even more distressing because the keeper is a woman and unable to fulfill her duties." In the early twentieth century, being a lightkeeper at a remote site like French River and the Bustards was tough. For a female lightkeeper, it was doubly hard.

There was much bitterness on the part of some of the men from French River. Together with several captains, they insisted that a man should be in charge. But Mrs. Borron had her own supporters. Each time there were complaints about the light not being lit, she would get signed depositions from local fishermen and others who insisted it had been. This battle went on for sixteen years, until one particularly damaging letter arrived on the desk of J.N. Arthurs, Superintendent of Lights, regarding Mrs. Borron's conduct:

Dear Sir,

I write to you regarding the matter of the Bustard Islands. I must inform you that I have been Assistant Keeper there for three years and so far have not been paid for the last year. In addition Mrs. Borron has only been out thrice in the last five months. At her lst visit she made me give her matches and some oil. I have a family and a wife and we are starving. I believe she is cheating the dept.

Your obedient servant,
Ignatius Bebamikawe

Others continued to complain the light was unlit, often for weeks at a time. Mrs. Borron disputed the allegations, but found herself in a corner when asked to furnish receipts for the assistant's wages and supplies for the Bustards. She had none. As it turned out, this was immaterial, as the Department had decided to split the Bustard and French River responsibilities. Mrs. Borron was left in charge of the French River set, receiving $300 per year, half her former salary.

In March 1918, Thomas Ullman took over as Bustards' keeper. Mrs. Borron showed him around, then rowed back to her French River home. On her return, she found her house burned to the ground and everything lost. Only her late husband's piano, smouldering in the wreckage, was recognizable. Devastated, she

French River Village in its heyday.
— Courtesy of the Borron family/ Willliam A.Campbell, Northeastern Georgian Bay and Its People

Bob Young

Robert Young was appointed lightkeeper in 1921, just as French River Village was on its last legs. The boiler for the mill had exploded, and with the mill gone, the town slowly died. A familiar man about the Village, Bob had come from Belfast, Ireland before the turn of the century to work at the Ontario Lumber Company mill. He lived in the village with his wife and rowed across the river each day to tend the light on Lefroy Island. A local paper reported what happened on one of these trips:

LIGHT KEEPER SHOT BY INDIAN
November, 1927
Robert Young was shot by an Indian while tending a range light on the French River. The 69 year old was critically wounded through the shoulder and hand but struggled on foot 12 miles overland to the railroad tracks and with the help of some hunters got on a box car to Parry Sound (50 miles.)

moved with her family into an old mill house in the village. Two years later, she took a leave of absence due to illness and went to Parry Sound to recuperate, planning to return the following year. When one of her sons returned to the house to collect some possessions, he found it had been vandalised and everything stolen. Emma Borron never returned to the town she had known for thirty-seven years.

For the next year, Young was on workman's compensation. When he returned to the job in June 1929, his bad luck continued. One evening on his way to Lefroy, he was attacked by a swarm of black flies. The infected bites were so severe, he became blind and again had to be taken to Parry Sound. This time when he tried to collect workman's compensation, he was turned down with this unsympathetic statement: "black flies are part of the country and are known to be worse than at the French River. Mr. Young must plan his trips more carefully and go after sundown. In addition, he should most likely row faster."

The 1930s were devastating for Robert Young. His wife died one winter early in the decade, but he could not leave because there was no one to attend the light. He made a coffin and kept her body in the back room, until lumbermen from nearby Bad River arrived in the spring and took the body to Parry Sound. He was now the last remaining resident of French River. His bad luck continued. One day while tending the light, thieves broke into his house (the last one in French River) and ransacked it. Discouraged, he let weeds grow up around the house and watched the town turn into a ghost town. Alone, he and his black and white collie sat on the dock waiting for ships to come in.

The Department received numerous complaints from passing captains that the keeper seemed to be destitute and was not taking care of himself. It was a sad end for French River Village and its lightkeeper. In 1934, Young was forcibly removed and taken to Parry Sound to recuperate. A year later, he returned to his birthplace in Northern Ireland. The light station was destaffed and automated.

William Pillgrem, who grew up at the Bustards fishing camp, remembers French River in the 1930s:

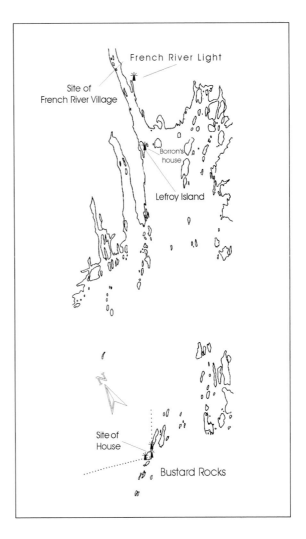

There were just a few empty buildings. McIntosh's store was still operating, and the church . . . I remember the church, big old rough lumber building — a building gets old fast when it isn't painted. In those days the buildings were put on wooden foundations, that's why those old towns disappeared.

Today, French River is a wild place full of poison ivy, rattlesnakes and thick bush, although the back range light in the former village remains. On Lefroy Island, the front range light is now on a pole. Nearby, only a few hooks and scars mark the site of the house that Emma Borron lived in for thirty-seven years. French River's sad past seems to have been washed clean from the rocks.

Bustards Lightstation
– *National Archives of Canada PA 172461*

THE BUSTARDS

+

Outer French River Range Lights

The Bustard lights were part of the French River range system, first built in 1875. When lined up, they guided lumber vessels past shoals and into the booming lumber village at the mouth of the French River. They also served as vital navigational aids to the local Bustard Island fishermen. During his Georgian Bay Survey, Staff Commander J.G. Boulton recommended adding another range light to the Bustards, and making the temporary structures permanent. This work was completed in 1893.

Edward Borron Jr. became the first keeper of the Bustards and French River in 1875. After his death, his wife Emma took over, until the Bustard lights and French River lights were separated in 1918. Thomas Ullman took over the Bustards (see French River) until David Mountnay was transferred from Badgeley Island the following year. He kept the lights until he became nearly blind, whereupon his wife took over.

By the time keeper Tom Flynn arrived on the scene in 1928, the fishing activity on the islands had changed dramatically. Instead of steamers picking up the catch and delivering it to Owen Sound, fishermen sent it by rail from Key Harbour. In the spring, Flynn would be the first to arrive, followed shortly by the fishermen and their belongings. Their arrival must have been quite a sight. Because of the threat of thieves, nothing could be left in their shanties over the winter, and so families like the Pillgrems arrived from Meaford, laden down with mattresses and bed springs in addition to the regular provisions.

THE BUSTARDS

Location: Three range lights on Bustard Rocks. Separate dwelling

1875
Description: Two trellis range towers (main light and inner range)
Height: Both 6.1 m
Lights: Fixed white (flat-wick lamps)
1893: Both towers rebuilt
Use: Two lights lead in clear of North Bustard Rock to intersect with the French River inner range

1893
Description: New outer range added
Height: 28 ft./8.4 m
Light: Fixed white catoptric
Use: Outer range and the main tower lead in clear of Isabel Rock on the north, and all the shoals south-west of Bustard Rocks on the south
Additional: Dwelling burned 1914, rebuilt 1916, then destroyed 1965
Present: Only the towers remain with green fixed lights; site of house overgrown

KEEPERS:
1875-1902	Edward Borron Jr.
1902-1918	Emma Borron
1918-1918	Thomas Ullman
1919-1928	David Mountnay
1928-1953	Tom Flynn
1951-1953	Reginald McIntosh

Thomas William Flynn, Bustard Rocks Lightkeeper (1928-53)
– Courtesy of Isabel Anderson/ William A. Campbell

when he first came up he had an outboard motorboat which was really a big square-sterned rowboat. He would put his family in there and when you saw them coming into the channel from the lighthouse all you could make out was the bow of the boat sticking up in the air and Tom's head peering over top of it trying to see. The motor used to catch on fire so he had to keep a blanket handy.

During his twenty-five-year tenure, Flynn worked diligently to make the Bustards a home.

The Flynn children spent summers playing with the Pillgrem gang. One of the lifeboats from a tug provided transportation to favourite fishing and watering holes.
– Courtesy of Pillgrem Family/William A. Campbell

Flynn was a colourful addition to the vibrant Bustards community with his flair for telling a story and coining a phrase — "holy jumping Nellie";" the hootenanny off the galloping rod"; "wouldn't that make you jump up and grab your eyelashes." William Pillgrem Jr. recalls his first memory of him:

Bustard Rocks residence and inner range tower, 1947.
– Courtesy of Jack Kennedy

Dozens of small vegetable and flower beds, laboriously created by transporting soil in bushel baskets from other islands, dotted the island. They kept chickens and sold the eggs to the fishermen. Flynn also built a series of wooden pathways to make it easier to move around the craggy island, and hopefully to prevent uninvited encounters with rattlesnakes which terrified him (hard to imagine of one who had earned a medal for bravery during the War.)

Following Flynn's retirement, the lights were automated using a battery system. William Pillgrem Jr., who by then was fishing out of the Bustards, recalled how strange it was not to have a lightkeeper. For the first few years, the job of recharging the lights was contracted out to Reginald McIntosh, then a local fisherman took it over. In May 1969, a 55-amp, 12-volt, 4-changer set was installed. Four bulbs were set on a wheel that automatically rotated once the bulb in use burned out,

replacing it with the next in line.

The small towers still stand guard on the wave-swept rocks, looking much as they would have a hundred years ago. Inside, it is a different story. Keepers would never have had to battle through spiderwebs as thick as gauze sheets to climb the stairs.

In 1875, The Bustard Islands were dotted with shanties housing independent fishermen and their families. The Booth Fish Company took over their operations after the turn of the century. In the 1930s, the families were hit hard by the Company's bankruptcy, as the Company had taken much of the season's catch but never paid for it.
– Parry Sound Public Library

Second Killarney East light erected 1909.
— *National Archives of Canada PA32546*

KILLARNEY
EAST AND WEST

---+---

Marking the east and west entrances to Killarney channel, these lights were among the first to be built following the era of the Imperial Towers. Constructed in 1866 to assist the Manitoulin Island area's developing fishing and shipping industry, the simple square wooden towers were quite a contrast to the earlier stone giants. It was not by chance this site was chosen, as the village of Killarney would, in the future, become home to a prize of up to a thousand boxes of lake trout and white-fish. The contest began at the Sault, and for twenty-four hours, ships would try any-thing to establish and maintain a lead, in order to be the first to arrive. With a two-hour headstart, the winner could pick up most of Killarney's bounty; anything less, turned the occasion into a spectator sport. Rival ships would leapfrog along the docks picking up crates. Sometimes, two ships would aim for the same dock at the same time, playing chicken until one relented. The air was filled with colourful lan-guage flying from wheelhouse to wheelhouse and dented fenders, guard rails, and docks were just part of the game.

The East and West lights were first tended by Philemon Proulx. In 1880, when his eyesight began to fail, Pierre Regis de Lamorandiere was appointed keeper. A blacksmith, cooper, gunsmith, sailor, farmer and fiddle player, P.R. shared the same industriousness which had characterized his grandfather, the founder of a trading post at Killarney in 1820.

While the Killarney East light was accessible by foot, the Killarney West light on Partridge Island could only be reached by water. P.R.'s solution to keeping the light burning in inclement weather? Hermits. He constructed a shack in a hollow near the light and furnished it with a wood-burning cookstove, small table, bench and

KILLARNEY EAST

Location: Red Rock Point, one
    mile east of Killarney
Built: 1866; rebuilt 1909
Description: Small square white
    tower; later square tapered
    "pepper-pot" design
Height: 20 ft./6.1 m
Light: Fixed white dioptric; then flashing
Visibility: 12 miles/19.2 kms
Fog Horn: Hand
Additional: Radio beacon; residence in town
Present: Aluminum siding hides cornice and ped-
    iments over door and window.

KILLARNEY WEST

Location: Partridge Island one mile N.W. of
    Killarney
Built: 1866, rebuilt 1909
Description: Small square white tower; later
    square tapered tower
Light: Fixed white catoptric
Visibility: 11 miles/17.6 kms
Present: Tower still standing

KEEPERS:

1866-1880	Philemon Proulx
1880-1904	P.R. de Lamorandiere
1904-1912	Frank Roque
1912-1946	Joseph Burke
1946-1950	Frank Sinclair
1950-1960	Ferdinand Solomon
1960-1960	Basil Roque (temp.)
1961-1979	Ferdinand Solomon
1979-1981	Brent Skippen
1982➤	Alfred de Lamorandiere

Early Killarney Village
– National Archives of Canada PA195255

snoring father, Herbie remembers elbowing him
with regularity. He often joined his father on
trips to the lighthouses after his mother's death
when he was seven. Soon he was helping with
tasks like pumping the hand cranked fog horn
during prolonged fogs. When Joseph began
working for a mining company, he could not
always arrive before sunset to light Killarney
East, especially late in the season when darkness
came early. The task fell to Herbie, who would
also return around 9 p.m. to crank the grandfather clock-type weights so that they would continue to rotate the flashing light until dawn.

*From a mile away, we could see the waves
crashing against the jagged shoreline and leaping*

P.R. de Lamorandiere at his Roche Rouge Farm
– Courtesy of Dorothy Hoyland

shelf. Oliver Pilon and Henry Solomon were
delighted to be its first occupants.

Many a night, Joseph Burke (1912-46) and his
son Herbie shared that ten by twelve foot room
with the hermits. Squeezed on a cot with his

P.R. and Virginia de Lamorandiere. Two weeks prior to his death in 1923 at age 80, P.R. travelled to Toronto to gain political support for a road in Killarney. He marvelled at the electric street lights, listened to jazz, and sat unmoved through his first moving picture until some ships came on the screen. – Courtesy of Dorothy Hoyland

Keeper Joseph Burke was presented with a medal from King George in recognition of his 34 years of service.
– Burke Collection/Huronia Museaum L995.0021.0002

over the lighthouse. The morning of our planned departure, we awoke to the sound of clanging rigging, and the sight of rows of fishing tugs tied snugly to the dock. Only a lone sailboat dared to test the waters. Past the protection of George Island, its mast began swinging wildly and the boat turned back. This stretch of water is renowned for the size and power of its waves. In a southerly wind, they build up along the entire length of Georgian Bay, until they explode against the steep rock below the Killarney East light.

Burke family standing in front of Killarney lightkeeper's house. Herbie Burke is the young boy.
– Burke Collection/Huronia Museum

Lightkeeper's house where Herbie Burke was born in 1917. Built in 1870 for $650, on what is now the empty lot beside 8 Charles St. in Killarney.
– Solomon Collection/Huronia Museum L995.0018.0001

Killarney West, 1890.
– National Archives of Canada PA 148783

A Prayer for the Sailors

From her kitchen window Margaret Burke looked out at the cold November day and watched the spray shoot over the East light. Placing breakfast on the table, she said to her children, "let's say a prayer for the sailors." Down the street, Merle Solomon sent her boys to fetch their father at the lighthouse. It was unlike him to be late. Before long Teddy returned, panicky and breathless, shouting, "the boat upset." Merle rushed out of the house but soon realized she needed a boat. Rushing back, she grabbed the phone and froze. Although Killarney was a town full of boats, she could think of no one to call! She rang the operator and begged for help.

Even though he knew the waves were going to be big in front of the East light, Ferdinand Solomon had decided to take the risk. As soon as he was in the open he knew he was in trouble. Huge rollers drove at him. One wave grabbed the Peterborough outboard and spun it into the air where the howling wind lifted it as effortlessly as paper in a breeze. Thrown into the lake, Ferdinand grabbed two lifejackets, pulling one over his head and pressing the other to his chest. As the waves pounded him, the second lifejacket was pushed suffocatingly against his face. He tossed it off and it was instantly snatched by a curling wave. Knowing that he would have no bone left unbroken if he were smashed against the rocky shore, Ferdinand swam with all his might until he blacked out from exhaustion. Waking, he saw Jackman Shoal and with arms and legs that felt cast in cement, propelled him-

Ferdinand Solomon
– Courtesy of Solomon family

self toward it. Turning his head, he saw a giant wave swelling behind. He held his breath and braced for the impact. The wave caught him and, with almost magical grace, placed him on the rock.

The Solomon boys watching on shore turned to see men running from town with a stretcher. Swimming out towards Jackman Shoal, the men could barely make out Ferdinand's crumpled, unconscious figure under the spray. Reaching the shoal, they hesitated to move him because his legs were frozen. On the difficult trip back to shore, Ferdinand regained consciousness. His first sight through the blinding snow was the lighthouse – still lit from the night before – mocking him from the cliff top. Ferdinand survived the shock and hypothermia, but never again challenged the sea in front of the Killarney East light.

The keepers were not the only area residents to be threatened by the cruel elements. While returning from Little Current, the local mailman Pierre Beauben, and his son, were caught in the ice as it rumbled and split apart. The son managed to swim to an island where he staved off hypothermia for three days. His less fortunate father was trapped on a drifting ice flow. Realizing he didn't have his son's stamina to swim to shore, he sat down on the mail bag, lit his pipe and waved good-bye, before drifting out of sight. Pierre Beauben was never seen again.

Since 1961, Killarney has been accessible by road, but its heart still faces out towards Georgian Bay and its channel still provides a welcome shelter for boats when the winds roar.

Killarney East, the original Red Rock light, 1908. First lit July 27, 1867– one of the first in the new Dominion.
– National Archives of Canada PA195254

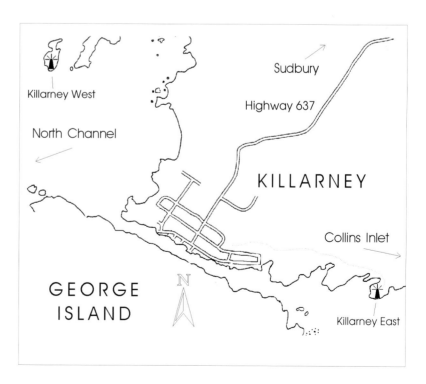

The Adventures of
Georgian Bay's
Lighthouse Tenders

FATE AND FOLLY
ON WATER

---+---

The lighthouse tenders were inextricably bound up with the story of the lighthouses. They delivered keepers and supplies, set and removed buoys and in some cases served as rescue vessels. Some of them were totally unsuitable for these tasks and most were poorly designed to face the unpredictable weather conditions for which Georgian Bay is famous.

(Information was compiled with the help of Pat Johnston. Between 1913-21 Pat's father George was lightkeeper on Lake Superior's Caribou Island. George Johnston left lightkeeping to become a lighthouse and fog alarm inspector for the Parry Sound Agency between 1921-47. Pat was hired in 1951, transferring his wartime diesel mechanic experience to the ships in the Agency. His brother, George Jr., also worked on the tenders, moving up the ranks from waiter to Captain. Many of these stories are from their family experiences.)

Simcoe *and* Lambton *tied at Parry Sound Base. CGS* Simcoe *foundered in Gulf of St. Lawrence Dec.7, 1917;* Lambton *foundered with all hands on Lake Superior, 1922.*
— *Parry Sound Public Library*

The First in a Long Line . . .
CGS *Simcoe*

Length: 180 ft.

Depth: 15 ft.

Beam: 35 ft.

Gross Tonnage: 913

Triple Expansion Steam Engine/217 hp

Built: 1909 Swan-Hunter, England

Demise: Foundered all hands, Magdalen
Islands, 1917

CGS Dollard *at St. John, N.B.*
— Courtesy of Pat Johnston

In 1910, the *Simcoe* became the first lighthouse tender to work out of the Parry Sound Base. Pat Johnston remembers her delivering his family to the Caribou Island Lighthouse each year and what excitement her return trip engendered. He and his brothers would dress in their best clothes to watch the men hustle about the island with sacks of coal for the fog plant and coal oil for the light.

In 1917, the *Simcoe* was on her way to St. John, New Brunswick to relieve the CGS *Dollard*, when she was caught in a November storm southwest of the Magdalen Islands, and went down with all hands. Years later, Magdalen Island fishermen claimed they could see her masts in deep water and in 1922, a life preserver from the *Simcoe* mysteriously washed up on Sable Island, Nova Scotia. The *Simcoe* was replaced by the *Dollard* from *St. John* for one season, before the *Grenville* took over.

Crew of the Simcoe *c.1910-13*
— Courtesy of Pat Johnston

The coffin-ship, the Lambton
— Parry Sound Public Library

CGS *Lambton*

Length: 108 ft.

Depth: 13 ft.

Beam: 25 ft.

Gross Tonnage: 323

Triple Expansion Steam Engine, 90 hp

Built: 1909 Sorel, Quebec

Demise: Foundered, all hands lost, Lake Superior, April 1922

"My father warned she was of dangerous design — the Government refused to listen."

In 1910, the *Lambton* was brought to Parry Sound to share duties with the *Simcoe*. One ship serviced Lake Erie, while the other serviced Lake Superior. Both tended Lake Huron and Georgian Bay. (Lake Erie was later transferred to the Prescott Agency.)

When George Johnston was training the new lightkeeper, George Penefold, for the Caribou Island light station in 1921, the new man was horrified to learn that the only way off the island at the end of season was in a 28-foot sailboat. This boat, with only a small cabin and a two cylinder coal-oil engine, to travel 65 miles across Lake Superior in December?! Mr. Johnston had nothing reassuring to say — two years earlier he and his assistant had been trapped in ice for seven harrowing days, and did not arrive on the mainland until New Year's Day. George Penefold subsequently started a letter-writing campaign, which eventually convinced the Canadian Government

The need to have lighthouse tenders capable of handling wintry Great Lakes weather was lost on the government.
—*Parry Sound Public Library*

Lightkeeper and fog alarm inspector George Johnston Sr., 1948.
— Courtesy of Pat Johnston

CCGS *Grenville*

Length: 164 ft.
Depth: 9½ ft.
Beam: 30 ft.
Gross Tonnage: 497
Triple Expansion Steam Engine, 900 hp
Built: Polson's Iron Works, Toronto
Demise: Crushed by ice

Only the tops of the CCGS Grenville's *masts are visible after she was crushed by ice against a bridge in December, 1968.*
— Ministry of Transport

to send the *Lambton* to pick up Lake Superior keepers.

That fall, in his new capacity as fog alarm inspector, George Johnston sailed on the *Lambton*, and was shocked to witness the crew chopping ice off the steering cable. Built originally as a tug, she rode low in the water, exposing the steering quadrant on deck to freezing spray. In addition, the lifeboats were on the roof. In a storm, the crew would be swept off before they could launch them. He immediately wrote a stern letter to the government, stating that the *Lambton* was dangerously ill-suited for the Great Lakes. Not surprisingly, his warning was ignored and so his wife took up her pen. In her letter to the government, she stated it was unconscionable that they would place anyone in such danger. Her husband had a large family and was not paid enough to purchase life insurance. Ottawa agreed and that spring George Johnston did not board the *Lambton* when she made her April tour of Lake Superior. The *Lambton* foundered and all hands were lost, including Caribou Island's new lightkeeper, George Penefold, the man who had first demanded her services.

The *Grenville* came to Georgian Bay in 1919, as replacement for the *Simcoe*. In December 1924, she ran aground on Burton Bank near Byng Inlet. Pumped out the following spring, she was delivered to the Collingwood shipyard for repairs, and was back in service by June.

For years the unflappable Captain Smith was at the helm. While anchored on Lake Erie, a strong squall snapped her lines and pushed her on shore. As he lit his pipe, Smith's only comment was, "there now, we'll have to see what we can do about that, now won't we." The *Grenville* plied the Bay for over a decade, before she was transferred to the Prescott Agency. In 1931, Pat Johnston's brother George helped deliver her to Sorel, Quebec, where the Prescott men took over the *Grenville* and the Parry Sound men returned to Georgian Bay with the *St. Heliers*.

One spring on the St. Lawrence River, ice clogged the *Grenville*'s water intake leaving her without steam power. She was grabbed by the current, slammed against the side of a cement bridge and slowly crushed under the force of the ice. The crew could only climb on the bridge and watch.

CGS *Murray Stewart*

Bought to replace the *Lambton*, the deep-sea tug the *Murray Stewart* was not entirely suited for the job, as she lacked a hoist for buoys. After service on Georgian Bay, she was moved to the East Coast and in 1939 was turned over to the Canadian Navy. She spent the war opening and closing the nets that protected the port of St. John from German submarines. Her military service ended in 1946, and she was sold.

In 1960, while driving through Port McNicoll, Pat Johnston spotted the old *Murray Stewart* along the bank. Having been sold for scrap, she was being cut up and a hoist was piling the metal along the shore. The still intact hull was bought by men in Penetanguishene, who rebuilt her as a tour boat under the name *Georgian Queen*.

Length: 119 ft.
Depth: 16 ft.
Beam: 26 ft.
Gross Tonnage: 234
Triple Expansion Steam Engine 156 hp
Built: 1918 Port Arthur
Demise: Scrapped; hull renamed
    Georgian Queen

Murray Stewart *in ice*
– *Courtesy of Pat Johnston*

CGS *St. Heliers*

The American Coast Guard crews would rib the Canadians, "Look! The Permanent Wave!"

The *St. Heliers* replaced the *Grenville* in 1931. A 130-foot deep-sea tug, she was built to clear shipwrecks around the British Isles following the First World War. The Canadian Government purchased her as a lighthouse tender, and in an effort to make her more suitable for Georgian Bay, they added sixty feet to her length. Despite the changes, the natural curve of a tug body was still visible at the stern, hence the nickname, the "Permanent Wave."

Length: 190 ft.
Depth: 16 ft.
Beam: 29 ft.
Gross Tonnage: 930
Triple Expansion Steam Engine, 116 hp
Built: 1919 Fergus Brothers, Port Glasgow
Demise: Sold in 1959

With a 29-foot beam and 190-foot length, the *St. Heliers* lacked stability. Several years passed before the crew learned how to balance her load so that she did not swing from side to side like a pendulum. She served on Georgian Bay until 1961, when she was bought by four Toronto

St. Heliers *lifeboat being lowered*
—*Courtesy of Pat Johnston*

St. Heliers, pre-1946.
— Courtesy of Rita Martin

men who dreamed of becoming Canadian shipping magnates.

St. Heliers: Mutiny, Gunplay and Piracy

Their dream was fueled by Carl Stewart, a man who made up in daring what he lacked in shipping experience. At one time, he had acted as a double agent, running guns for Fidel Castro while reporting to the U.S. Coast Guard. Later he was hired by Bahamian police to pose as a gunrunner in order to help overthrow an illegal gun and narcotics ring.

The newly purchased *St. Heliers* set sail on the first of many calamity-filled voyages. After running aground twice, she ran out of fuel and the captain ordered her deck planking ripped off and burned. While anchored at the mouth of the Don River in Toronto, the Panamanian flag was hoisted and she was renamed the S.S. *Tropic Sea*, in order to avoid carrying a Canadian crew at unionized wages. As soon as a replacement crew was flown in from Central America, the ship departed. Days later, the steering gear slipped a pin and Captain Brown ordered "all hands on deck." The crew ignored him. They had been

working a straight 36 hours and refused to leave their cabins. Somehow, the ship reached Halifax, on her way to the Bahamas. Captain Brown's log entry for that day read: "dense fog, no radar, no radio direction finder, no echo sounder. Sailed 1700 for Nassau." When the hapless vessel arrived in the Bahamas, no agent would unload her cargo of flour. Because of Stewart's reputation as an undercover agent, no one would deal with the Captain. Immediately, the unpaid crew began smashing tanks and barrels with fire axes. The ship had no alternative but to set sail for another port.

Cursed By a Ghost

In Spanish Honduras (now Honduras), they were able to take on a cargo of yellow pine. As the *Tropic Sea* had no ballast, the lumber made her top-heavy. Predicting the ship would sink within 48 hours, the Captain walked off. Suddenly, the *Tropic Sea* rolled to one side, her gunwales smashing the dock. A number of the crew jumped off. Then, she started to right herself. Nervously, the seamen clambered back on. Immediately, she swung thirty degrees in the opposite direction and again regained an even

S.S. Tropic Sea, *formerly the* St. Heliers, *moored at Kingston, Jamaica, after the ride of her life.*
— Maclean's, *May 19, 1962.*

keel. As if possessed, the *Permanent Wave* performed this peculiar side to side dance for the rest of the day. Four of the deckhands, convinced she was cursed, packed their bags and ran. After the cargo was shifted, the *Tropic Sea* was forced to anchor in the middle of the bay.

Several episodes later, the ship was being towed to Jamaica, when heavy winds caused her to roll. The crew donned their life jackets and lashed themselves together. As the gunwale touched the water, one man tried to untie himself but Stewart threatened to shoot if he continued. By some miracle, the crew and ship survived and were towed into Kingston Bay. (The *Permanent Wave*'s tropical adventures, which included charges of piracy, sedition, contempt of authority and armed robbery, are recounted by Ken Lefolii in his 1962 article for *Maclean's*, "The Slapstick Saga Of The S.S. *Tropic Sea*.")

CCGS *C.P. Edwards*

Length: 144 ft.
Depth: 10 ft.
Beam: 27 ft.
Gross Tonnage: 338
Triple Expansion Steam Engines, 375 hp
Built: Collingwood shipyards 1946
Demise: Sold by crown assets

The *Ottawa Mayerhill* was built at the Collingwood Shipyards as a small coastal freighter for the South China Sea. However, the Second World War ended before she saw duty. Purchased in 1948 by the Ministry of Transport, the *Ottawa Mayerhill* was modified to serve as a lighthouse tender and was renamed the *C.P. Edwards*. Like other tenders, she was not entirely suited for service on the Bay, as evidenced by Jack Kennedy's experience. Because of a storm warning, the former Superintendent of Lights, chose to take the North Channel route eastward instead of heading across Lake Huron. All went well, until the ship encountered ice just past Strawberry Island. The thought of having to go all the way around Manitoulin Island was too much for Kennedy and so he decided to proceed.

CCGS C.P. Edwards
— Courtesy of Pat Johnston

But because the ship lacked power, the only way they could make any headway was to turn the ship around and back through the ice.

One can imagine the feelings of relief when she was taken out of service in 1970, but before long she was refitted as a bulk carrier for the supply route from Montreal to Frobisher Bay! Subsequently, she operated in the more hospitable climes of the West Indies, then vanished from record.

CCGS *Alexander Henry*

Built in 1959 to replace the *St. Heliers*, the *Alexander Henry* was the first real ice-breaker commissioned by the Coast Guard for the upper Great Lakes. On the one hand, her construction included massive one inch thick, steel bow plates, especially designed for the purpose. On the other hand, her two General Electric stationary diesel motors were ill-suited to power the rapid shifts in direction needed to break through ice.

Her first assignment was to maintain access to the grain elevators on Lake Superior. Georgian Bay ports like Midland and Collingwood were furious because they too needed her services. To appease them, the Ministry of Transport sent a replacement ship, the

Length: 210 ft.
Depth: 16 ft.
Beam: 44 ft.
Gross Tonnage: 1,674
Twin G.E. diesels, 3550 hp driving into hydraulic gear boxes, twin screw
Built: Port Arthur shipyards 1959
Currently: Museum, and bed and breakfast, Kingston, Ontario

Vercheres. (In 1985 the *Alexander Henry* was purchased for $1.00 by the Marine Museum of the Great Lakes at Kingston, Ontario.)

Alexander Henry, *now a museum in Kingston, Ontario.*
– Arthur Collection/Huronia Museum L995.0009.0035

Vercheres

Length: 104 ft.
Depth: 11 ft.
Beam: 26 ft.
Gross Tonnage: 198
Steam compound engine, 54 hp
Built: 1901, Polson's Iron Works, Toronto
Demise: Sold in 1963. Scrapped 1967

CGS Vercheres, *breaking ice in Midland Harbour, 1959-60.*
– Courtesy of Pat Johnston

Pat Johnston chuckles at the mention of the *Vercheres*, "in typical government style they sent us this old ship that wasn't even fit to be commissioned." Among those who knew her, the *Vercheres* was known as a coffin ship because water poured freely through her rivets. En route to Georgian Bay from Sorel, Quebec, the ship docked at Toronto where the captain walked off and left the mate, George Johnston Jr., in command. George called the base to explain the situation. "I guess you're going to bring her up," they replied. "And if I don't?" queried George. "I guess you're not going to have a job," came the cool response.

Today, the work of servicing the Georgian Bay, Manitoulin, and North Channel lights is done by the Coast Guard's two helicopters, with additional help when needed from their ships: *Cove Island, Caribou Island, Griffon,* and *Samuel Risley.*

Coast Guard Ship Captains on Parry Sound Coast Guard Day, 1962. Left to right: George Johnston, Jr., Jerry Masales, Jack Kennedy, Basil Dubé.
– Courtesy of Pat Johnston

Passage broken through ice by St. Heliers *returning to Midland.*
– Courtesy of Howard Warner

PART III

LIGHTHOUSES OF MANITOULIN ISLAND AND THE NORTH CHANNEL

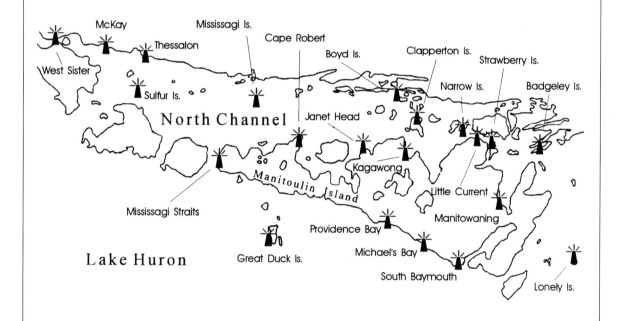

McKay

West Sister

Thessalon

Mississagi Is.

Cape Robert

Boyd Is.

Clapperton Is.

Strawberry Is.

Sulfur Is.

Narrow Is.

Badgeley Is.

North Channel

Janet Head

Mississagi Straits

Manitoulin Island

Kagawong

Little Current

Manitowaning

Providence Bay

Lake Huron

Great Duck Is.

Michael's Bay

South Baymouth

Lonely Is.

BADGELEY ISLAND

✛

As early as the 1850s, Badgeley Island was considered so important to shipping along the North Channel, that it was one of the locations chosen for an Imperial Tower. Unfortunately, the government ran out of money and it would take another 60 years before a lighthouse and back range tower were built to assist the lumber and fishing traffic from Killarney, Collins Inlet, and Little Current.

Frank Fowler— Making a Living

The lumber industry was booming and so lightkeeper Frank Fowler started a steam-powered sawmill on the island to help support his family of eight children. The mill produced fish crates and board lumber, both in great demand, until the August day in 1935 when a spark from the smokestack set the mill on fire while the men were having lunch. Before the alarm could ring, the building had disappeared in flames.

That was just the beginning of the Fowlers' misfortunes. Hubert, one of the younger children, fell in the water while climbing into a boat. When Mrs. Fowler yanked him out by the seat of his pants, he wasn't breathing! She and Frank tried without success to revive Hubert, including rolling him on a barrel. In desperation they set out for Killarney with the unconscious child. Nearing town, Hubert suddenly sat up and blinked at his shocked parents. They later learned that at that moment he had burst a lung, allowing him to breath.

It Looked Haunted

March 1946 – the day Merle Solomon first came to Badgeley. As the team of horses pulled the sleigh onto the frozen lake, their hooves splashed in the slush along the shore. Merle held her breath until they were safely on solid ice. With a lump in her throat, she looked back at her young boys, Jimmy and Teddy, and tightened her arms around the baby. There was no turning back. The house in Sudbury had been sold and they had said their goodbyes to all their friends. She couldn't meet her husband Ferdinand's eyes, nor those of the father-in-law she hardly knew. How could this strange world of snow-covered islands ever become familiar? When Ferdinand nudged her, pointing ahead at their new home, Merle tried not to cry. The icicle-covered lighthouse appeared so stark and inhospitable.

As the upstairs was not insulated, Ferdinand set up beds in the living room. Pulling back a flannel sheet, Merle was greeted by a scrambling insect. "Bed Bugs!" she shrieked. Ferdinand cleared his throat "Oh that — that's a cockroach. There's a few." (Years later Merle laughed, "a few cockroaches — a few million!") Later that night, after the children were asleep, the silence of the house was thick and suffocating. "It's a prison," Merle whispered to herself.

With only a rowboat, the trip to Killarney for supplies and food was laborious and slow and so it was a banner day when the Department of Transport upgraded the Solomons to a sailboat.

BADGELEY ISLAND

Location: Point on south side of island
Built: 1912
Description: Square white wooden dwelling with light rising from roof
Light: Fixed white catoptric
Visibility: 10 miles/16 kms
Additional: Dock and marine railway, sawmill
Automated: 1965
Dynamited: 1981

Back range:
Built: 1912
Location: Southeast point of island
Description: Steel skeleton tower
Light: Fixed white 4th order dioptric
Visibility: 13 miles/21 kms

KEEPERS:

1912-1916➤	Patrick Proulx
◄1919	David Mountnay
1921-1937	Frank Fowler
c.1938-1945	Frank Sinclair
1946-1950	Ferdinand Solomon
1950➤	Frank Sinclair
◄1981	Lauly Beaucach

Front lighthouse, July 4, 1912.
— National Archives of Canada PA148784

Fowler family c. 1936. Children left to right: William, Lloyd, Hubert, Marie, Dorine, Florence, Roland, and Gerald. Parents Winnifred and Frank.
— Courtesy of Marie Hall

Badgeley back range light.
— Huronia Museum L995.18

Ferdinand and his son Jimmy towed the new boat to Killarney and had Joe Roque give them a sailing lesson. It took longer than planned . . . .

As darkness fell, Merle's concern grew. An unlit light could cost Ferdinand his job. She lit it, but then realized she would also have to light the 65-foot range tower. She had refused to learn how, reasoning it might give Ferdinand an excuse not to return home on time. Her panic grew as the tower's silhouette faded in the gloom. What would she do? When Ferdinand finally appeared, Merle reminisced, "I lit into him something fierce. He left immediately to light the tower light and when he came back I said, 'oh I was so glad to see you coming.' 'Well,' he said, 'you would never have known it.'"

Over the years, Merle's lack of lightkeeping skills continued to provide some amusing family stories. On one occasion, when Ferdinand was in Killarney, ". . . the fog rolled in and a ship started blowing," recalled Merle. She began to pump the fog horn. The ship blew again. Merle pumped again. And so it continued. When Ferdinand returned, he found his wife with raw, blistered hands. Trying not to laugh, he explained that vessels signal steadily in fog to avoid collision with one another. As the ship sailed on, the amused captain gave a noisy salute to Merle's dedication.

"My God Merle! There's a ship on our verandah!"

Settling back for a quiet evening, Merle reached for her knitting, while Ferdinand filled out the logbook. Suddenly the house shook and the windows rattled as if the island were struck by an

The dock where Hubert Fowler nearly drowned.
— Courtesy of Marie Hall

The Burlington *grounded in front of the lighthouse, 1949.*
— *Solomon Collection/Huronia Museum L995.0018.0010*

Great Lakes history. He added a whole new chapter when he turned his ship to line up with the range lights a half mile too soon! Merle later told her husband that she had noticed the *Burlington* in the vicinity of the light, but had thought nothing of it. Perhaps if Ferdinand had known this, he might have averted the disaster.

Merle Solomon, "it was the fastest move they ever made."

earthquake. "My God Merle! There's a ship on our verandah!" The sight was stunning. A huge ship, the *Burlington*, ablaze with lights, loomed up against the night sky. Ferdinand's first impulse was to check that the lighthouse was operational — it was. Sometime later, the Captain admitted he had not navigated this route for years and had taken the Turkey Trail (the old North Channel shipping route named for the sight of ships dodging back and forth around islands and shoals) in order to let his crew experience some

Three days after his second birthday, October 17, 1950, the Solomon's fourth son, Terry, tragically drowned. After the funeral, Merle could no longer bear to be away from her children who were attending school in Killarney. The lighthouse and the island had once more become a prison. Since Frank Sinclair, the former keeper, had always wanted to return, he gladly exchanged the Killarney lights with Ferdinand. It was the fastest move the Department ever approved.

Merle and sons, Ted, Leonard and Jim.
— *Solomon Collection/Huronia Museum L995.0018.0006*

We weren't expecting to find much as we pressed through the tangled bushes on the island. In 1981, the lighthouse had been dynamited by the Coast Guard and replaced with a metal tower. Yet in a clearing, we stumbled upon an elaborate series of stone walls, once used to enclose animals and a garden. Beside the metal beacon, we found the lighthouse's rubble-filled foundation, along with a jumbled pile of rusted door knobs and twisted bed frames. We later learned some items had been salvaged, including the staircase and some of the wainscotting which now grace a house in Killarney.

Badgeley lighthouse destroyed in 1981. The Coast Guard waited until a Sunday when the Badgeley mine dynamite expert was free. Photo, 1995.
– Lynx Images

When the Burlington struck the shore in front of the Badgeley Island lighthouse, Merle Solomon remembers it felt like an earthquake.
– Bev Keefe Collection/Huronia Museum

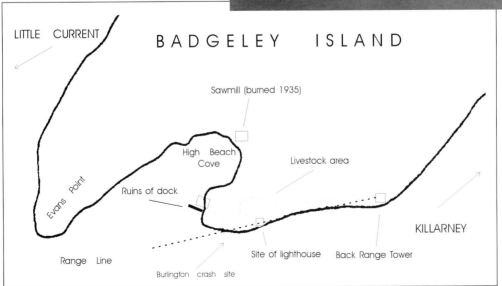

202

Manitowaning

The *Manitoulin*

Before a lighthouse ever came to Manitowaning, freight and passenger boats made it their first port of call on Manitoulin Island. Its deep harbour at the end of Manitowaning Bay welcomed them with the promise of a safe anchorage.

On a clear May day in 1882, the new steamer *Manitoulin* headed toward the small farming village. Her Captain, "Black Pete" Campbell, was enjoying his noon meal with the first-class passengers, while a young family, the Tracys, looked with anxious excitement at the land that would soon be their home.

At the Manitowaning dock, a cheer went up when the steamer was spotted rounding Phipps Point. Then, David Young, a young man on the dock, saw red flames and clouds of smoke shooting out of the ship. The cry went out, and "everyone who could pull an oar jumped into some boat or canoe to go to the rescue . . . the vessel was over two miles away and I never worked so hard in my life for that quarter of an hour."

On board, a terrified man burst into the salon shouting "Fire! Fire!" The Captain ordered the crew to man the hose and called for full steam ahead. A coal-oil lamp had exploded in the lower engine room, and the fire was spreading with wicked speed. In the wheelhouse, the First Mate, anticipating the Captain's order, was already steering the boat towards the Wikwemikong shore, a mile and a quarter away. Some panicked and jumped overboard, but most just waited and held their breath. By the time the ship ran aground, the flames had reached her bow. The rescue boats saw the passengers clamber down the ropes to safety, then everyone watched as the boat burned to the waterline. The Tracys lost all their possessions, but were looked after by a Mr. Lehman and the kindly villagers, until they were able to start out on their own. Others were not so fortunate. Eleven people died and many more were injured.

The ship itself fared surprisingly well. The hull, the engine and the boilers were towed to Owen Sound, and rebuilt into the steamer *Atlantic*, which served for twenty years before she too faced a fiery end. (The ship that replaced the *Manitoulin* was the *Asia*, which lasted only four more months before meeting an untimely end.)

The Lighthouse

More and more steamers coming to Manitowaning arrived at night and so it became obvious that a lighthouse was needed to mark the port entrance. In 1883, tenders were let for its construction, but according to the Manitoulin papers, the process did not go smoothly:

LET THERE BE LIGHT
September 20, 1884
When the contractor for the construction of Manitowaning light house arrived here early in July, he announced that the building was to be completed by the 15th of August. We are now well on into September and the building is still far from completion. Is the construction of this edifice being purposely delayed, that the position of keeper may be once more held out as a bait during an election contest? The previous history of this concern would point to the probability of an affirmative answer proving correct.

DAWSON'S MONUMENT
August 8, 1885
Dawson's monument, otherwise known as the Manitowaning light house, is to be completed at last. But perhaps we should not prophecy too early as we made the same announcement a little over a year ago.

John Waddell of Kingston, Ontario was the unpopular contractor who failed to complete

---

MANITOWANING

Location: East of St. Paul's on the hill in the village
Built: 1885
Description: Square white wooden tapered tower, red polygonal lantern
Light: Fixed white 7th order dioptric; later fixed green
Visibility: 14 miles/22.4 kms
Present: Newly shingled with cedar shakes

KEEPERS:

1885-1886➣	Benjamin Jones
1900-1906➣	John Gourley Jr.
1912-1916➣	J.J. Morrow
1936-1964	Jack Clark

---

the job as scheduled. The Department of Marine and Fisheries took the job over, and, despite some skepticism, did complete the tower in 1885 and appointed its first keeper, Benjamin Jones.

Over the years the dock remained the centre of Manitowaning's activity. In the early thirties, it hosted a giant celebration, a surprise party in honour of Captains Batten and McCoy's twenty-five years of service as masters of the steamers *Caribou* and *Manitou*. For many seasons, the two steamers had shared dock space at Manitowaning every Wednesday afternoon. As each man knew almost everything that transpired on their vessels, party arrangements had to be made in secret, in an effort to keep them in the dark until the last moment. Apart from explaining the unusual number of VIPs on board, at Manitowaning, the trick was to get Captain Batten away from the ship as preparations were made, and to find an excuse to bring Captain McCoy, who lived in Manitowaning, back on the ship for the party. Everything worked out, and the event was a huge success.

Manitowaning lighthouse.
— *National Archives of Canada PA148100*

The Manitoulin *burned in Manitowaning Bay, 1882.*
— *Archives of Ontario*

These men were friendly rivals who relished a weekly race over the first eight miles after leaving the dock. Even while unloading freight at the dock, the fires were kept stoked so the ships could be hot off the mark. On Wednesdays, resident housewives knew enough not to hang laundry, because of the thick smoke that poured from the funnels. Captain McCoy of the faster *Manitou*, revelled in getting upwind of the *Caribou* and engulfing it in a choking black cloud. The stubborn Captain Batten remained unfazed, until the day someone on the *Manitou* tossed oil and rubber tires into the boilers. The soot-covered *Caribou* pulled away, and never raced again. Even Captain McCoy was not amused when he discovered the paint on the *Manitou*'s funnels had blistered. Both men served for several more years on this route, one of the most demanding on the Great Lakes, and completed their remarkable careers with many close calls, but no loss of life.

The lighthouse still stands and in 1995, the Coast Guard gave her a facelift by covering the exterior with new cedar shake shingles — just in time to celebrate the Municipality of Assiginack's 125th birthday in 1996.

"Black Pete" Campbell, the Manitoulin*'s captain.*
— *Collingwood Museum*

STRAWBERRY
ISLAND

———— ✛ ————

*D*ramatic shafts of light broke through the heavily overcast sky as we approached *Strawberry Island. By the time we came alongside, the sky was a flaming orange, and the lighthouse seemed to be on fire. It was too late to land and set up our film equipment, so we regretfully continued on to Little Current for the night. The following morning under clear blue skies, we returned to Strawberry to film and to search for a set of initials carved by a young boy with a jackknife. They were DM, for Donald McKenzie, the son of William McKenzie, one of Strawberry's early keepers.*

Like many lighthouse families, March was the month the McKenzies, William and Mary Jane, would gather their children, their belongings and their animals and set out across the ice to begin another season of tending the light. This routine was one their son, Donald eagerly awaited. He had been born at the lighthouse on April 6th, 1883, with no doctor in attendance. For assistance, his parents had had only a small medical manual included with the rules and regulations for lighthouse keepers.

The medical advice covered a wide range of topics such as: management of acidity of the stomach — "if the food sours on the stomach, as much rhubarb powder as will lie on a five cent piece, mixed with three times as much cooking soda should be taken twice a day;" bronchitis and inflammation of the lungs — "begin by giving a teaspoonful of ipecacuanha wine two or three times until vomiting is produced. Then put on the chest a cloth soaked in hot water and sprinkled with turpentine. If this does not bring sufficient relief replace the hot cloth with a hot linseed meal poultice . . . "

There were also clear instructions covering infancy and childhood, including precautions to be taken by the Mother.

William and Mary Jane McKenzie. Photos taken c. 1919 shortly before retiring from Strawberry.
– Courtesy of Don McKenzie

STRAWBERRY ISLAND

Location: Northern tip of
    Strawberry Island (3.5 miles
    east of Little Current)
Built: 1881; last altered 1984
Description: Square tapered
    wooden tower with attached
    dwelling. White with red trim.
Height: 44 feet/13.2 m
Light: Fixed white catoptric; 1916 (4th order
    dioptric
Visibility: 11 miles/17 kms
Fog horn: Hand fog horn
Present: Leased as a cottage

KEEPERS:
1881-1882	Bryan McKay
1883-1919➤	William McKenzie
◂➤	Roxy Smith
1930-1963	Alvin Stewart

After Confinement and during Nursing: As a general rule the mother should not leave bed, or even sit up in it, for four or five days after delivery. If all goes well, after that period, the mother may dress, but she should still lie down all day, and only after a few days more should she begin to go about, doing very little at first. . . .

Suggestions if a baby would not nurse included, "the infant should suck the milk from the bottle by means of an artificial nipple, which may be either a cow's teat, or made of washed chamois leather or folds of linen, pierced with a small hole. . . ." Much emphasis was placed on the importance of milk in the diet, ". . . although no marked immediate bad effects may appear to result to children from a deficiency of milk, it is probable that delicacy of constitution, or even consumption and other diseases in after life may be often mainly due to this cause."

Strawberry Island, North Channel, 1881.
– Courtesy of William Ritching

William and Mary Jane McKenzie and their children.
Standing left to right: George, Minnie, and Charlie; seated
left to right: Donald and Bill c. 1887-88. Donald was born
at the lighthouse in April 1883.
— Courtesy of Don McKenzie

"Curly" and Jean Stewart celebrated their 25th wedding
anniversary at Strawberry. Photo, 1963.
— Courtesy of Vicki Raisbeck

The present light is lovingly tended and leased during the summer months. Plans are underway to have it declared a heritage building.

Thanks to their own good sense, the McKenzies successfully raised seven children at the light, before retiring to Little Current after the First World War. Years later, Donald McKenzie's son made a visit to the lighthouse and found his father's initials still carved into the back door. Unfortunately, we did not.

The Strawberry light is a well-known landmark for those who cruise the North Channel. One visitor was so entranced that he had a replica built on his inland property in southwestern Ontario!

Strawberry, 1935.
— National Archives of Canada PA14891

STRAWBERRY
ISLAND

Shed

Camp
Cove

Boat House

N

LITTLE CURRENT

---✦---

By the time the town plot was surveyed in 1866, steamers had been visiting Little Current (then called Shaftesbury) on a regular basis. That same year, the Department of Public Works constructed two range lights: a front one on Spider Island, and a back one on the Little Current waterfront. These early lights were simple square boxes, similar to the original ones at Killarney.

Little Current's first lightkeeper, Donald McKenzie, arrived at Manitoulin in the 1850s. He and his wife Margaret settled in Wikwemikong, where they taught Natives to make packing boxes for the burgeoning fish trade. After Margaret died, leaving him with three children, Donald married her sister and moved to Manitowaning. Sadly, she died in childbirth and the McKenzie family moved to Chicago. In 1866, they returned to take over the new light. At that point, the McKenzies were one of only four white families in Little Current — the influx of white settlement was still to come. Donald later married a widow with three children. In all, he raised 13 children during his long tenure as lightkeeper.

As a stopping point on the main steamer route between Lake Superior and Georgian Bay ports, Little Current thrived on shipping and most of its activity centred around the wharves. Tom Reid, the town's first teacher, moonlighted as a bartender at a saloon on the steamboat dock, and so at the first sound of a ship's whistle, he would dismiss the students as quickly as he could tie his bartender's apron. It is doubtful his actions raised many eyebrows, as this was a town where the toot of a ship's whistle was enough to bring an entire congregation rushing out of church, leaving the minister high and dry in the pulpit.

The story of Spider Island (now connected to the mainland by land bridge), where the first front range tower was located, can be read in the nicknames it acquired over the years: Lighthouse Island, naturally, but also Knockerville, in reference to a brawl that once rocked the island; Potter Island after William Potter who built a sawmill in 1886; Center Island; Indian Island; and Pollackville, after the immigrants who lived on the island while building the spur line from Espanola on the CPR main line, to Little Current. In the 1950s, the Spider Island lighthouse was demolished. Little Current's former lighthouse on the main street is now the site of the waterfront War Memorial, erected in 1922.

Little Current light from the water.
– National Archives of Canada PA195256

Little Current light hidden by shed.
– National Archives of Canada PA195256

LITTLE CURRENT

1866
Location: Front range, east extremity of Spider Island
Description: Square white wooden tower
Height: 43 ft./12.9 m
Light: Fixed white, 16" reflectors
Visibility: 6 miles/9.6 kms
Location: Back range, Little Current
Description: Square wooden tower
Light: Fixed white, 16" reflectors, later fixed red, then fixed green
Visibility: 6 miles/9.6 kms

1907
Front range: Former back range lantern moved to roof of Byron H. Turner's warehouse, becoming front range lantern
Visibility: 6 miles/9.6 kms
Back Range: Pole light
Light: Fixed red 7th order dioptric
Visibility: 1 mile/1.6 kms
Purpose: 1907 range lights led into Little Current wharves

KEEPERS:
1866-1901➤ Donald McKenzie
1902-1907➤ David Boyter
c.1920➤ William McKenzie

November 1907, shifting currents caused log booms to trap ships in harbour. Foreground: the Iroquois; *background left to right:* Minnie M., City of Midland, Caribou, Telegram, *and* Lulu Eddy *with dredge.*
– Frank Hamilton Collection, Rutherford B. Hayes Presidential Centre neg 6346

Little Current light, 1910.
– *National Archives of Canada PA172448*

Early Little Current, light can be seen on right side of street.
– *Courtesy of Don McKenzie*

NARROW ISLAND

---+---

In 1884, Staff Commander J.G. Boulton recommended a lighthouse be built on Rabbit Island, (as Narrow Island was known locally) to guide mariners on the western approach to Little Current and "to facilitate navigation in this intricate portion of the channel." Six years later, a light was constructed which lasted another twelve before burning down. The new lighthouse continued to operate with some modifications but without incident, until 1954.

At that time, a recommendation was made to automate the light and approval was sought from the captains of the Owen Sound Transportation Company. They agreed, but the Department was still reluctant — 55-year-old Carl Dieter, who had tended the light since just after the First World War, should be given special consideration as he was the sole support of his children. Automation was therefore delayed until 1958.

Among some bureaucrats, there was a conviction that automation of lighthouses would reduce costs while increasing efficiency. However, there was little recognition that even an unwatched light needs maintenance. Only five years after the Narrow Island automation, District Marine Agent F. K. McKean wrote, "the Narrow Island lighthouse looks as if it is abandoned since it has not been painted. Like many of our automatic installations, we do not have the time and crew to keep them in proper condition." One answer was to lease the lighthouse, but this was easier said than done. In a second memo, the frustrated McKean wrote,

> . . . there has been criticism of the Department [of Transport] for the practice of renting lighthouses, but I think there has been much more criticism arising from the sight of beaten up buildings which have been vandalised in a disgusting manner . . . We ask that the subject should be reviewed before a final decision is made, and we think there will be considerable outcry if some of these buildings are torn down, and yet they cannot be maintained without some sort of occupancy.

The B.B. Buckhout *stranded on a reef west of Narrow Island in November 1912. The wood boards can still be seen scatterred around the wreck.*
— *Courtesy of Cris Kohl*

Many potential tenants came forward, but each deal fell through. In 1976, a sailing club applied to use the lighthouse and island as a marina, yacht brokerage, charter boat depot and sailing school. Their dream was to make Narrow lighthouse the base for North Channel cruising. The government declined, saying it was against their policy to lease lighthouses to companies. As the property continued to deteriorate, concerns grew about possible personal injury liability. These were well founded. A Coast Guard employee remembers a large hole had been chopped in the floor just inside the front door. Anyone entering could easily have fallen through to the basement.

In 1978, the Department proposed a solution. They would retain ownership of the property, raise a metal beacon, and tear down the old building. In November 1979, after twenty years of failing to find a solution, a Coast Guard crew hired a local man to take them out to the island. Little did he know that when he came back to pick them up, the lighttower would be gone.

Narrow Island, 1890. This lighthouse was destroyed by fire in 1902.
— *National Archives of Canada PA172493*

New lighthouse at Narrow Island, 1907. When a Manitoulin man was hired in 1979 to take a Coast Guard crew out to the lighthouse, little did he know it would be gone when he returned.
— *National Archives of Canada PA172492*

TRIPLICATE FOR PAYOR.

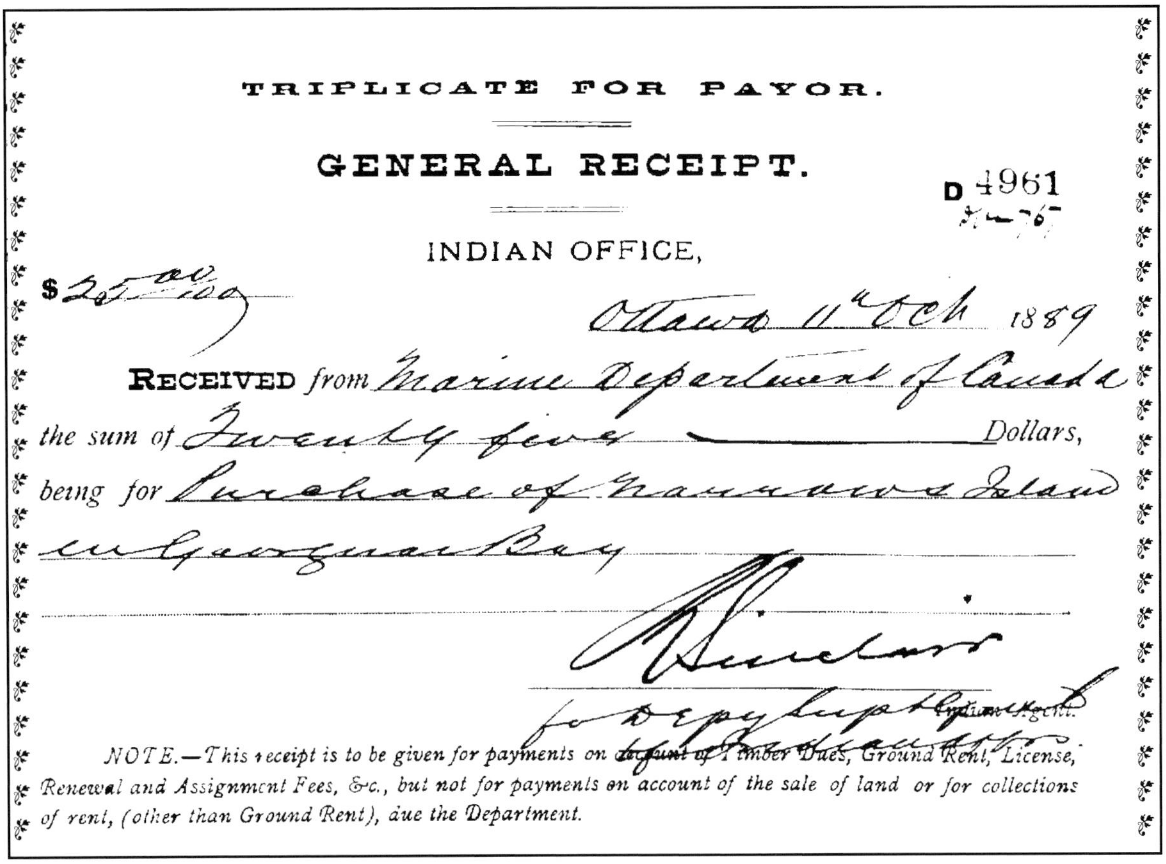

GENERAL RECEIPT.

D 4961

INDIAN OFFICE,

$ 25 00/00

Ottawa 11th Oct 1889

RECEIVED *from* Marine Department of Canada

the sum of Twenty five ——— *Dollars,*

being for Purchase of Narrows Island in Georgian Bay

R Sinclair

for Depy Supt Genl of Ind Affairs

NOTE.—This receipt is to be given for payments on account of Timber Dues, Ground Rent, License, Renewal and Assignment Fees, &c., but not for payments on account of the sale of land or for collections of rent, (other than Ground Rent), due the Department.

$25 receipt to Marine Department of Canada from Indian Office for purchase of Narrow Island, 1889.
– Canadian Coast Guard

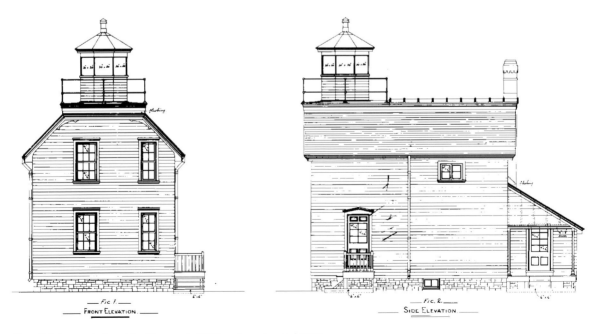

FIG. 1. FRONT ELEVATION.

FIG. 2. SIDE ELEVATION.

New lighthouse designed for Narrow in 1902 and constructed 1903.
– National Archives of Canada NMC162341

CLAPPERTON ISLAND

✛

The story of Clapperton light can be seen through the eyes of the Baker family who lived on the island over a period of 88 years between 1875 and 1962. It began with Benjamin Baker, Clapperton's second lightkeeper.

Benjamin Baker — Murdered?

George saw his father's sailboat coming down the channel but took no particular notice, until the boat continued past the lighthouse. He could see his father's dog running back and forth on the deck barking excitedly, but where was his father? George's heart began to pound as he jumped into the row boat. Maybe his father was napping . . . maybe he wasn't feeling well. After all, he was returning from a night out with the boys in Gore Bay, where the men always enjoyed a good stiff drink with their card playing. George rowed faster.

When he reached the boat, the dog jumped at him trying to lick his face, but he pushed the animal away. There was no sign of his father, only a whiskey bottle and his pocket book. George opened it. No money. Benjamin always carried money. Something was wrong — his father couldn't just disappear. Had he stumbled over the side? Had he lost heavily at cards? Benjamin Baker's body was never found after that September day in 1894, and no explanation was ever offered by anyone in Gore Bay.

At age 30, his son Henry took over as keeper of Clapperton Island light. Years later, an incident occurred which made the family begin to suspect that perhaps Benjamin's disappearance had been no accident. Henry's wife Jenny developed an

Benjamin Baker (1875-94) left for a game of cards and never returned.
— Lloyd Collection/ Huronia Museum .0007

Below: This wallet, a bottle of whiskey, and his dog were retrieved from Baker's drifting sailboat.
— Lloyd Collection/ Huronia Museum .0001

excruciating toothache and her husband suggested a nip of whisky might soothe the pain. This was the same whiskey that had been found in Benjamin's boat and the bottle had been sitting on the shelf ever since. Jenny poured an ounce, swished it over her inflamed tooth ... and immediately became intensely ill.

Benjamin Baker's great grandson, Norman Lloyd, relates the family's concerns about the suspicious whiskey,

the feeling was the bottle had been doped up somehow. Now, had he been lucky at the table and someone drugged his bottle, rolled him and in the act, he was killed and his body disposed of and the boat set adrift? Had he been unlucky, lost everything, and was ashamed to go home, and jumped overboard? Did he have too much to drink and was knocked or fell overboard? Why was the wallet lying open and empty on the seat? We'll never know.

Life On Clapperton

Henry Baker was no stranger to the position of lightkeeper, nor to the secondary jobs the family took on in order to eke out a living in tough times. In the island's interior, they kept a farm where they grew hay, and tended sheep and cattle. Then they took on the maintenance of the channel buoys, fur trapping, fishing and later guiding and lumbering. They

Clapperton's dwelling and second tower built after the first was struck by lightning. Remains of this Clapperton dwelling are lying behind the Bakers' farmhouse in the island's interior. Photo taken c. 1919.
— *National Archives of Canada PA172467*

Robertson Rock ——— x — Range Lights

Lighttower

Cartwright Pt

Site of House

Baker's Bay

Site of Farm

CLAPPERTON ISLAND

Little Current

At the age of nine, Norman Lloyd cooked meals for the Bakers' farmhands.
– Lloyd Collection/ Huronia Museum .0004

Salvage crew on the Western Star.
– Great Lakes Marine Historical Collection, Milwaukee Public Library

would take their fishing catch out to the steamer *Normac* and in return pick up their barrels of coal oil. This was accomplished by tossing the *Normac*'s crew a line which was tied around the barrel before pushing it out the gangway. From there the Bakers towed the fuel to shore.

Some duties were happily given over to Henry's grandson, Norman Lloyd, who spent summers

Western Star – infamous for being one of the most difficult salvage jobs on the Great Lakes. A giant coffer dam had to be constructed for on-site repairs before the ship could be towed to the Collingwood shipyard.
– Lloyd Collection/ Huronia Museum .0012

on the island. Polishing brass, cleaning the prism, dropping the curtains in the morning so the lens would not start a brush fire, and replenishing the fuel for lighting, were well-suited to keeping a boy busy. Norman also logged all the ships that passed. The Bakers became so familiar with the sound of their engines and whistles, they could make accurate entries in the log book even during the middle of the night. During the Second World War, the Department of Transport required all lightkeepers to keep a complete log of ships in their vicinity. As there was only one form for all of Canada, the Bakers found themselves filling out a report tallying how many submarines they had seen in the North Channel!

Shipwrecks are a part of lighthouse lore. Robertson Rock, a treacherous shoal off Clapperton, can take credit for several disasters, including the *Western Star* in September 1915, and the *North Wind* on July 1st, 1926. The Bakers believed the latter was wrecked for insurance purposes. Apparently, the skipper ordered all the crew except the engineer, to abandon ship, then gave instructions to ram into Robertson Rock. As the *North Wind* sank, the open bridge broke away, eventually drifting onshore along with her pinnacle compass and a hurricane lamp. The lamp and compass became part of the lighthouse decor.

Henry Baker—
Struck By The Range Light

Like his father Benjamin before him, Henry had to contend with the problem of tending the range lights in extreme weather. He would tie a rope around his waist, attach the other end to a tree and with this umbilical cord, carefully work his way across the ice. This solved half the problem. The range lights were illuminated by coal-oil lamps inside heavy brass lanterns, which were refueled by lowering the lantern from the thirty-foot pole using a block and tackle. Coated by icy spray, the brittle lines strained under the weight of the lanterns and Henry feared they would snap. He complained bitterly to the Department and suggested the ranges should be moved back from the water's edge. The freighter

Henry Baker (1895-1946), the North Channel's longest serving keeper.
– Lloyd Collection/ Huronia Museum .0003

captains vehemently disagreed. Moving the lights would force them closer to Clapperton's shore and nearer to treacherous Robertson Rock. As a gesture to placate Henry, the Department built a protective shed, which at least provided enough shelter for him to successfully strike a match to light the wick. Eventually however, his prediction proved correct. While hoisting the lantern one evening, the rope broke and the falling lantern crushed Henry's shoulder and broke his ribs. Despite his agony, Henry managed to mount his horse and ride the one and a half miles back to the lighthouse. Taken to the hospital in Little Current he died soon after, on September 17, 1946, at the age of 82.

William Baker – The Man For The Job

Four days after Henry's death, the Department of Transport wrote a letter of condolence, but not wanting to waste paper, they tacked on an acknowledgment of William as Clapperton's next keeper. Soon after, the range lights were moved back and lowered.

The Bakers took this picture to show the Department the dangerous conditions of the range light at Cartwright Point. Before lighting it they had to secure themselves with a rope.
– Lloyd Collection/ Huronia Museum .0008

Bill Baker in front of the third lighthouse with two of the pure-bred horses they used for transportation.
— Lloyd Collection/Huronia Museum .0015

Bill Baker went through some difficult years. The year after his father's death, his brother Earl was shot in the head while hunting on Clapperton Island with Grant Rogers, owner of the Harbour Island Tourist Resort. Apparently Mr. Rogers took him for a deer. Bill himself had more than his share of close calls. He narrowly escaped drowning when a deadhead bashed a hole in his 32-foot tug. Not being a swimmer, Bill had to propel himself to shore by clinging to a life preserver. The second mishap came when he was cutting ice. He was kicked by a horse, but escaped with broken ribs and a punctured lung. The third incident is a testament to Bill Baker's character.

It was a Friday when Bill's appendix ruptured. He was alone at the lighthouse and didn't know what to do. In such acute pain, he certainly could not manage the boat. By Saturday, the poison had spread through his system and he began to drift in and out of consciousness.

By Sunday the situation was desperate. He looked up at the lighthouse — it was dark. The light had been burning all weekend and had run out of fuel. Bill tried to crawl the 30 or 40 yards to the lighthouse but collapsed. Nearly five hours later, Harold Hutchings and Bert Bailey of Kagawong appeared. On a whim, they had decided to return a few items they had borrowed. Within moments they discovered Bill's crumbled figure. As they hovered over him, Bill whispered, "I'm done boys. Get Norm Lloyd out of Kagawong to look after the light. It's out of oil."

The men rowed as fast as they could to Kagawong, then drove Bill to the Red Cross Hospital in Mindemoya. Bill was lucid enough to request a telegram be sent to Mr. McKean the Superintendent of lighthouses, informing him the lighthouse duties had been passed to Norman Lloyd.

Upon receiving the telegram, McKean's first question was, who is Norman Lloyd, and does he know how to operate a lighthouse? He chartered a float plane from Parry Sound to Little Current, then took a boat out to Clapperton, where he saw the light blazing in the night sky. Norman was officially appointed assistant, thus becoming the fourth family member to tend the light. Bill survived the surgery, and worked another twelve years before retiring in 1962.

Today, the only evidence of the Bakers' long sojourn on the island is their nineteenth-century log house and barn, discernible from the air among the overgrown fields of their farm in the interior. As for the Clapperton light, it was rolled down the rocks and towed to Spanish, where it stuck on a sandbar and sat for a considerable time until the water level dropped enough for it to be retrieved. The site where it once stood proudly, is now occupied by a metal beacon.

The Bakers raised cattle and sheep at their farm and winter home on Clapperton Island.
— Lloyd Collection/Huronia Museum .0006

KAGAWONG

———— ✦ ————

Kagawong's original light was set up on the dock, while a second light, a simple lantern on a pole, was erected further back in town. A nearby shed stored the coal oil. In 1892, a fire raged through town, burning the hotel, several houses, the light pole and shed. The building of a third light was delayed until 1894 as the tenders submitted were too high, according to the 1894 Canadian Parliament Sessional Papers report:

> Mr. Noble [from the Department of Marine and Fisheries] was sent to Kagawong in September last, and erected a lighthouse to replace the temporary light maintained since the mast and shed were destroyed by fire. This tower was completed for the sum of $293.81, thereby justifying the department's action in refusing to accept any of the tenders received for the work, the lowest of these having been $925.

Austin Hunt, who cared for the automated light in the 1960s remembers its exceptional craftsmanship. "Whoever built the light did a good job; the timbers are well done. It's more than a shell by inexperienced carpenters." The elegant curved supports that grace the tower once harmonized with an ornate circular catwalk (now a square one). On the wall inside the tower, 1890s ship arrival and departure times, probably penciled by keeper William Boyd, can still be seen.

In the late 1800s a ship's safe arrival was never taken for granted. Norman Smith (now age 93), a former wheelsman on the *Manitou*, recalls how Captain Batten of the *Caribou* would dock at Kagawong in a thick fog:

> they were going slow. He asked them to stop the boat so he could listen. Batten says, "we are about five minutes from the dock, I can hear the echo of the water lapping on shore — go ahead just a little bit." In five minutes they were at the dock and they couldn't see it until they were there. That's how they navigated. The captain

would say "steer on that there big pine tree for ten minutes." I'd do that. Then he'd say "steer on that big point of land there." They didn't use their charts.

Roads around the village were more like trails, and as "crooked as a dog's hind leg" and so it was the steamers that kept the residents in touch with the outside world. Even in the 1930s they were poor and unusable. When a plume of black smoke and a trail of hungry seagulls were spotted, villagers would flock to the wharf to greet the *Michipicoten*, and later the *Caribou* and the *Manitou* which called two or three times a week during the 1930s, to pick up fish from the Graham Bros. Fishing Co., and lumber from the Henry/Carter Lumber and Grist Mill. The two Henry brothers who founded the village, both died tragically in 1882 – Robert from a fatal heart attack after rescuing passengers from the burning Manitoulin (see Manitowaning) and William, a victim of the *Asia* disaster (see Why Were They Built.)

For several years following the construction of a paper mill by the Green Bay Wisconsin Pulp Company to supply paper for the Sears Roebuck

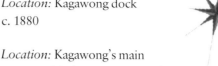

KAGAWONG

Location: Kagawong dock
c. 1880

Location: Kagawong's main
    street, Mudge Bay, Manitoulin
    Island
1888: Pole light (destroyed in town fire 1892)
1894: Square tapered wooden tower, wooden
    lantern
Height: 27 ft./8 m
Light: Fixed white catoptric, later fixed red
Visibility: 11 miles/18 kms

KEEPERS:
1893-1916➤   William Boyd
◄1930-1950➤   William McKenzie
◄1960s➤   Austin Hunt

catalogues, lumber tugs and packet freighters filled the harbour. Local men were hired as day labourers to load the lumber and a favorite social event was gathering for the hot meal served onboard. The children too would hang around, hoping for a bowl of fish soup, or if they were really lucky, a piece of pie.

After the mill's closure, the village became a favourite stopping place for excursion steamers en route to Lake Superior. In 1939, the week-long trip from Owen Sound to Michipicoten and back cost $35. Up-bound tourists could enjoy a pleasant stroll through the village or a visit to nearby Bridal Veil Falls and on their return, a choral service at the tiny St. John the Evangelist Anglican Church. The church has a nautical theme, enhanced by a pulpit made from the prow of a foundered 32-foot ChrisCraft yacht. While cruising the North Channel, the captain of the *Rhu* struck a spar

Early roads on Manitoulin Island.
– Archives on Ontario ACC9912-12

buoy just past Clapperton Island and ran onto a shoal. The group of four adults and two young girls stayed on the boat overnight hoping they would be spotted, but by morning, high winds and rain had developed, and they made the fatal decision to leave ship. The two girls did not last long in the cold water, and in the end, only two of the group managed to reach the Manitoulin shore. Five years later the bow of the *Rhu* was restored as a pulpit and placed in the church, and was officially dedicated in 1970.

In the early 1960s, the delivery of freight shifted from water to land transport. Today, the government dock built to accommodate the passenger boats and freighters, and the white lighthouse on the hill remain to speak of the time when ships regularly visited the small village harbours on Manitoulin Island.

William and Florence McKenzie. Along with keeping the lighthouse, William ran a hardware store and the dock.
– Lloyd Collection/ Huronia Museum .0014

Kagawong light in winter
– Courtesy of Lottie Chapman

BOYD ISLAND

✠

Floeing Through the Night

As the pink dusk faded into purple night, Elizabeth Martin became more and more concerned about her husband William. Pulling her coat tightly around, she crossed the bridge from her house to the light on the big island. She trimmed the wick and lit the lamp, all the time her eyes searching the ice-mottled channel. Back at the house she continued to peer out from the kitchen window.

William, who had been late in leaving for the light, jumped into his punt and started to row to the island. As he headed into the channel, it was clear he had underestimated the strength of the wind. He rowed harder. A huge ice floe hit the punt, sending it spinning off to one side. William tried unsuccessfully to push himself free with an oar. Just then a second ice floe smacked the other side of the punt. He was a prisoner! Stunned, he sat back, his oars resting on the ice. The boat was rapidly approaching the lighthouse and William prayed his wife was watching for him. It was his only chance. As the punt drifted under the lighthouse beam, William stood, waving furiously. From the window, Elizabeth spotted him and ran outside waving and shouting encouragement. They both stared helplessly as they vanished from each others' sight.

That night Elizabeth paced the floor. She hung a distress signal from the tower and prayed it would catch someone's attention. The mill manager, Mr. Hiesordt, was the first to notice it and immediately sent a tug to ascertain the trouble. A search party was organized and the *Fanny Arnold* tug dispatched. Tell-tale pieces of ice pushed up on islands and rocks led the crew toward the Clapperton lighthouse. As they neared the island, Clapperton's keeper, Benjamin Baker, and William Martin rushed onto the beach.

The *Manitoulin Expositor* of May 7, 1892 completes the tale:

He, Mr. Martin, having arrived there [Clapperton Island] at day break, was able to shout and awake Mr. Baker, who immediately came to his assistance and got him off the boat. Though much used up and his hands badly frost bitten, he was able to walk, and you may be sure it was a joyful sight a few hours later when he perceived the *Fanny Arnold* and many of his neighbors on board in search of him. It was Sunday, but you would have thought of Donnie Brook fair if you had heard the whoop that went up when they saw Mr. Martin on the shore. He was soon on board and homeward bound, and the tug whistle told the news to his loving wife long before they were in hailing distance.

In the 1960s, the Boyd Island lighthouse met an ugly end. A Coast Guard crew poured forty-five gallons of gas into glass jars and set them on the window ledges. A fire was lit at the bottom of the house and the glass jars at the top were ignited by a bullet shot from a boat offshore. The end was mercifully quick. As with the Narrow Island light, the community found out after the fact.

BOYD ISLAND

Location: Boyd Island
Built: 1885
Description: White square
   wooden tower
Height: 39 ft./11.7 m
Visibility: 6 miles/9.6 kms
Additional: Bridge led to residence
   (on neighbouring rock)
Abandoned: Before 1955
Present: Skeleton tower with white flashing light
Destroyed: 1960s

KEEPERS:
◄1889-c.1905   William Martin
1905-1916►   Elizabeth Martin

Boyd Island lighthouse and dwelling on adjacent islands, 1896.
– National Archives of Canada PA195248

JANET HEAD

---+---

As so few of the early keepers' log books have been preserved, the Janet Head log books are invaluable in giving a glimpse into the lightkeepers' daily routines and into the world in which they lived. Entries are most often straightforward notations about the weather and the time of lighting and extinguishing the light, but some allude to their joys and sorrows.

Janet Head's log is infused with the character of its first keeper, Robert Boyter. In his quarterly report of 30th June 1885, he relates a series of terrible events:

> I am sorry to say any remarks this time are of a very melancholy nature. My wife and eldest son left here on the 11th [of April] to go to his farm on the North shore with a yoke of oxen but owing to the depth of snow and water on the ice the oxen tired and they had to stay on Dart Island all night and did not reach Spanish river Mills until one oclock next day. She was so badly chilled and frozen that she died on 19th, the boy is still living but if he gets over it will be crippled for life . . . .

As soon as he heard of the tragedy, Boyter along with a Mr. Thorne, a Mr. Lewis and two young girls, drove across the ice along the planted line of trees which marked the mail route to Spanish River. In an affidavit to the District of Algoma, Boyter continued:

> Mr. Thorne arrived with his team at my place at one o'clock, p.m., and with him were Mr. Lewis, [and eleven-year-olds] Miss Baxter and Miss Shea. There was besides, a carcass of beef and three satchels. There was also a bag containing bottles. Mr. Lewis also carried a bottle of whiskey in his pocket, which I saw and tasted. We then started from my place at about a quarter to two o'clock p.m., and struck immediately for the bushes.

Before long, the snow was so thick the horses balked. In order to get them to move, the men discarded three-quarters of the beef. At some point, Boyter's compass was lost from his vest pocket. When darkness fell, the horses refused to go any further and so they wrapped the girls in bed ticks and buffalo blankets, and settled in for the night.

The next morning, the girls and Mr. Lewis pleaded to return to Gore Bay. The group headed back . . . only to be caught once again in blinding snow. Again the horses refused to proceed, so the group made camp beside the sleigh, huddling together through the afternoon and evening. As the weather worsened, frostbite and desperation crept in. At 10 p.m., the storm abated and they were able to coax the horses to move, but only for a short stretch. Despite being severely weakened, Thorne and Boyter left the party to find help. In the morning, they met a search party, who continued on to the stranded group. An account, written much later, describes this encounter:

> The team was found stationary, facing a big snow drift about half way between Burnt and Clapperton Islands, ten miles from Gore Bay. Lewis and Miss Baxter were on the sleigh almost speechless and entirely helpless, the latter covered with a frozen quilt and her hands and arms frozen to the elbows as hard as

JANET HEAD

Location: End of Water Street, 2 miles northwest of Gore Bay. Western entrance point into Gore Bay

Built: 1879

Description: Square white wooden tapered tower, dwelling attached. Octagonal red lantern

Light: Fixed white catoptric; then 7th order dioptric

Visibility: 11 miles/17.6 kms

Fog horn: c.1888 – Hand crank

Additional: 1885 – Boat house

Present: Year-round occulting white light, 5 sec. intervals. Lighthouse leased. 3⅓ acres of land retained in case new lighttower is required on bluff.

KEEPERS:

1879-1895	Robert Boyter
1895-1903	James Kinney
1903-1913	Captain Angus Matheson
1913-1934	Robert Lewis
1935-1955	George A. Thorburn

ice. Miss Shea had fallen off the sleigh and was unable to get back again.

Janet Head lighthouse, erected 1879.
– National Archives of Canada PA172483

May Baxter and Mr. Lewis were so severely frost-bitten that their feet and hands had to be rubbed in ice water for five and a half hours to draw the frost. May died a few days later and Mr. Lewis' feet were amputated. While Boyter's account emphasised his own responsible, selfless actions, Boyter and Thorne were accused by many of drunkenness and negligence. It was said they appeared, at least part of the time, to have been so intoxicated, they almost

Photo of Lydia May Baxter taken after her death, 1885, age 11 – a common practice in the Victorian era.
– The Manitoulin Recorder, *September 8, 1982*

came to blows, and they were accused of sheltering themselves at the others' expense. It was a horrifying event for the community.

Official Records

During his tenure, Boyter left other records of a more mundane nature that reveal interesting aspects of lightkeeping, 1880s-style. His supply lists attest to the amount of scrubbing and painting expected of a keeper; while his quarterly

reports reveal his growing frustration in trying to convince authorities to respond to requests for equipment. His signature, which is rather modest in 1879, becomes quite florid by the late 1880s. Needless to say, punctuation was not a priority!

31 December 1882
Quantity of oil required for next Sesson about One hundred and fifty gallons. One doz of iron tubes about forty lbs of Soap Six brooms Six towls six box of matches two hair dusters One Chois[chamois] Skin two Scrubbing brushs . . . One pickaxe about four gallons of pint Oil and One . . . ledder about thirty feet long

30 September 1884
I Require a boat house at this Station

30 September 1885
At the end of last year I requested a stove and coal as the house is verry cold in winter everything freezing in it with all the warmth I can apply it has not come will you kindly bear it in mind. The water comes into the cellar spring and fall and I have dug a ditch from it I should have plank to cover it. No fog horn yet the Captains passing here are grumbling.

31 March 1886
No remarks this time except to again remind you of a fog horn

31 December 1886
N.B. I have also in store 1 boat 1 boat house and dock 2 sets of blocks 2 pick axes 1 barrel of cement 1 ladder 20 fathoms rope 1 keg black paint. And now I want 1 set of curtains for lantern windows [so that lens did not start brushfire] 7 panes 3 kegs white lead 1 of Yellow 2 of iron clad (?) 5 Gal Linseed Oil 1 large paint brush 2 white wash brushes 2 scrubbing brushes 40 lbs soap 6 boxes matches ½ Doz brooms ½ Doz Towels 2 Iron pails 1 Ton

Coal 1 pr Siscors 2 Doz lamp glasses 1 Chamios skin 2 lbs putty ½ Coil ½ inch rope 1 Box Rouge [for polishing reflectors.] Leakage of tank beyond my control.

31st March 1887

In making remarks I would say seven Gal of Oil I have consumed but lost 30 Gal by leakage next would call your attention to the necessity of a winter light the travel from the North Shore on the Ice now exceeds the summer travel and there is really more danger of loss of life in the winter and having been requested so long and so often to lay this nesicessity before you consider it a part of my duty to do so I am just out of Blank sheets.

30th Sept 1888

You may think I should have measured the oil every night but knowing the quantity consumed for this quarter I have put the short and long nights at the same quantity and hope it will meet with your approval as I am anxious to do what is right and give a satisfactory account of my expenditures.

31 December 1888

[The long-anticipated fog horn was listed among the stores]

Records show that the Janet Head light was generally lit between March or April and December, although between 1910 and 1924 it was tended throughout the winter, to serve the high volume of winter traffic crossing the ice to the North Shore. In many of the logs written by succeeding keepers, mail emerges as a major preoccupation:

Cover of Robert Boyter's Janet Head log book for 1882
— Western Manitoulin Historical Society Museum, Gore Bay

James Kinney:

Jan 15, 1902	First Mail to cross the Ice
Mar 25, 1902	Mail by dog train
Mar 28	Ice getting bad
April 5	Tug went through the Ice with Mail
April 6	Ice all brok up
April 13	First Boat – Telegram

Captain Angus Matheson:

Winter Servis commences 15 December

Last mail by boat today 7 January

first mail over Ice 23 January

March 1913 – the nights the light was not in operation were clear moon light nights and I did not think it was necessary to light it.

Robert Lewis:

April 1913 – last Mail Over Ice 14. Came with in four miles of the Light house on the 13 and the horse Broke through and had to Leave the Mail On the Ice untile the Next Morning

Dec 23, 1914 – Last trip of Mail Boat. Lake froze all Over and Mail Boat had to Brake Ice

(Excerpts from keepers' log books courtesy of the Western Manitoulin Historical Society Museum, Gore Bay)

DEPARTMENT OF MARINE AND FISHERIES, CANANDA.

LIGHTHOUSE SERVICE.

Name of Station *Gore Bay* Type of Apparatus *Droptric*

Type of lamp or burner *Duplex*

RETURN of Stores for quarter ending *December* 1915

ARTICLE.		Brought forward from previous quarter.	Received during the present quarter.	Consumed during the present quarter.	Carried forward to next quarter.	Requirements for next fiscal year.	ARTICLE.		Brought forward from previous quarter.	Received during the present quarter.	Consumed during the present quarter.	Carried forward to next quarter.	Requirements for next fiscal year.
Petroleum	Gals.	155		57	103	150	CORDAGE.						
							Manila, size 1/4 in	Ft.	59		59		50
BURNERS.							" size	"					
Duplex	No.			7		7	" size	"					
Mammoth, No. 2	"												
" No. 3	"						**DRY GOODS.**						
							Cotton	Yds.	5		5		5
							Flannel	"	5		5		5
CHIMNEYS.							Ticking for blinds	"					
Duplex, red	No.						Towels	No.	4		4		4
" white	"			5	4	17							
Mammoth, No. 2, red	"												
" No. 2, white	"						**GLASS, HOUSE.**						
Mammoth, No. 3, red	"						10 inches by 14 inches	No.	14		7	17	
" No. 3, white	"						inches by inches	"					
							inches by inches	"					
WICKS.													
Duplex	Yds.					6	**GLASS. LANTERN.**						
Mammoth, No. 2	"						36 inches by 36 inches	No.				3	
" No. 3	"						inches by inches	"					
							inches by inches	"					
BRUSHES.													
Blacklead	No.			7			**HARDWARE, TOOLS, &c.**						
Chimney	"				7		Axes	No.	1		1		1
Dust	"	1		1	1		Axe handles	"					7
Paint, flat	"				7		Block. single. size	"	7			1	
" round	"						" " size	"					
Sash	"						" double, size	"					
Scrub	"						" " size	"					
Whitewash	"						Door locks	"		7	7		7
Window	"				1		Files, flat, size 6 in	"					7
							" " size	"					

2

ARTICLE		Brought forward from previous quarter	Received during the present quarter	Consumed during the present quarter	Carried forward to next quarter	Requirements for next fiscal year
HARDWARE, &c.— Con.						
Files, ½-round, size	No.					
" " size	"					
" round, size	"					
" " size	"					
Hammers	"	1			1	
Hatchets	"					
Hinges, size	"					
Monkey wrench	"	1			1	
Nails, size 3	Lbs.		10		10	
" size 2½	"		10		10	
" size	"					
Padlocks	No.		1	1		4
Pails	"		2		2	
Putty knife	"	1			1	
Saws, hand	"	1			1	
" cross cut 1 small	"		1		1	
Scissors	"	1			1	
Screwdrivers	"	1			1	
Solder	Bars	1			1	
Soldering irons	No.	1			1	
PAINTS, OILS, &c.						
Black	Gal.		1		1	
Blue	"					
Boat varnish	"					
Clock oil	Qt.					
Dryer	Gal.					
Green	..		1		1	
Ironclad	..		6		6	
Linseed, boiled	..		1		1	
" raw	"					
Machine oil	"					
Mercury	Lbs.					
Methylated spirits	Gal.					
Red	"	4	4		8	
Soda	Lbs.		5		5	
Turpentine	Gal.		½		½	
White	"	3	3		2	
Whiting	Lbs.					
Yellow	Gal.	2			2	
Umber	"					

ARTICLE		Brought forward from previous quarter	Received during the present quarter	Consumed during the present quarter	Carried forward to next quarter	Requirements for next fiscal year
MISCELLANEOUS.						
Blacklead 1 Bot	Lbs.			1	2	4
Boat, anchor	No.	1			1	
" chain, dia.	Ft.					
" davits	No.					
" hook	"					
" oars, size 7	"	1			1	
" " size 8	"	1			1	
" rowlocks	"					
" row, size Small	"	1			1	
" sail, size	"					
Brooms	"	2	3	1	2	
Chamois skins	"	1			1	
Clock cord						
or wire, dia.	Ft.					
Hand horn reeds	No.					
Hand lanterns	"	1			1	
" globes	"	4			4	
" wick	Ft.	2			2	
House lamps, bowls	No.	2	2		2	
" burners	"					
" chimneys	"			2	4	
" wick	Ft.	3			3	
Ladders, size	No.					
" size	"					
" size	"					
Lantern blind cord	Yds.					
Lime	Bbl.					
Matches Boxes	Doz.	4		1	3	
Metal polish	Cans.	1			1	
Putty	Lbs.					
Rouge	"					
Rust scrapers	No.	1			1	
Soap	Lbs.	40		5	35	
Sponges	No.	2			2	
Stoves, cook	..	1			1	
" heating	..	1			1	
" oil	..					
" pipe, size 7	..		12		12	
" " size	..					
" elbows, size	..					
" T-pieces, size	..					
" tie wire	Yds.		10		10	
" shovels	No.					
" scuttles	"					
Waste, cotton	Lbs.					

Keeper Robert Lewis, 1913-34.
— Courtesy of Stanley Johnson

Unofficial Records

On September 7, 1979, the present occupant of the lighthouse, Stephen Fletcher, was preparing to wallpaper one of the rooms. He discovered a letter in a stovepipe hole, that had been written on Department of Transport letterhead by keeper George Thorburn in 1941. It read:

I am papering this room today July 16 finished N.W. room yesterday. The Russians & Germans are in a big battle, Germans trying to capture Moscow. The British RAF are bombing Germany and German held countries hard causing heavy damage.

I am just curious to know how long it will be when someone repapers these rooms.

George A. Thorburn
Light-Keeper

It continued:

July 20/1953
I am papering this room again North East room downstairs. 12 years since I papered it before, and we are heading for another war with Russia. The United Nations are fighting in Korea now trying for nearly three years to get a settlement.

I won't be looking after light much longer. Dominion Election on August 10th this year and I may lose my job. I am not feeling too good. Very hot weather and my heart is troubling me.

George A. Thorburn

(Thorburn's fears did not materialize. He continued to work until 1955, when the Department recommended automating the lights, retiring him as lightkeeper, but keeping him as caretaker.)

Janet Head lighthouse.
— Lynx Images Collection

GORE BAY TOWN POINT LIGHT

---+---

Gore Bay was a hub of activity. In the spring and fall, packet steamers such as the Northern Navigation Company's *Midland*, *Pacific*, *Atlantic*, and *Germanic* brought supplies to the permanent residents and in the summer, tourists, to fill the village's three hotels. On their return journeys, the steamers loaded grain, hay, and livestock for shipment to the railhead at Owen Sound.

The point chosen for the new light was known locally as "Fish Point," because of the giant stacks of fish boxes, and rows of net-drying racks. Around the harbour stood saw mills, grist mills and cattle pens. (Manitoulin Island had developed into a significant cattle-raising area.) One evening, the *Caribou* pulled into port many hours behind schedule. Freight was unloaded on the port side, then the steamer switched docks and cattle was loaded on the starboard side. The cattle walked up the gangplank, across the deck, and out the open gangway. Someone had forgotten to close the gate. Chaos ensued. Crew members attempting to round up the cattle by rowboat, had first to rescue some other prospective cowboys from a sinking boat. Cattle landed all along the shore and began running amuck through streets and gardens. It took the townspeople and the passengers about an hour and a half to round them up.

Keeper Robert Lewis' grandson, Stanley Johnson, remembers the lighthouse tender the *St. Heliers* sitting in Gore Bay harbour for three days in the early thirties without any activity. Apparently the crew was waiting for the construction plans for the lighthouse to arrive from head office. The Town Point light was kept by the Janet Head keeper. Johnson recalls helping his grandfather with the lightkeeping duties at Janet Head and at Gore Bay during his ailing years. They travelled between the lights by horse and buggy, horse-back, and by motorcycle if the road was dry. The road to the lighthouse consisted of three tracks which wound around various large rocks and stumps — two from the buggy wheels, and one from the horse. The next keeper, George Thorburn, bicycled out each evening after having lit Janet Head. In the early years, he was said to have received an extra ten dollars for his trouble.

GORE BAY

Location: Town Point
Built: c.1931
Description: 6-8' square tower. Pulley on 10-12 ft. steel pipe to raise and lower light.
Height: Approx. 8 ft./2.4 m
Light: Fixed red dioptric
Replaced: c.1949, light on pole
Automated: c.1956

KEEPERS:
c.1931-1934   Robert Lewis
c.1935-c.1955   George A. Thorburn

Location: Head of Gore Bay
Built: Before 1955
Description: Triangular range towers with white daymarks
Lights: Fixed red

CAPE ROBERT

✦

The tender for erecting the Cape Robert light was awarded to John Waddell of Kingston, Ontario in 1883. When he failed to complete the job, the Department of Marine and Fisheries took over and made it operational in 1885. But despite the presence of the lighthouse, the trading schooner *Nellie* met her fate off this rocky promontory a year later, completely unnoticed by anyone.

Even though the *Nellie* was a "coffin" ship, her captain, Noble T. Jolliffe assured his partner, Mr. Wright, that as long as he sailed in smooth weather, he would be fine. He was wrong. On a sunny June day in 1886, with the Cape Robert lighthouse on the horizon, the *Nellie* suddenly sprang a leak and started to list. Jolliffe scrambled toward the lifeboat, but it broke loose and drifted away. Climbing onto the side of the ship, Jolliffe waited through the night for a passing ship to spot him.

On the second night, the *Nellie* lost her masts, enabling the captain to right her. She was a pathetic sight as she slowly settled up to her deck. Weakened and badly sunburned, Jolliffe remained submerged in this drifting "swimming pool", finding some solace in a bottle of whiskey he had salvaged from the cabin. By now he was famished, exhausted and delirious. This torture continued until the *Nellie* grounded on John Island on the sixth day. Jolliffe attempted to build a raft, but was too confused.

In his lucid moments, he realized boats were passing, but none showed any interest. Seven days after the boat sprang a leak, locals in Gore Bay began to question the puzzling wreck. Jolliffe's partner, Mr. Wright caught wind of the story but it took another two days before he could hire a boat. When he finally reached the submerged *Nellie*, Jolliffe had disappeared. Shortly before Wright's arrival, some curious fishermen had found the unconscious captain, sitting up to his neck in water, his head precariously balanced on the bulwarks. Though blind, with his body swollen like a balloon, Jolliffe was alive. He was a survivor.

Cape Robert after the road went in.
— Courtesy of Marie Hall

The Way In

Lightkeeping at Cape Robert might have been easier, if there had been road access. Each day, Norman Matheson had to sail some 15 miles from Elizabeth Bay on Manitoulin Island to tend the light. One evening when his wife wanted to get word to him about a death in the family, she had to send their nine-year-old son. The only way he could get to the Cape was by taking a horse and buggy along a trail to the beach, then walking the four or five miles along the rocky shore with only the light of a small lantern to guide him. By the time he reached the eight-foot-high clay banks below the lighthouse, he was spooked. Glancing up, he saw a pair of gleaming eyes moving towards him; he was terrified. Yelling and hollering, he waved the lantern hoping to frighten the "monster" away. Instead, it lunged and hit the water beside him. He was so badly shaken, he could hardly climb up to the lighthouse. Surely the deer had been just as terrified.

A rough horse and buggy trail was cleared in the early 1900s and each new keeper did his part in keeping it open. But it wasn't until the 1940s, that the road was improved enough for keeper Frank Fowler to drive a Model A to the lighthouse. Use of a car made life much easier, as

CAPE ROBERT

Location: Northern extremity of promontory dividing Bayfield Sound from Vidal Bay, Manitoulin Island
Built: 1885
Description: Square white tower with attached dwelling
Height: 41 ft./12 m
Light: Fixed white double burner oil light
Visibility: 14 miles/22 kms
Fog Horn: Hand pump
Destroyed: 1950s
Present: Skeleton tower with flashing white light every 4 secs. Now visible only 5 kms.

KEEPERS:
1885-1885	A.K. Nesbitt
1886-1895	William Nesbitt
1896-1916➤	Norman Matheson
◄1937	Frank Sinclair
1937-1944	William Rumley
1945-1949➤	Frank Fowler

Cape Robert lacked a protected harbour. Generally, the lake was too rough to keep boats at the dock and they had to be pulled into the boathouse by windlass and roller. The water could get so rough, that on one occasion, the government ship had to anchor off the Cape for

Bungalow built c. 1948 was towed to Silver Lake to be used as a cottage.
— Courtesy of Marie Hall

days, before it was calm enough to unload the coal oil and other supplies.

Getting drinking water at Cape Robert was another problem. Gerald Fowler recalls that after a storm, clay would wash down from the bank near the lighthouse and muddy the water. In answer to complaints, the Department of Transport constructed a cistern which filtered rainwater collected on the roof. The only hitch was that some chemical in the shingles ran into the cistern and contaminated the water. Somehow, the murkiness of the lake water didn't seem so terrible after all.

The clay bank may have been responsible for

Lightkeeper Frank Fowler.
– Courtesy of Marie Hall

dirtying the water, but it also gave Gerald hours of entertainment. "It was about 80 feet high and I rolled boulders over the edge and watched them bounce down the bank and splash in the lake." He admits, he was a little concerned the day one of the boulders just missed their 16-foot cedar skiff.

Despite its drawbacks, the Cape Robert light had been a welcome change for two of the keepers who had previously worked at the Great Ducks – William Rumley and Frank Fowler. After years of climbing that 90-foot tower, William Rumley's damaged knees welcomed the change. The Cape's fixed light meant there were no weights to wind, and with a hand-operated fog horn, there was no need to stoke fires in the fog plant. It was practically like being on vacation.

The years were hard on the Cape Robert lighthouse and by 1948, it was obvious a new dwelling was needed. A builder from Gore Bay, his son and Gerald Fowler were hired to construct a bungalow. When the station was discontinued, the lighthouse was destroyed and the bungalow began a new life as a cottage at Silver Lake. Today a skeleton tower marks the spot where the house once stood and the Cape Robert lantern room now adorns the guardhouse at the Parry Sound Coast Guard base.

Cape Robert was one of the North Channel lighthouses razed in the 1950s. Its lantern room now sits atop the guardhouse at the Parry Sound Guard base. Photo, 1935.
– National Archives of Canada PA195266

Mississagi Island

✤

The Mississagi Island lighthouse is often associated with the macabre story of the fishermen who were windbound on the island while the lightkeeper was absent. One of the party found the keys to the fuel shed, and spying a container of alcohol, decided to quench his thirst. Unfortunately, it was the wood alcohol used to start the vapour light. By the time his companions found him, he was dead, his body turned black.

Mississagi Island lighthouse, 1907. Moving to the lighthouse every spring, the MacDonalds took a cow with them in the open sailboat. On one snowy trip to Blind River, Lauchlin MacDonald became lost and drifted for over a week before he was found, suffering from severe exposure.
– National Archives of Canada PA14878

Mississagi Island looking northeast showing complex, 1935
— National Archives of Canada PA195261

Dwelling and light after fire, Aug. 1948
— National Archives of Canada PA195262

MISSISSAGI ISLAND

Location: South end of island
Built: 1884
Description: Square white
    wooden tower, dwelling
    attached
Light: Revolving white catoptric;
    then flashing
Visibility: 12 miles/ 19 kms
Burned: August 1948

KEEPERS:
1885➤   James MacDonald
1896-1916   Lauchlin MacDonald
    ◄➤   Alfred Clark
    ◄➤   Captain Roque
1940s   Foster Morris

Foster Morris,
keeper, 1940s.
— Courtesy of Jack
Kennedy

View looking west, 1935
— National Archives of Canada PA195260

BLIND RIVER

When the American lumber baron, Senator S.O. Fisher, realized his original sources of timber were almost exhausted, he turned his greedy eye on the North Channel and Manitoulin's virgin forests. In 1900, the same year that the Blind River range lights were set up, he established the Michigan Land and Lumber Company and built the Blind River Company mill. The former was essentially a holding company for the large tracts of land he controlled between Blind River and the Mississagi River. Soon mammoth log booms filled Mississagi Straits heading toward American mills in Michigan and Canadian mills in Penetanguishene, Victoria Harbour and Midland. Other lumber companies, such as Eddy Brothers, also saw the potential in the area and set up business. Adding to all this commercial activity, Blind River became a fish depot for stations at Burnt Island, Meldrum Bay, Gore Bay, the Grant Islands and later Lake Superior's Booth Fish Company.

To relieve some of the resulting dock congestion, the Department of Public Works built a Government wharf at Harriette Point in 1904. The following year the range lights were moved: the front onto a wooden storehouse at the end of the Government wharf, and the back — a lantern on a pole — to the west side of the river mouth. A second set of range lights was established by placing a lantern on a pole, and behind it a lamp on the Eddy office building.

BLIND RIVER

1900: Established
Front range: Beach east of wharves, 15-foot-high post
Back range: Post on verandah of M.L.L.Co.
Lights: Fixed red incandescent, reflectors in front lights, then dioptric
Third Light: Pole with white electrical light, end of east wharf
Additional: Dep't of Marine and Fisheries paid M.L.L.Co. $80/year to tend the lights

1905: Range lights moved

THESSALON

---------------- ✦ ----------------

The Dyment Lumber Company welcomed the replacement of their small private light by the Thessalon lighthouse in 1898. Little did anyone suspect that this light would have a rather woeful history.

Following the death of her husband in 1915, Esther Harvey took over as keeper for the next twenty-five years. To the passing captains, she was known as "the brave little lady of the light," and certainly her mettle was tested the day she heard screams coming from the water. A gas boat was on the rocks. Despite the danger, she saved one of the men by throwing him a clothesline. The other man had already drowned.

During her tenure, the lighthouse was kept in good order, although a 1939 inspection mentioned structural problems such as a cracked kitchen foundation, a twisted boathouse, and rotten floors, door frames and sills. Nothing was done to improve the situation and so in his 1950 report, H. Tait, the Inspecting Officer noted:

> . . . The interior of the dwelling . . . presents a very drab appearance to anyone entering the station. Apparently the present occupants, discouraged at finding the rooms of the dwelling in such poor condition, have accomplished little towards remedying the condition . . . . The lighthouse lantern leaks badly and this condition only adds further discomfort to the otherwise neglected condition of the dwelling . . . .

The following year, the report showed that nothing had changed, except the need for a new rowboat was added to the list of deficiencies. It also noted that supplies had been stolen from the lighthouse over the winter. The report ended with a recommendation that the light be made unwatched.

Instead of improving the situation, this development seemed to make it worse. One police report listed ten battery jars broken, 28 panes of glass smashed, the lantern glass smashed, doors and locks broken. Every window in the lighthouse had been destroyed and stones, B.B. pellets, and spent .22 calibre bullets were found scattered on the floor. The police were surprised to learn the caretaker, Francis Valley, inspected the light only when it failed. According to the report, that must have been two years earlier.

The problems with the Thessalon Light became so severe, the District Marine Agent, F.K. McKean wrote the Mayor of Thessalon in 1957,

> . . . we believe that it is in the best interests of the town to have better supervision over public property and we solicit the best co-operation from your citizens and police force for our installation at the point . . . . If vandalism continues as in the past, I must recommend that the old lighthouse be torn down and that a simple steel mast should be installed, similar to that at the town dock.

Apparently nothing could curb the vandalism and so in 1961, the beleaguered lighthouse was taken out of service. That did not stop the destruction. A 1969 report stated, "vandals have removed doors, windows and stairs, the remainder is being torn down board by board for campfires, some of which are being lit inside the building on the wooden floor." Shortly after, the lighthouse was put out of its misery.

THESSALON

Location: 60 ft. from extremity of
   Thessalon Point, North
   Channel
Built: 1898
Description: Square white
   wooden dwelling, lantern
   rising from middle of roof
Height: 30 ft./9 m
Light: Fixed white 7th order dioptric
Visibility: 10 miles/16 kms
Fog Horn: Hand horn (discontinued 1952)
Automated: 1952 white flashing; electrified
   1958; discontinued 1960; 1970 skeleton
   tower

KEEPERS:

1897-1915	James Harvey
1915-1940	Esther Harvey
1940➤	James Harvey Jr.
c.1950-1951	Clyde Lewis
c.1952-1955	William Thompson (caretaker)
1955-1959➤	Francis Valley (caretaker)

Thessalon lighthouse. Between them, James and Esther Harvey kept the light for over forty years.
— *National Archives of Canada PA172521*

Thessalon lighthouse, Sept. 1915 — the date Esther Harvey, "the brave little lady of the light" took over lighthouse duties.
— Courtesy of Jack Kennedy

SULPHUR ISLAND

---✦---

In 1868, a light was recommended for Sulphur Island, which lies on the North Channel route between Georgian Bay and Sault Ste. Marie. A square white wooden lighthouse was built in 1869 and replaced in 1906 with a freestanding octagonal tower.

When the Sulphur Island lighthouse ceased to have a permanent keeper, it, like many of the other North Channel lights, became the target of repeated vandalism. In 1944, William Thompson, sent out to check complaints about the unlit light, found the lantern thickly coated with carbon, a result of vandals tampering with the light. This mischief continued for several years, until the tower was demolished in 1968.

When a Coast Guard crew cut the lighthouse at its base and pulled it over they thought it would collapse . . . .
— Courtesy of Bob Parr

With the increasing traffic on the North Channel, Sulphur Island light, was one of the first lighthouses built.
— Top: Archives of Ontario
— Bottom: Thunder Bay Historical Museum Society

SULPHUR ISLAND

Location: South end of Sulphur Island

Built: 1869; rebuilt 1906

Description: 1869 square white wooden tower; 1906 white octagonal tower, red octagonal lantern

Height: 43 ft./13 m

Light: Fixed white catoptric, 4 lamps, 15" reflectors; then 5th order dioptric

Visibility: 12 miles/19 kms

Fog Horn: Hand horn

Present: Tower replaced by skeleton tower in 1968

KEEPERS:

◄1871-1883►	William Shepherd
1890-1902►	Mrs. Shepherd (acting keeper!)
1905-1906►	J.J. King Jr.
1910-1916►	W. Birch
1944►	W. Thompson (caretaker)
1955►	F. Valley (caretaker)

First Sulphur Island lighthouse c.1903.
— National Archives of Canada PA172524

BRUCE MINES AND McKAY ISLAND

✛

In 1902, a lantern on the wharf's freight shed helped guide ships into Bruce Mines' new 1,000-foot public wharf. McKay Island's lighthouse was built in 1907 to serve the timber industry which had replaced copper mining as the main commercial activity at nearby Bruce Mines. By the 1920s, the area boasted 23 mills. Like many company towns, Bruce Mines was subject to strict regulations governing private enterprise. An inventive Thomas Marks, barred from opening a shop, took to selling his goods from a store he built on a barge in the harbour. The town was also home to many colourful characters, such as Mr. Lawrence, the mill owner, who brought his opera singer wife to Bruce Mines (the marriage didn't last.)

Joseph Harvey, McKay Island's first keeper served for nine years until 1915. In October, he caught a cold while attending his brother James' funeral in Thessalon (James had been keeper of the Thessalon light.) Back on McKay Island, Joseph,

> in company with Percy McNeish, rowed to Bruce to consult the doctor. On the way over he was taken worse and on reaching the shore was unable to walk without assistance. He was taken to the home of Mrs. McNeish but gradually grew worse and about ten o'clock his spirit passed to the great beyond . . . [As lighthouse keeper] he has been a faithful servant. Night after night the lights were kept trimmed and burning, and not until the lamp of his own life ceased to shine did he relinquish his office.
>
> *The Bruce Mines Spectator*, October 28, 1915

His successor was Angus McNeish, whose Cornish family had lived in the area since the early days of Bruce Mines. Unlike most of McKay's keepers who travelled

SS Premier *at dock in Bruce Mines. It later burned at this very spot in Oct. 1927.*
— *Courtesy of Merritt Strum*

BRUCE MINES

Location: Bruce Mines govern-
    ment wharf
Installed: 1902
Description: Anchor lens lantern
    on shelf, southeast corner of
    warehouse
Light: Fixed white dioptric; then red
Fog horn: Hand pump
Visibility: 5 miles/8 kms

McKAY ISLAND

Location: East end of McKay Island, 2 kms
    from Bruce Mines
Built: 1907
Description: Square white wooden dwelling,
    tower rising from roof
Height: 34 ft./10 m
Light: Fixed white dioptric, coal-oil vapour
Visibility: 11 miles/15 kms
Visibility: Fog horn: Hand crank
Present: Private cottage, skeleton tower, white
    flashing 4 secs.

KEEPERS:

1907-1915	Joseph Harvey
1915-1946	Angus McNeish
1946-1947	Merritt Strum
1947-1953	Gordon Inch
1953➤	Harold Wing

daily to the light from Bruce Mines, Angus, a rugged loner, and a divorcee, only ventured into town when supplies ran low. On his retirement in 1946, the job was offered to war veterans such as Merritt Strum. Returning, after twelve months in a Toronto tuberculosis sanitarium, Merritt tended the light for one year before taking a job in a mine at Noranda, Quebec. In 1947, Gordon Inch, who had served with Merritt in the Sault-Sudbury Regiment and who also contracted TB, took over.

In order to serve the light, Merritt would leave each day at noon, row from the mainland to French Island, cross on foot, row his cedar skiff to McKay, and return to town in the morning. When wartime restrictions eased, he was given a permit to purchase a 5 hp Johnson motor. No more roundabout routes — he headed straight across the two kilometres to McKay Island. He remembers on one stormy day, catching the attention of the Captain from the steamer *Caribou*. When Merritt told him he was on his way to tend the light at McKay, the captain hollered, "you're crazy!"

Keeper Harold Wing's wife Eva, wasn't so crazy. She refused to allow her three children to go all the way by boat in rough seas. While

Bruce Mines light was on top of the wharf's freight shed.
— *Courtesy of Merritt Strum*

Harold motored around French Island, she and the children would walk the half kilometre across the island. They would meet at the other side for the final leg. It is not surprising therefore, that Harold Wing and Merritt Strum built the first causeway between the mainland and French Island. (Both gaps now have causeways.)

Harold Wing, McKay keeper 1950s.

Merritt Strum, McKay keeper 1946-47

Gordon Inch, McKay keeper 1947-53

— Courtesy of Merritt Strum

Eva and Harold Wing with their children Eddie, Douglas, and Donna in the 1950s.
— Eva Wing Collection/ Huronia Museum L995.0047.0002

Work crew at McKay Island, c. 1908.
— National Archives of Canada PA172505

Merritt Strum, a former light-house keeper at McKay, was responsible for having the freight shed moved to the agri-cultural grounds.
– Author's Collection

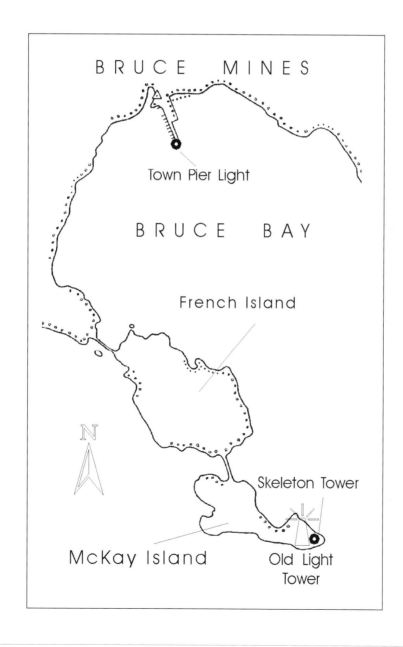

WEST SISTER ROCK

Moving light from North Sister to West Sister, 1905.
— *National Archives of Canada PA195267*

West Sister, 1995.
— *Lynx Images*

WEST SISTER ROCK

Built: 1885 on North
Sister Rock
Moved: 1905 to West
Sister Rock
Description: White
hexagonal wooden
tower on pier with red lantern
Light: Fixed white 7th order dioptric;
then flashing
Visibility: 11 miles/17.6 kms
Fog horn: Hand fog horn
Present: Still standing

KEEPERS:
1885-1902➤ William Weightman
1905-1916➤ J. Thibault
◄1949➤ Thomas Jondreau

MISSISSAGI STRAIT

—— ✛ ——

As early as the 1850s, plans were made to build a stone Imperial tower on Mississagi Strait, but it took until 1873 before the Manitoulin light was actually constructed. The Strait was filled with lumber ships heading to the United States and the mariners welcomed a light to help them navigate this perilous passage which harboured the dangerous Magnetic Reef and Castilian Shoal.

Magnetic shoals and islands were a navigator's nightmare. At the turn of the century, compasses responded to all magnetic sources whether it was the North Pole, minerals in the soil or a wrench in one's pocket. A reef, such as the one off the Mississagi Strait lighthouse, could create a compass deviation significant enough to direct a ship's crew to founder on the very shoal they wished to avoid. (Although the mechanically-operated gyrocompass was introduced in 1910, it was not used on the Great Lakes until 1922.)

After several ships ran aground on Magnetic Reef in foggy weather, a compressed air fog horn was installed at the light in 1881. Ten years later, following complaints from ship captains, the horn was replaced with a screeching "wildcat" steam whistle. In 1908, the whistle was upgraded to a diaphone type. D.N. Sullivan (keeper 1946-70) recalls arriving at the station after World War II, to find the machinery worn out:

> You had two machines to run air for the fog plant, and if you had a long stretch of fog you would always have one machine down, and you would be working on it, trying to get it ready. Everything was kerosene lights, I remember my wife standing down there half the night holding the lantern for me. I had an assistant, but he thought I would never get the machine running so he wouldn't stay down there.

The Griffon
– John Ross Robertson Collection/Metropolitan Toronto Reference Library

MISSISSAGI STRAIT

Location: Extreme westerly point
    of Manitoulin Island
Built: 1873
Description: Square white
    wooden tower, red octagonal
    lantern; attached dwelling
Light: Fixed white 4th order dioptric
Visibility: 15 miles/24 kms
Fog horn: 1881 – compressed air; 1891 – steam
    whistle; 1908 – diaphone

KEEPERS:

1873-1876	John Miller
1877-1900	William Cullis
1900-1913	J.H. Ball
1913-1946	William A. Grant
1946-1970	D.N. Sullivan

The *Griffon* Controversy

Long before the advent of the lighthouse, this area proved to be a graveyard for ships. The most famous foundering is said to be that of the *Griffon*. Having gained official sanction to follow the Mississippi River to its mouth, and to

In 1930 Roy Flemming of Ontario inspected the Mississagi wreck. The report on a hand-threaded iron bar with nut and washer, sent to Paris, France for analysis at the Laboritoire d'essais du Conservatoire national des arts et métiers *stated, "the threaded bar which we have been studying represents all characteristics of antiquity for a piece of iron manufactured by a process used in France before the 18th century. In particular it could have been manufactured some time before the 1679 when the* Griffon *disappeared." This has added to the controversy over the site of the wreck.*
– Mississagi Lighthouse Museum/Huronia Museum L995.0062.0016

set up a string of fur-trading forts along the way, René-Robert Cavelier Sieur de La Salle commissioned a barque, the *Griffon*, to be built at Niagara Falls in 1678. By September 1679, he was in Green Bay, on Lake Michigan with the ship full of furs. Chronically in debt, La Salle ordered the cargo to be taken back to Niagara, in order to pay off the expedition's financial backers. The *Griffon* sailed with a skeleton crew of five under the command of the pilot, a giant nicknamed "Luc the Dane." She was last sighted from the north shore of Lake Michigan, running eastward before a gale. Some said she made it into Lake Huron. In any event, she never reached her destination. Debris, including an ensign staff, a hatch, and bales of beaver skins washed up on Mackinac Island in the Straits of Mackinaw, but no one knew the spot where she had gone down.

For years, local Indians had been aware of an early wreck on the beach a half mile north of the present lighthouse. It was often used as a source of recycling material. During World War I, when

Mississagi Strait lighthouse
—Mississagi Lighthouse Museum/Huronia Museum L995.0062.0001

fishermen could not purchase lead, the metal used to caulk the ship's planks, was pried out and melted down to make excellent net sinkers. Farmers used the iron bolts to make harrow teeth. Around 1927, when he was thirteen, keeper D.N. Sullivan recalls visiting his cousin John Grant. The bow of the *"Griffon"* was sitting on the beach. The two boys set it on fire, plan-

ning to sell the iron to Jimmy McColeman — "Jimmy the Devil" — from Thessalon, who collected metal. Sullivan remembers the wreck smouldered for weeks under the cobble beach — "we thought we were going to get a bush fire going."

By the time an official investigation was ordered, what was left of the wreck had been

The Griffon *wreck?*
— *Mississagi Lighthouse Museum/Huronia Museum L995.0062.0009*

carried out into deep water. Nevertheless, there seemed to be enough evidence to make identification possible. The wood samples corresponded in age, rings, fibre and consistency to samples of seventeenth-century Niagara growth; the Musée de la Marine in Paris, France confirmed the Mississagi wreck followed French ship design of La Salle's era; the lead caulking used in the hull was typical of ships of the period. (Caulking was necessary to fill the cracks which appeared when the green lumber used in construction, dried and shrank.)

A less scientific discovery added to this evidence. Mississagi's keeper William Cullis and assistant John Holdsworth came upon some old buttons and coins. On searching further, they discovered a cave entrance. Entering, their hearts stopped. Leaning up against the wall were four skeletons, one so big, its skull would have fit over an average man's head. Further exploration revealed two more skeletons, six in all — the exact number of men believed to have been on the *Griffon's* last voyage. For years, the buttons and other trinkets were kept in a baking powder can in the fog plant, while the skulls were lined up along the boathouse dock, until someone kicked them into the water one night.

Not everyone believes this wreck is the *Griffon*. The hull is said to be too big; the large amount of iron is questionable and threaded bolts point to a later era. Orrie Vail of Tobermory came forward with another potential *Griffon*. His grandfather, William Vail, one of the first white men on the Bruce Peninsula, had been told by Indians of a wreck on an island they called "Wabus" or Rabbit Island, about two miles northwest of

Above: Mississagi Strait lighthouse, 1907. After the wooden lantern room was replaced by a steel unit, lightkeeper William Grant took the original to his home in Meldrum Bay where it served as a gazebo.
— *National Archives of Canada PA182870*

Left: Keeper William Cullis, 1877-1900.
— *Mississagi Lighthouse Museum/Huronia Museum L995.0062.0005*

The *Burlington* and the *Green*

Not all ships that were lost at Mississagi were victims of natural disasters. Between the years 1913 and 1915, the *Burlington* burned at anchor right in front of the lighthouse. D.N. Sullivan has his own opinion about the ship's fate: "I think she burned for the insurance to tell the truth. She was steam . . . an old wooden barge. It was in the days that they were getting obsolete." The wreck is fifty feet offshore and is a popular diving site.

Another ship, the lumber barge *Green*, grounded on Magnetic Reef in broad daylight. The lightkeeper William Grant went to its assistance. Warning that a heavy blow was headed their way, he suggested the captain remove a number of items such as the ship's swivel chairs and several 31-day clocks. The Captain refused, insisting "they were going to come and pull her off." The crew and Captain spent the night at the lighthouse and as predicted the storm destroyed the *Green*. "There was nothing left of her," recalled Sullivan. "Everyone knew it was for the insurance, in those days that's what people did. It was understood."

William Grant and the Bootleggers

Grant's 33-year tenure at Mississagi covered the period of Prohibition in the United States, 1919 to 1933. Prohibition created an instant underground economy, as Canadian bootleggers and rum-runners cashed in on the American thirst for illegal booze. Communities along the North Shore with liquor stores, like Thessalon and Blind River, became key suppliers. Canadians

Fog Alarm machinery, 1907. During a prolonged forest fire on the south shore, the fog horns blew for so many days they ran out of fuel.
— National Archives of Canada PA148186

Tobermory. When Orrie showed this wreck to a reporter and two *Griffon* experts in 1955, it was still in good condition, with the keel, bow, stern, thirteen ribs, and quite a bit of planking intact. Its length and shape matched the *Griffon's* . . . and the bolts were hand-hammered. Although these experts affirmed their belief that the Tobermory wreck was the *Griffon*, the controversy still rages.

Keeper William Grant, 1913-46.
— Mississagi Lighthouse Museum/Huronia Museum L995.0062.0006

Keeper John Miller, 1873-76
– Mississagi Lighthouse
Museum/Huronia Museum
L995.0062.0004

delivered the liquor to prearranged islands and shoals, where it was retrieved, under cover of night, by Americans in high-speed boats.

In the Mississagi Strait area, Green Island was the drop-off spot. On one occasion, the Straits liquor boat, which was fitted with an airplane engine for extra power, ran aground on Magnetic Reef. After unloading the beer, the crew managed to bring the damaged vessel alongside the lighthouse. The rum-runners said a bearing had burned out, after they ran aground on nearby Cockburn Island. Grant fashioned a new one, and did not question their story. Perhaps he was influenced by the Captain's artfully exposed gun, or maybe he had heard the rumour that the Captain had shot a man and thrown him overboard on a previous trip.

Afterwards, Grant, on a hunch, went out to the Magnetic Reefs and found the sacks of beer hanging from a buoy. "I don't know how many cases he got but he had an awful slew," recalls his nephew Sullivan. Word about the free liquor outlet soon spread through the community. Cockburn Island residents took to rowing out, and after setting their nets, fishermen would take their daily constitutional swims at the reef. If they were lucky, they found some of the beer on the lake bottom, chilled and ready to serve. Fearing the return of

the Captain and his gang, Grant hid his share of the contraband in a hole cut into the wall of one of the upstairs bedrooms. Eventually, the rum-runners were arrested. D.N. recalls, "they wanted to give the head of the gang a good trip. He was locked up, I don't know for how long. But Mr. Grant was always worried he might come back." As it turned out, Grant set up a little business of his own with the contraband, selling it to a local hotel which soon after was raided by the police. (Grant not only got off scott-free, he earned enough money from the sales to buy himself a car!)

The Land Link

D.N. Sullivan took the job as Mississagi's keeper when he returned from the war in 1946. For the first ten years, he hiked the seven miles to Meldrum Bay with a packsack full of supplies. Thankfully, unlike his uncle, William Grant, he didn't have to walk backwards pounding a metal pan to discourage a bear from stealing his food. By the late 1940s, the road was improved enough so that Sullivan could drive his Model A to and from the lighthouse –

Keeper J.H. Ball, 1900-13
– Mississagi Lighthouse Museum/Huronia Museum L995.0062.0003

the road was so bad, but it was a lot better then carrying the supplies on your back. It was 12 miles by water and I never had a boat for heavy weather. It was just a bush trail. I worked on it until the last two years I was there, you would get it to pretty fair shape in the spring, the tourists came, get it fair shape again, then the hunters would come and the wet weather. No end to it.

As the economy changed, traffic through the Strait, once filled with barges carrying lumber, pulp wood and coal, declined. In 1968, an automatic beacon was erected beside the old Mississagi light, and the station was offered for lease. Happily, the Meldrum Bay Historical Society

Keeper D.N. Sullivan and family, 1946-70. "Sullivan's Deluxe Taxi Service"
– Courtesy of D.N. Sullivan

turned the lighthouse into a Museum. The lease is now held by the Manitoulin Tourist Association and the lighthouse is part of the Mississagi Lighthouse Heritage Park.

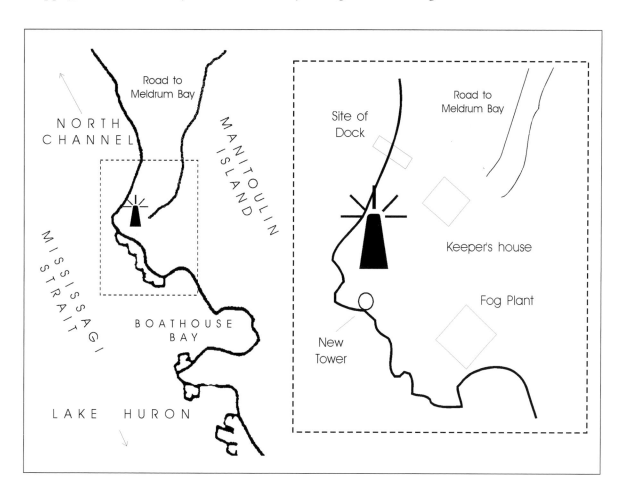

First lighthouse on Great Duck Island. "All risk of scurvy is prevented by the use of milk and potatoes, or turnips, carrots, cabbages and onions. Hence the importance of cultivating and improving the gardens, and of keeping cows . . . the most important vegetable is the potato, but the other vegetables named above are excellent antiscorbutics, and onions, from the ease with which they can be stored, would be found of great service in the event of unexpected deficiencies of the other kinds." (Excerpt from "Medical Directions for the Use of Lightkeepers," 1875.)
— Western Manitoulin Historical Society Museum, Gore Bay

GREAT DUCK ISLAND

---+---

After anchoring on the east side of the Island, it took awhile to find the two-mile road that cuts through the woods to the lighthouse. Early lightkeepers traveled along this trail by horse, although later ones were able to drive. Here and there, hand-painted signs: "This way to the Great Ducks Lighthouse", "Enchanted Forest", reminded us of the many lightkeepers' children who must have played in this thick forest: 12 Purvis', 7 Boyles, 9 Rumleys, 8 Fowlers, 6 Rourkes and 6 Hopkins'. Lured on by the sound of the surf and the fresh smell of Lake Huron, we emerged from the shadowy, shelter of the trees into the lighthouse complex. By day it was filled with colour — red trimmed windows highlighting the stark whiteness of a soaring, classically inspired tower; yellow wildflowers and a multitude of greens, brilliant against steel grey skies and water. When the storm rolled in, the verandah around the old 1931 house gave us shelter and a marvelous vantage point from which to view the sweeping beam from the original Fresnel lens cutting through the driving rain.

Guarding the main shipping route across northern Lake Huron, Great Duck Island was considered one of the most important lighthouse sites on the Bay. So important that during the First World War, its tower was heightened to almost ninety-feet, making it the tallest in the region. In the early years, there was a boat house in front of the lighthouse into which boats were winched, but in the 1920s, a harbour was created on the east side of Great Duck Island facing Outer Duck Island, the result of gravel being extracted and sold in the United States to make concrete. Beside this harbour, two shipwrecks lie just beneath the water. Orton

Original Great Duck lighthouse, built in 1877.
— National Archives of Canada

GREAT DUCK ISLAND

Location: SW point of Great
   Duck Island
Built: 1877
Description: Square tapered
   tower, dwelling attached
Height: 54 ft./16 m
Light: Red and white revolving catoptric,
   6 circular burners with 22" reflectors
   (upgraded to 10 lamps by 1878)
Visibility: 20 miles/32 kms
Fog Alarm: 1888 — steam powered siren;
   later diaphone (discontinued 1989)

New tower built: 1918
Description: Octagonal reinforced
   concrete tower
Height: 89 ft./26.7 m
Light: 3rd order Fresnel lens, coal-oil
   vapour
Dwelling: 1931

KEEPERS:
1877-1897	William Purvis
1898-1911	John Purvis
1912-1919	Norman R. Smith
1919-1930	William Boyle
1931-1936	William Rumley
1937-c.1944	Frank Fowler
1945-1947	William Rumley
1948-1949	Bob Leeson
1950>	John D. Grant
1959-1965	Frank Rourke
<1972	Jim Rumley
1972>	Joe Thibeault

Rumley, the son of lightkeeper William Rumley, grew up on the Ducks in the 30s, and recalls that one was the *Chattanooga*, the other the *C.F. Bielman*. The *Chattanooga* was a three-masted schooner that worked the coal, grain and iron ore trade. She ended her days at the Ducks, filled with gravel and used as a dock. The *Bielman* was a bulk cargo steamer, sunk to make a breakwall. (The local twist to this story suggests both vessels were seized by the Canadian Government and subsequently abandoned by their American gravel company owners.)

As well as being home to a gravel enterprise, Great Ducks was the site of several other fledgling industries. Early in the century, cattle and pigs were raised on a farm located on the island's high ground, while around 1932, someone had the brilliant idea of building an oil rig. No oil was discovered, only a lot of sand. In the mid-thirties, logging of the virgin maple and beech on the island was carried out by Murphy and Young Co.

However, the industry for which the Ducks is best known, had its beginnings with Great Ducks' first lightkeeper.

Lightkeeper William Purvis and wife Annie with their children.
— Purvis Collection/Huronia Museum L995.0056.0001

someone asked, "aren't you going home to fire up the boiler?," Boyle shrugged, "oh, just another hand."

The Purvis boys went on to build a small fishing empire: William, operating on Lake Winnipeg; John, lightkeeping and fishing in Providence Bay; and Jim fishing first in Gore Bay, then Lake Superior. Alexander's operation on Burnt Island (on the southwestern part of Manitoulin Island) still survives. (The Great Ducks fishing station was razed by vandals sometime in the 1920s.)

The William Purvis Legacy

Born in Aberdeen Scotland, William Purvis, emigrated to Canada at age 29 and became a policeman in Kincardine. No doubt, his Liberal Party leanings helped him gain his appointment to the —Great Ducks light in 1877.

When William set out to teach his sons how to fish, he was probably unaware he was laying the groundwork for the largest family-owned fishing operation in Ontario. After his retirement from lightkeeping, he established a fishery on Great Duck Island, across the channel from the Gauthier fishery on Outer Duck. According to his grandson, George Purvis, the fishing station stood on the shore near the gravel operation, with a dock stretching along the front. It was a lively spot, from which lightkeeper, William Boyle (1919-30), often had trouble pulling himself away. One foggy night, hearing ships signaling for the fog alarm,

The Ducks fishing station.
— Courtesy of George Purvis

Few can believe a boathouse once stood in front of the Great Ducks lighthouse, exposed to the full force of Lake Huron. Photo, 1910. Note original tower in background.
— National Archives of Canada PA182858

William Boyle, keeper 1919-30, who used his felt hat to strain the fuel when his motor failed out on the open lake.
– Courtesy of Sandy McGillivray

The lighthouse suited William's wife, the irrepressible Annie Purvis. After her transatlantic voyage from Scotland, she took a boat to Hamilton, rail to Guelph, and stagecoach to Goderich. Unable to find transportation at Goderich, she began to walk to Kincardine until a kindly farmer picked her up. Her hardy spirit was often needed. Hearing a panicky "Bring a skiff! Bring a skiff!", she raced to the shore to find a capsized boat and her sons, William, Jack, James, and Alex struggling to keep the youngest, Edward's head above water. In a matter of minutes, she had flipped over a heavy skiff, dragged it down the rocky shore and rowed to the rescue of her young children.

William Boyle brought his wife Rosalie and seven children by skiff to the lighthouse in 1919. Manitoulin Island historian, Sandy McGillivray remembers many of his grandfather's stories. One of Sandy's favourites concerns his mother, Bernice. For Bernice, climbing the tower's 97 steps to wind the weights was a pleasure, not a chore, as it allowed her to admire the wonderful soft amber and purple sunsets and the view of Lake Huron that seemed to stretch to the ends of the earth. One evening, she heard — one, two, three — distinct knocks. She turned in terror. Three sharp knocks were supposed to be an omen of tragedy — the bony tap of the Grim Reaper. She rushed down the steep iron stairs and into the house. Who had played this cruel prank? Seeing his daughter's genuine fright, William confessed to the deed. Satisfied it was only a joke, Bernice bravely returned to the tower to finish her chores . . . shortly afterward, her grandmother died.

Building new tower, 1918, a rare lighthouse-building project in a time of wartime austerity.
– National Archives of Canada PA148778

Wooden railroad for bringing in supplies.
– National Archives of Canada

1949: Before Radio-Phones . . .

It was December 15th and John Grant, a future Ducks keeper, noticed the Great Ducks light was unlit. Nothing to worry about. The Ducks normally closed for winter on the 12th. But then, why wasn't assistant keeper Raymond Hughson's boat at the Meldrum Bay dock? Grant notified the Department of Transport, which decided a quick fly-over was in order. As the plane circled, pilot Ian Watt and Dick McKean were silent.

The sight below said it all — a beached skiff rocking on the snowy shoreline, a half mile from the lighthouse, with no sign of keeper Bob Leeson or assistant Raymond Hughson. "Give it another minute," they thought, "they'll come running out of the forest," but the men didn't appear.

Raymond Hughson relieved to be home.
— Manitoulin Expositor, *December 22, 1949*

December 12, 1949 –
The Journey Home

The two lightkeepers loaded their 22-foot boat, then piled suitcases, a mattress, blankets, and a pail of salted herring into the 16-foot sailboat they were towing behind. Although it was blowing hard, both Bob and Raymond were anxious to return to their families, whom they had not seen in months. Raymond manoeuvred through the waves, regularly turning to check on their belongings. Near Middle Duck Island, he felt a lurch, then nothing. The line shaft had broken inside the housing. In an effort to get the boat pointing into the waves, Raymond threw out the anchor. Before long, mounting seas began swamping the boats. They had to get in to shore, but the anchor had became lodged

Bob Leeson — after 3 days and 3 nights wrecked on Middle Duck Island, his wife would not let him in the house.
— Manitoulin Expositor, *December 22, 1949*

between two boulders and there was no raising it. Pulling the smaller boat alongside, they untied it, and while Raymond held the sides, Bob began to toss the mattress and other bulky items overboard. Waves were hitting with such force that one pulled the rope out of Raymond's frozen hands, and sent Bob's dingy spinning away towards shore. As Raymond scrambled to release the length of anchor chain in order to get himself closer to shore, another giant wave smashed the boat against a boulder, and threw him into the frigid water.

He managed to crawl onto the beach of Middle Duck Island and saw Bob lying face down about 200 yards away. With great difficulty, Raymond pulled him under the shelter of some trees. As Bob drifted in and out of delirium, his friend tried to build a fire. Although both the kindling and his pack of matches were wet, he somehow succeeded.

The following day, Raymond collected any belongings that had washed on shore. Wool socks became makeshift toques. Two feet of snow had fallen and Raymond struggled to build a tent out of some blankets. It was still blowing on the third day, but Bob was coherent enough for them to attempt to cross to Great Duck. Raymond reminisced, "the first thing we did was hit the larder, and boy did we make ourselves a pot of stew!" Hoping to attract attention, they lit

Classically-inspired architecture, popular in the early years of this century, adapted well to lighthouse design. Placing the windows in a vertical line creates an illusion of greater height.
— *Lynx Images*

the light. No response. Only after several days, did they hear the welcome sound of a plane. Their worries weren't over however, even when they were safely stowed inside, as the plane had a hard time taking off. "It just kept bouncing against those big waves. Then the pilot turns to us and says casually 'the engine's not working too well today.' I remember Bob and I didn't say anything — we just looked at each other." The following year, 1950, Robert Leeson and his new assistant John Charlton received a radio-phone link at the Great Duck lighthouse.

A Vision Of The End Of Season

All lightkeepers agreed — late fall was the most difficult time to be at the lighthouse. As November

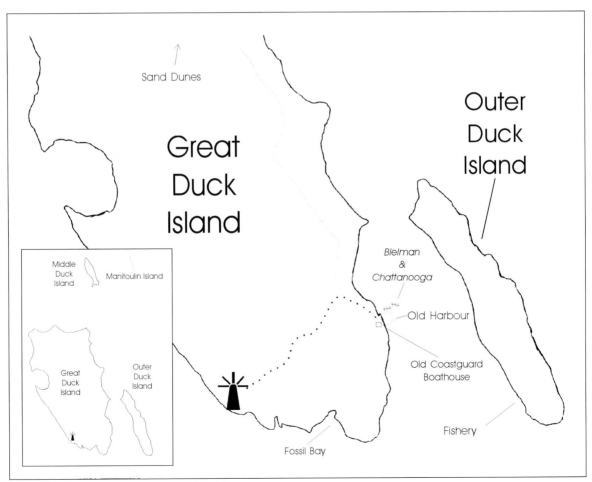

Fog alarm building, 1957, where many foggy nights were spent baby-sitting the machinery.
— National Archives of Canada PA195253

drifted into December, they would think of friends and family starting Christmas preparations, while they would be anxiously scanning the lake for a sight of the lighthouse tender. Juanita [Rourke] Keefe (1959-65) has some vivid memories of the government ship that would arrive at night to pick up the Rourkes and their assistant.

After carrying their belongings down to the shore, their last chore would be to extinguish the light. In the enveloping darkness, the ship, coated with almost two feet of ice, would glow

Great Ducks house, demolished 1995.
— Keefe Collection/ Huronia Museum L995.0006

like a ghost ship. Because the whole shoreline was ice-covered, the crew would put a plank across to the punt, but the moment the plank hit the water it too turned to ice. Juanita chuckles, "that was all right for me, the guys just took my hand but Lena, well . . . ." Apparently the assistant's wife was heavy set and could not balance on the ice-covered board. After a few failed attempts, "they actually rolled her to the punt – she didn't seem to mind." On board, they would be greeted by a hot meal: "steak and everything – what a warm feeling!"

Save for the lighthouse and a bungalow, this once proud station has been stripped of all its buildings. The fog plant, where more than one lightkeeping couple kept close vigil, is reduced to a crumbling ruin. Within the last year, the Coast Guard burned the old house. The lighthouse complex, first cleared by James Purvis, is becoming overgrown with rhubarb, lilacs, and tall grasses. Will the lighthouse eventually join the gravel operation, the farm, and the fishery, as just another memory on Great Duck Island?

Providence
Bay

✛

Lightkeeper Controversy

During the Depression, competition for jobs was intense. When political considerations were added in, the resulting furor sometimes tore communities apart. After the death of the Providence Bay lightkeeper Thomas Ellis, circa 1930, the Liberals hastily handed the lighthouse keys to Milton Buie, a staunch party supporter, unemployed, with a large family. Tory feathers were ruffled. The job should be open to all. Under pressure, the Liberals agreed to a qualifying examination and five local men wrote the test. To the chagrin of the Liberals, Alonzo Buck, a First World War veteran, scored highest. Not only was Buck a Conservative, but he already had a small pension. The town polarized — Buck had won fairly, yet Buie needed the employment. Given the unpleasant task of having to go to the Buie residence to retrieve the lighthouse keys, Mr. Buck was greeted at the door by a furious Mrs. Buie who blasted him for "taking food directly out of the mouths of the children" etc, etc. The Liberals had egg on their face; the town was bitterly divided, and both Buie and Buck were humiliated. Wisely, the politicians worked out an amicable solution: Buck was offered a comfortable increase in his pension if he would return the lighthouse keys to Milton Buie. The compromise was accepted, and peace was restored.

In the 1950s, the Department of Transport looked at ways to cut costs at Providence Bay and other less important lights. Through automation, they calculated they could eliminate a keeper's annual wage (less than $1,000 including $48.00 to operate the fog horn) in favour of paying a caretaker a mere $50.00 per

Providence Bay dock
— The Little Schoolhouse and Museum

annum. The last lightkeeper resigned in April 1953, and by 1955 a hydro cable was laid.

On October 14th, 1973 the lighthouse caught fire and burned to the ground. Some say the tower was struck by lightning; others believe the fire was intentionally lit. Because the building had been subjected to repeated vandalism, and trespassing had become a nuisance for adjacent property owners, there was no strong support for a scheme to reconstruct the light.

PROVIDENCE BAY

Location: West extremity of
    Providence Point
Built: 1904
Height: 42 ft./12.6 m
Light: Fixed white dioptric with duplex burners,
    hydro in 1955
Visibility: 11 miles/17.6 kms
Burned: October 14th, 1973
Replacement: Steel tower, November 1973

KEEPERS:

1904-1905	J.J. Roussain
1906-1911	John B. Sinclair
1912-1930s➤	Thomas Ellis
◄1938-1949➤	Milton Buie
◄1973	Jack Cornish (caretaker)

Wharf Light: Fixed red light lantern on
    23-ft./6.9 m pole

KEEPER:

1948-1960➤	Delbert Pattison (caretaker)

Providence Bay lighthouse boasted a library of books from the Upper Canada Tract Society, and a bed for the keeper on long foggy nights. The library burned with the lighthouse.
— Courtesy of Leland McIntyre

MICHAEL'S BAY

---✦---

It was 1866 when Robert A. Lyon bought 22 square miles of Tehkummah Township at Michael's Bay on the south shore of Manitoulin Island. Within a short time, it had a thriving lumber mill and over sixty residents. Known as "Stumptown," Michael's Bay began shipping wood products to the U.S. and southern Ontario.

In 1870, a lighthouse was built by the Department of Marine and Fisheries and the timber company to guide the schooners and barges in and out of port. It was the second lightstation on Manitoulin after the range lights at Little Current, and the only one on the south shore.

The first keeper listed in the 1878 Parliamentary Sessional Papers was John W. Chisholm. His official appointment was recorded in an Order-In-Council dated June 1883 and signed by Prime Minister John A. Macdonald and Governor General, the Marquis of Lorne.

During the village's heyday in the late 1870s and early 1880s, the ill-fated *Asia* was one of many ships that called in regularly. But despite the village's economic boom, Lyon did nothing to eliminate debts he had accumulated — an oversight which caused his Michael's Bay Timber Company to go bankrupt in 1888. The village began to decline and in 1899 the light went black. It was relit in 1901 and continued in service until 1909, when it was permanently discontinued. A 1910 fire destroyed much of the village, and subsequent fires finished the job. Out on the point, the light escaped the fires, but because of rotting timbers, it eventually collapsed around 1930.

Michael's Bay keeper, H.R. Bowerman
— Courtesy of Richard Bowerman

MICHAEL'S BAY

Location: West extremity of point
    forming the south shore of
    Michael's Bay
Built: 1870
Description: Square white
    wooden building surmounted
    by octagonal red iron lantern
Height: 25 ft./7.5 m
Light: Fixed white catoptric, mammoth flat-
    wick lamp, 33" reflectors
Visibility: 11 miles/17.6 m
Fog horn: Hand fog horn
Discontinued: 1899; back in operation 1901;
    permanently discontinued 1909
Present: No light

Keepers:
◄1878-1883►	John Willson Chisholm
1901-1902	H.R. Bowerman
1902-1906►	Edward Martin
◄►	Alexander Murray Chisholm

SOUTH BAYMOUTH

---+---

Just past Rattlesnake Harbour on Fitzwilliam Island, one of the engines exploded. Limping along on the other, we failed to notice the fog thickening around us. Increasingly nervous, we surveyed the shoal-filled chart showing the approach to South Baymouth and pulled out the GPS (Global Positioning System) for the second day in a row. Space-age equipment notwithstanding, we were tremendously relieved to hear the reassuring blast of South Baymouth's fog horn, and to catch sight of the buoys that mark the harbour channel entrance. The news that the damage to the engine was worse than we had anticipated, left us with mixed feelings — disappointment, but also pleasure at the chance to explore a community which had weathered many changes, from typical Great Lakes fishing village to ferry terminus.

South Baymouth Light: Keeping It In The family

South Baymouth's first settlers were Jim Ritchie and Val Wilman and their families, from nearby Walker's Point. Around 1878, they set up a partnership in a fishing station which lasted forty years. During the summers, other fishermen from Collingwood, Southampton, and Goderich joined them. The catches were salted in barrels, then shipped to Killarney to the Buffalo Fish Company. In 1879, the Booth Fish Company started to market fresh fish, and so they contracted with Wilman and Ritchie to build a dock and an icehouse at South Baymouth.

As nearby Michael's Bay began to decline, South Baymouth took on the role of the south shore's main port. Two range lighthouses were built in 1898. Jim Ritchie was the first lightkeeper, followed by his cousin, John Ritchie. At that time, the front light was on an island. John would row out each night and morning, then fish all day — a perfect arrangement. As he grew older, his daughter Pearl often tended the light. She later married Harry Chisholm, a First World War veteran

SS Graham *in two pieces, east point of South Bay*
– The Little Schoolhouse and Museum

who, as both a veteran and a relative, was a shoe-in for the job. The family tradition continued when Len Leeson, another of John's sons-in-law replaced Harry in the late 1950s. He stayed until the light was automated.

The SS *George A. Graham*

October 6, 1917
Soon after passing Detour light on the St. Mary's River, on her way to Midland with a load of grain, the SS *George A. Graham* was hit by a furious storm. The watchman, seventeen-year-old Mark Russell, described the frightening waves "sweeping over the back of the ship and raking the deck to the bow."

At Cove Island, the cargo shifted, pulling the ship under. She righted, but listing substantially to port, fell helplessly into trough after trough. Despite a broken stern cable, the Captain managed to head the *Graham* back towards South Baymouth, but before she could reach safety, her stern piled up on the east point with such tremendous force that she buckled like an accordion. Fishermen rowed out to rescue the crew mem-

bers, and billeted them in town. Retired fisherman, Ivan Sisson, recalls the following days, when a steady stream of farmers came to load up their wagons with the abandoned grain. The wreck was a favourite haunt for local children until the start of WWII when the valuable steel was salvaged.

Johnnie Ritchie mending nets, South Baymouth
– The Little Schoolhouse and Museum

Back range tower.
– Courtesy of Lottie Chapman

This was not the only grain bonanza in the tiny port. Sisson also recalls the leaking *Agawa* being towed to South Baymouth from Michael's Bay:

> there were pumps going all the time, and these pumps were pumping out grain. There was great heaps of grain down here at the bottom of the bay, and we'd go out, we had a big hoop and a bag on it and a great long pole and a rope, and one fella'd be in the back of the boat digging it into the grain, and the other fellow would be pullin' it up, and you'd pull up this bag full of grain and dump it in your boat, see. And come in and sell it to the farmers for 50 cents a bag . . . and 50 cents was still something then.

The Fishing Village

In the 1920s, South Baymouth was a Booth Company fishing village. Net drying reels lined the waterfront along with the Company's docks, ice house, fish house, and net shed. The fishermen were divided into two groups: the captains who stayed all winter and were paid to mend the nets, and those who sailed up only for the season, spending their winters in the lumber camps.

It was a sad day in the late 1920s, when the skippers heard the Booth Company tugs weren't coming back. But with such an abundance of fish, the vacuum was soon filled by small open gas fishing boats belonging to fourteen different individual operators. Even the Indians trolling from sailboats with hand lines, brought in catches of 150 pounds of trout. For all these vessels, the range lights were absolutely vital if they were to navigate the channel into the harbour safely.

As a way of making a living, fishing has always been risky. When autumn gales raged for four or five days, the South Baymouth fishermen would congregate at the docks, fearfully scanning the water, and discussing where each of their nets was set. Each man usually had three "gangs", or fifteen sixty-yard nets, and because of the expense, there were no back-ups. If nets were lost, or the web was torn away, they would have to wait for winter to make new ones. That meant no income to purchase provisions. Aside from equipment

South Baymouth dock, 1927.
– The Little Schoolhouse and Museum

South Baymouth front range in a SW storm, 1900. In 1898 a Manitowaning social news column effused: "this harbour is now as easy to access as it is safe and snug — the lights being range lights so that one can be sure of his course."
— The Little Schoolhouse and Museum

cents a pound for trout, but at other times they might be forced to sell for three cents a pound.

As the fishing industry declined, ferries and tourists became South Baymouth's bread and butter and the harbour was redesigned to accommodate them. Nevertheless, the two range lights lost none of their importance. Little maintenance is required, except when the unpredictable fog horn refuses to shut off, and exasperated locals have to summon a Coast Guard helicopter crew from Parry Sound to service it.

losses, the fishermen were also at the mercy of the laws of supply and demand. In the late '30s and early '40s, they were paid as much as fifty

Wide shot taken from rear lighthouse before 1900. Keeper John Ritchie, and Mr. Green in boat.
— The Little Schoolhouse and Museum

Lonely Island's second tower is squat because of its site high on a bluff.
— National Archives of Canada PA172503

LONELY ISLAND

— ✦ —

As we approached Lonely Island, grey mist rolled over the distant lighthouse, a gleaming white sentinel on the summit of a wooded bluff. Thousands of years ago, only the highest points of this two-mile-long island stood above the glacial waters. Receding waters left remnants of ancient raised beaches in the forest and along the white cobble shoreline. A cracked cement path leads to a white two-story house built in 1907 after a fire decimated the former tower-house on the hill. The new house was constructed on the beach for easier access to drinking water. Further along, a 1960s bungalow looks almost suburban in this unlikely setting. A cedar bridge behind this house points to a moss-covered pathway carved out of the woods 126 years ago. To reach the tower, one must climb a rickety wooden staircase clinging to the cliff face, its 100 faded green steps wrapped with branches and vines.

Johnny Adams remembers the climb well:

> Used to climb those steps every day. I had to carry the oil up there. We had a yoke to carry five gallons on each side. The first year I was there the steps were in terrible shape, snow piled half up the cliff in winter, and in summer, rattlesnakes, that hell wouldn't have.

One Big Graveyard

"Lonely is one big graveyard from one end to the other" asserts former assistant keeper, Orton Rumley, and many are the tales passed down from keeper to keeper about some of these burials. Aldene Strand (daughter of Aldon Brethour): "There is an old Indian burial mound beyond the lighthouse. Whenever Indians stopped at the island, Dad would invite them up to the house. He told me they refused to

*Old Lonely
Island tower
– National
Archives of
Canada
PA195259*

LONELY ISLAND

Location: Lonely Island on
    summit of north bluff
Built: 1870
Description: Square wooden
    tower, dwelling attached
Height: 42 ft./12.6 m
Lantern: Fixed white catoptric, 5 flat-wick
    lamps with 15" reflectors
Demise: Burned

Rebuilt: 1907-8
Description: Octagonal tapered wooden tower,
    red circular lantern
Height: 57 ft./17 m
Light: Group flashing white 3rd order dioptric,
    coal-oil vapour
Visibility: 20 miles/32 kms
Fog Horn: Hand horn, then fog alarm building
    housing acetylene gun 1944
Additional: Foursquare dwelling on beach and
    boat house, 1907-8; bungalow in 1961-2
Automated: c.1987 converted to solar power,
    generator building
Additional: 1907 house, bungalow, and other
    out-buildings destroyed 1995

KEEPERS:
1870-1872   John Egan
1872-1872   Henry Solomon
1872-1885   Domonic Solomon
1885-1914   Jean Haitse
1914-1916   Louis Roque
1916-1942   Harry Loosemore
c.1943-c.1958 Edward Rousseau
1959-1965   John Adams
1966-1978➤   Aldon Brethour
c.1982-c.1986 Lorne Gibson

move away from the dock. For them, Lonely
Island was sacred ground."

Several stories relate to a keeper who decided
to stay at the light over the winter but did not survive his ordeal. Frank Butler (assistant 1980-81):
"There are several mounds of a peculiar nature
on the island. Six in total. Two of these mounds
are rumoured to be from the keeper who got
stuck over the winter. He was ill, ran out of food.
He smashed the furniture for fuel. The dog and
keeper are supposed to be buried there." Orton
Rumley (assistant 1978) fills out the story:

> Apparently when the tug came in the fall, the
> assistant went on, but the old guy said no, he
> had nothing to go in for and wanted to stay for
> the winter. He said that he would put on the
> light at certain dates in the winter. He put it on
> Christmas and another day, but the next one
> towards spring, the light didn't come on.
> When they went out, he was dead on the
> kitchen floor, and his dog had starved to
> death. He is buried behind the old oil shed.

On the east side of the island, folklore has it
that crew and passengers from the *Asia* are said
to be buried. Newspaper articles corroborate
this story.

Accusations of Robbing the Dead

For eleven days, the crew of the tug *Kendell* had been scouring every bay and beach for bodies and wreckage from the steamer *Asia*. She had foundered with over 120 passengers during the hurricane of September 14, 1882 (see Why Were They Built?). On October 6th, the tug crew landed on Lonely Island. Approaching light-keeper, Domonic Solomon, as he was setting fish nets, the Captain inquired if any dead had floated onto Lonely's shores. "None," he was assured. Captain Richmond pressed the matter. Finally, Solomon conceded there had been one corpse, an unclothed woman, so badly decayed he had felt it best to bury her. The Captain demanded to see the grave but at first, Solomon stalled. Tension mounted.

A report in The *Manitoulin Expositor* continued the story:

> The [group] found the body of a woman clothed and having a life-preserver on. It was near the water's edge, and a board laying on top of it. No efforts had been made to bury it. On examining the corpse the name of Mrs. Woods was found on the corset and stockings . . . . The corpse had been badly decayed and was unrecognizable. The party removed the body further inland, and scraped gravel off a large flat rock and placed the body on it with a board for covering. This was the best form of burial they could make, as it was too decayed to be taken aboard the boat. They returned to where the lighthouse-keeper was fishing and told him the body had been robbed.

The search party had noted impressions of a necklace and finger ring on the bloated body. Domonic confessed to taking a pearl broach, two dollars and 10 cents in silver, and a gold watch. Except for the watch, which his wife had taken to Manitowaning for repairs, he turned over all the items to the Captain. Just then, one of the search party, Mr. Ten Eyck, arrived with an empty wallet which he had discovered in the brush.

The keeper admitted taking it from the corpse and tearing the clasp off but said there was nothing in it, and that he simply dropped it down at the head of the corpse. Mr. Ten Eyck then told him where it was found, and accused him of throwing it as far as he could after taking its contents. The keeper seemed much confused, and finally admitted throwing it away, and said the reason he did so was because he was afraid it would be discovered. He then produced a clasp that had been torn from it.

A thorough search of the lightkeeper's premises was carried out and brought to light several more items from the *Asia*: stools, chairs, axe-handles, a cabin door, a trunk and valise (both opened and empty), block and tackle, a water tank, a pillow-case, and a picture of a girl

The 100 steps to the Lonely tower.
– *Courtesy of Rosalind Zamiska*

in a gilt frame. The discovery of three more life preservers, with a "disagreeable smell pervading", led the search party to believe more bodies were "secreted away on the island."

On October 16th, the Department of Marine and Fisheries stated that an inquiry into the alleged conduct of the Lonely keeper would be held. The local newspaper began to defend Mr. Solomon, saying the lack of regular communication between Lonely Island and Manitoulin or the mainland, prevented him from reporting the bodies. The paper also cleared him of wrong doing because he had returned all the possessions, asserting that "his version puts quite a different face on his conduct."

It's Not Lonely for Nothing

In spite of the extreme distance from Lonely Island to Manitoulin and the mainland, many of her keepers risked supply trips to Killarney and Tobermory. One of them was Domonic's father. According to the 1873 *Canadian Parliamentary Sessional Papers,* his trip ended in tragedy and was the reason Domonic became keeper:

John Adams, 1941.
– Courtesy of John Adams

Mr. Henry Solomon, keeper of the lighthouse at Lonely, was drowned in the month of June last, while proceeding from Killarney, near the mainland, to the island with supplies. He had nearly reached the island, in company with an Indian, when the boat was upset in a squall, and both Mr. Solomon and the supplies were lost, but the Indian was saved. He left his wife and a large family of young children, and the Government considerately appointed his son, Dominick Solomon, lightkeeper in his place, in the 17th of last [1872], at a salary of $450 per annum, which will no doubt prove to be a great relief to the family, as they were in extremely poor circumstances.

Lonely Island lightstation from the air.
– Courtesy of Aldene Strand

Several years later, another keeper's supply trip added an amusing chapter to the Lonely Island folklore. Approaching Yeo Island in the Coast Guard issued 16-foot molded plywood boat, John Adams switched gas tanks. The boat would not start. Flipping up the motor, he found the entire bottom had fallen off. Armed with two oars (and two rifles), John began to

Standing: Sister Ignatius, Margaret, Dorothy, and Dell Loosemore. Seated: Margaret de Lamandiere, Edgar Loosemore.
— Hoyland Collection/Huronia Museum L995.0037.0002

Vernon, Norbert, and Harry Loosemore on the dock
— Hoyland Collection/ Huronia Museum L995.0037.0005

row, and row, and row. His intuition told him Cove Island's keeper Bill Spears was watching through his binoculars and having a good chuckle. "After five hours of rowing I thought, if I get close enough to that lighthouse, I'll start shooting the windows out — they won't be so smart then!" Bill Spears was indeed watching and after a good laugh, he came to John's aid, brandishing a bottle of whiskey as a peace offering. John recalls, "I couldn't have lifted [the whiskey] if I wanted to. I had blisters on my hands, everywhere! I was so mad!"

The Loosemores — Stranded for Days

Usually, mail was delivered to the island courtesy of the Killarney fishermen, but one July day in 1926, Adelaide (Dell) Loosemore, decided to surprise her husband Harry by going out to see him at the light rather than writing a letter. With

her children and two others, she set off from Killarney. After an hour's run, the boat's engine died and before the driver could fix the motor, a storm broke and pushed them onto a shoal. Fortunately, the water was shallow enough for the driver to carry Dell and the children to nearby West Rock, a small island one mile from Squaw Island. They sat on the treeless rock, patiently waiting for a boat to leave the commercial fishing camp at Squaw. None passed, and so they fashioned a lean-to out of a blanket, to protect the children from the wind and spray overnight.

The next day the children tied towels to sticks, ready to wave them if someone came into view. Later that afternoon, they caught sight of a

John David Roque and Justin Low on tower. Spending summers at Lonely was a child's dream.
— Courtesy of Rosalind Zamiska

Wedding portrait of keeper Edward Rousseau and wife Margaret, c.1928-30.
– Courtesy of Rosalind Zamiska

man walking along the shore of Squaw Island, but nothing they did could capture his attention. On the third day, a fisherman, Joseph Trudeau, did notice the distant commotion. He brought the chilled and bedraggled group to Squaw and from there the tug *Papoose II* returned them safely to Killarney. From then on, Dell wrote letters to Harry.

Childhood Memories

Each summer, Rosalind and Blake Roque waited with anticipation to learn if they could stay with their uncle, lightkeeper Edward Rousseau, on Lonely Island. There was much for them to do: picnics at Club Island, long hikes, hiding inside the wooden life-boats hanging from the boat house ceiling, and beachcombing to decorate their "tree house", a clearing in the middle of a thick clump of cedar bushes. Their most precious finds were light bulbs thrown from passing ships. (They had never seen such things, as Killarney had not yet received hydro.) On the island the children were given complete freedom – only the rattlesnakes posed a danger, and the children rarely saw any of these. Rosalind was later shocked to learn that when the cedar trees

were bulldozed to clear land for a bungalow, the rocks were found to be infested with rattlesnakes – "that's where we played!"

Rabbits not rattlers were lightkeeper Edward Rousseau's nemesis. More often than not, the only reward he received for his hours of gardening, were gnawed stumps of lettuce. Despite the rabbits, Lonely Island's fertile soil and moderate temperatures were ideal for growing apples, strawberries, sand cherries, sugar plums and raspberries, from which several keepers made wine and preserves. Rousseau also kept goats and chickens. One day, he spotted a hawk making off with one of his prized chickens. The children were amazed when their enraged uncle took a shot at the bird, putting a hole through the window screen.

Each evening on the dot of six, Edward would sit down at his desk that folded out from the wall. "He wrote down anything he did in his log book, the weather, emergencies . . . one time a plane had to make an emergency landing on the beach," remembers Rosalind. It turned out to be a Miami millionaire taking his two young sons to Camp Adanac. Pushed off course by high winds, and with only a few minutes of fuel, the pilot spotted Lonely Island. Despite nicking a few treetops on his steep descent, the pilot safely

Standing left to right: Julian Low, Cecil Low, Margaret Rousseau, Edward Rousseau, William Low, Justin Low (in front of Edward). Seated: Regina Rousseau, John David Roque.
– Courtesy of Rosalind Zamiska

landed the plane on a 200-yard strip of beach.

Like all rotating lights, Lonely had clockwork that needed winding. Since there was such a long walk to the tower, the department built a tiny cabin on the bluff, furnished with a bed, table, armchair and large alarm clock. The assistant had to wind the weight at midnight and again at 3 a.m., then shut it down at dawn. When light-keeper John Adams came to Lonely in 1959, the cabin was quite dilapidated. "That shack wasn't my cup of tea," John Adams recalls with a shake of his head. Accidentally or intentionally, it was later pushed over the side of the bluff while he was clearing trees around the tower.

Another of Rosalind Roque's happy memories centers around the steamships out of Killarney. "We would try our best to stay awake because we knew around 12:30 they would come past Lonely – they would look so marvelous all lit up. As children it was the most wonderful place. It was all we anticipated – being able to go. It was like a dream."

Dismantled piece of Lonely's Fresnel lens.
– Author's collection

Mermaids Sighted

For one of Lonely's last assistants, Rudy Payerl, a visit to the light was sometimes truly like a dream. The *Toronto Star* printed an interview with Rudy in which he reported climbing the tower during a storm. In between the noise of crashing trees and screaming wind, he swore he heard strange voices. Turning to look out the window, he saw a strange sight: five mermaids! "If there's a strong wind you hear them," said Payerl, "It's a different sound."

On our first visit, we had discovered the tower's beautiful Fresnel lens, dismantled and lying in pieces just inside the entrance, waiting to be crated. A month later, we flew over the island and were saddened to see raw scars on the shore-line where the houses had recently been burned by the Coast Guard. In a few years, foliage will choke the path to the tower, and the tired stair-case will collapse, leaving the lighthouse isolated on its lonely bluff – a haunting memorial to a forgotten era.

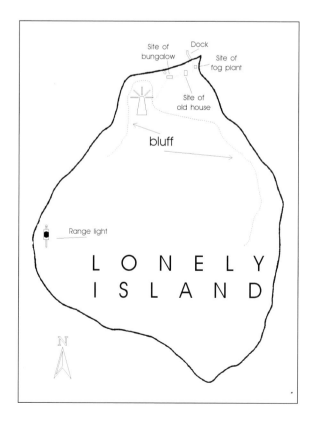

THE NATURE
THAT SURROUNDS

---✦---

Whether a keeper and his family lived on the mainland, a wooded island, or a bare rock, they were intimately connected to the seasonal changes and to nature. Asked whether he ever became bored with such an isolated life, Orton Rumley of Lonely Island shook his head and replied, "I never got lonely. I never got bored. You're right out there with God's creation, how can you get bored?"

For many, the varied wildlife was a constant pleasure. Juanita [Rourke] Keefe spent three years on the small, barren Western Islands, followed by seven years on the large, lush Great Ducks:

> The Westerns — the wildness of the water, the wonderful rocks — such big strong headlands that have been there all these centuries. In the fall at the Great Ducks the snow geese come. The island had rabbits. Rabbits by the hundreds! Lots of water snakes, big coiled water snakes. I had my pet crow, my pet chickadees, and my dogs. The crow and I fell in love with each other. He never flew off the island. The others would fly off across Lake Huron but he was always there in the spring. When I would walk in the woods the Chickadees and Blue Jays would fly with me.

Lonely Island: "Snakes Until Hell Wouldn't Have Them!"

Locals say that the first rattlesnakes drifted to the shores of Lonely Island on a log from the mainland. However they arrived, they liked it, stayed — and multiplied.

Snake pit camouflaged in grass on Lonely Island.
— Courtesy of Pat Johnston

Stories of Lonely's snakes reach legendary proportions. Each evening, before John Adams took the long path through the woods to the lighthouse, he donned rubber boots, grabbed a flashlight, and slung a shotgun over his shoulder. "The rattlesnakes would be laying on the board walk on the way to the lighthouse. They would be waiting for birds to hit the lantern and fall to the ground. I would walk along there with my flashlight and shotgun and, 'Bang! Bang!'"

The next keeper, Aldon Brethour, took an entrepreneurial approach to the problem. He caught and crated the rattlers and shipped them to scientists at the Royal Ontario Museum, or to a laboratory for the production of anti-venom serum. One night, just after Aldon's wife went outside to throw a bag of garbage away, she

rushed back, huffing and puffing after a run-in with a sizeable rattler. Orton Rumley, Aldon's assistant, laughs, "I remember it took us three days to find that garbage bag (it was twenty feet up a tree!"

(In April 1991, the Massasauga rattlesnake was added to the "endangered species" list by the Committee on the Status of Endangered Wildlife in Canada. As of May 1990, they are protected by law everywhere in Ontario.)

Nuisance on the roof.
— Spears Collection/ Huronia Museum L995.0017.0001

Cove: Bears!

Dora and William Spears (keeper 1949-76) remember a bear they nicknamed Nuisance, who helped with the home renovations by tearing a door off the house and picking shingles off the roof. A second bear, Gentle Ben, was tamer. On grocery trips to Tobermory, the Spears would

Aldon Brethour, Lonely Island.
— Courtesy of Aldene Strand

Gentle Ben gets fed.
— Spears Collection/ Huronia Museum L995.0017.0005

Buller, Presqu'ile's assistant keeper!
— County of Grey-Owen Sound Museum

pick up "bear bones" rather than the customary "dog bones" as treats for them. Nevertheless, these bears were not trained animals. When assistant Lou Brandon tried to get a tow from one of them, the bear decided it would rather ride and started to climb into the boat. Hastily, Lou sped away.

Presqu'ile: The Dog Who Helped To Run The Lighthouse

There was one animal who was trained. In fact, John Mackenzie called his dog, Buller, his lighthouse assistant. Each morning at precisely 5 a.m., Buller would enter the bedroom with the lighthouse key in his mouth and rouse his master with a gentle touch of his paw. If Mackenzie wanted

The key to the Presqu'ile light.
— County of Grey-Owen Sound Museum

an extra snooze, Buller left him for another fifteen minutes.

This collie performed a variety of duties, from learning to recognize individual ship whistles, to delivering notes in town, just by being told the recipient's name. His intelligence was evident from an early age. When only a year, he was ordered to take a heavy pail of apples to the house. Without taking the handle from his mouth, Buller tipped the pail and rolled out just enough fruit to lighten the load.

Henry the gull, a friend for eight years.
— Madigan Collection/ Huronia Museum L995.0015.0008

Pointe au Baril: Henry The Seagull

Another creature that became a favourite companion was a seagull named "Henry". No matter the time of day, as soon as Emmaline Madigan called, the gull would appear. Their friendship lasted eight years. Henry knew who to trust, and it certainly wasn't the Madigan children. They devised a plan to catch him by tying a string around a piece of bread. They figured they could reel the bird in after he swallowed the food. However, the scheme didn't work, and after that Henry refused to touch any of their offerings. He was almost like another child to Emmaline and so when she found him limping one day, she put baby aspirins into his food. But the biggest excitement came the day Emmaline had to reassess her belief that Henry was a male. One spring morning, he appeared with a baby gull in tow! After the initial shock, Emmaline decided it didn't really matter whether the gull was male or female. Henry was Henry. Henrietta just wouldn't fit.

A tub of dead birds collected after one night at the Westerns.
— Keefe Collection/Huronia Museum L995.0006.0004

Hope Island: Dorthea Doolittle

Dorthea Herron grew up on the Hope Island light in the mid 1940s. Without companions her own age, she developed a deep fondness for nature. All creatures were worthy of her affection: mice, snakes, crayfish, turtles, and her favourite, frogs.

When her father, Alex Herron (1940-63) was invited by two well-known hockey players to go fishing, he decided to bring his young daughter. It was a perfect day. Dorthea sat quietly in the bow while the men chatted, until one of them

grabbed a live frog from the bait pail and pierced it with a hook. What! They were torturing and killing frogs! She looked at each man. They seemed engrossed in their conversation. Surely they wouldn't notice one missing frog. Not moving her eyes from the "killers", she slipped her hand into the bucket, grabbed a frog, and tossed it into the lake. Then she surreptitiously released another, and another, until the pail was empty. In mid-conversation, Alex Herron reached into the pail. No frogs. At first he was confused, then his face turned red as he looked at Dorthea. The fishing trip was over. "Oh, he was mad!" Dorthea laughed, "he just went quiet. That was the worst."

James Kineen (Nottawasaga) had two mischievous pet crows, Handsome and Charlie, who were skilled pickpockets.
— Mazur Collection/ Huronia Museum L995.0003.0002

Skipper and Jiggs on Great Duck.
— Charlton Collection/Huronia Museum L995.0020.0008

When asked by her older brother Bob why she threw a garter snake away, Dorthea Herron shrugged, "Oh, that one bit me."
— Arthur Collection/ Huronia Museum L995.0009.0012

Destaffing and destruction
✛
The Future

Early one morning in May 1969, while the inhabitants of Lion's Head slept, a Coast Guard crew arrived from Parry Sound. They demolished the lighthouse that had been a fixture for years, and took the remains to the dump, before any in the village became aware. To the surprise of the Coast Guard, the villagers were enraged. Why, they wondered, was there an outcry now, when there had been next to none over the demolition of Cape Robert light, or Sulphur Island light? Mindful of this reaction, when it came the turn of the beautiful old lighthouse on Flowerpot Island, the Coast Guard scheduled the destruction for the fall, in the belief it would draw less attention. They were wrong. This time the outcry did result in a temporary suspension of the project. The reprieve was brief, however, and the demolition resumed at Narrow, Badgeley, Clapperton, and Boyd on the North Channel. Time after time, communities only learned of their loss as the lighthouses came tumbling down. Many, including Coast Guard personnel, were heartbroken as the demolition program inexorably continued.

How did matters get to this point? The destaffing process began in earnest, on Georgian Bay and the North Channel in the 1950s and 60s. A bureaucratic initiative outlined to the Coast Guard that savings of tens of millions of dollars could be achieved if the system were to be automated. This projected financial advantage proved to be irresistible. Natural attrition and staff reductions achieved savings at the outset, while automation of the smaller stations resulted in additional savings. Records of significant dates in the destaffing process are incomplete and scattered. With humour and perhaps some defensiveness, it has been suggested by the Coast Guard, that the incomplete nature of the records just adds to the mystery and romance of the lighthouses.

Stations with fog alarms were able to postpone their destaffing somewhat longer, because the solar panels installed in the stations were not able to supply enough power for the alarms. Someone was needed to ensure their operation. The department's solution was to install automated fog horns. By eliminating fog plants, they could simultaneously eliminate the last of the keepers. But how could they convince the mariners of the efficacy of the new fog horns?

The bureaucrats invited the Coast Guard operations personnel to come to the East Coast to take part in a test. New horns were placed at various locations, and each participant was given a checklist on which to indicate whether they heard a horn. Jack Kennedy remembers how biased he and the other operations people were against the new "car horns", and how their bias frustrated their hosts: "he'd say, 'you hear them, don't ya'?' We'd go, 'yeah'. He'd go, 'well if you hear them they must be okay, right?' And we'd go, 'we hear them but they're not grunting.'" A little grunt noise was added on the end to appease the old-timers, and on the Great Lakes, the new horns were brought in. Jack Kennedy feels, "the moment we accepted the new fog horn, that was it . . . but we dragged it [destaffing] out twelve years. The East and West Coasts refused the new horns, and that is essentially why they still have keepers."

There were other factors, of course. While the Coast Guard attempted to reduce operating costs, the keepers were unionized. Their demands were for better working hours and conditions, and the result was upward pressure on budgets. It would be less expensive, the Coast Guard calculated, to automate the stations, and hire a caretaker at a minimal salary to replace the keepers. However, in many cases the caretakers were not on site, and it still fell to the Coast Guard in Parry Sound to maintain the stations. The short season, combined with the many other pressures on ship time, left little time for such work, and so the structures fell into ruin. A few of the lighthouses were leased as dwellings, and the Parry Sound base planned to use some of that revenue to maintain other stations. Unfortunately, they were not permitted to keep the revenue, and in some communities, the leasing itself created problems. Vandalism soon followed and concerns arose as to the legal liability for injury to trespassers. Demolition was the inevitable solution. Badgeley Island, automated in 1965, and dynamited in 1981, is a typical example.

It is the communities who most lose by having these historic lighthouses disappear from the landscape. Although the Coast Guard's mandate does not include the preservation of structures for heritage reasons, the current policy regarding lights is to maintain them for at least two years after the date of destaffing. During that time, if other uses can be found at the federal, provincial, municipal, or private level, no building will be torn down. If no suitable purpose is found, the structure will be deemed obsolete, left to deteriorate, and eventually demolished.

Because these historic lights no longer fall within the mandate of the Coast Guard, there will need to be some mechanism whereby their stewardship can be transferred to the local communities. This has been successfully done at a few sites: the Cabot Head light and Mississagi light are now operating as successful museums. Lighthouses such as Brebeuf, Strawberry, and Janet Head have been leased with good results, and other lights such as Pointe au Baril and Cove Island are watched over by local groups. But the destruction continues at more remote stations such as Lonely Island and the Great Ducks. Only last year, houses were razed at those locations, despite the fact they were in good condition. It is too late to save many of the lights on Georgian Bay, Manitoulin Island, and the North Channel, but they do sound an alarm for other parts of the country where demolition is still being defended as the solution to a perceived problem. Lighthouses on Lake Superior are slated to go this summer. And the East and West Coasts, now undergoing the destaffing process, will not be far behind unless the public intervenes.

Destaffing and destruction of lighthouses are sensitive issues worldwide. Advances in navigation like GPS, (Global Positioning Systems), enable ships to manoeuvre through storm and fog with ease. So what is to become of these structures? For many lighthouses, it is already too late, but if this significant element of Canada's marine heritage is to be preserved for future generations, those for whom preservation is important will have to identify and establish a basis on which to coordinate their efforts. The lighthouses that once assisted those in peril on the water, are now themselves in peril.

Selected Bibliography

─────────── ✦ ───────────

Appleton, Thomas. *Usque Ad Mare: A History of the Canadian Coast Guard and Marine Services*. Ottawa: Department of Tranpsort, 1968.

Barry, James P. "The First Georgian Bay Steamers," *Inland Seas*. Vol. 23., 1967.

_____. *Georgian Bay: an Illustrated History*. Erin: Boston Mills Press, 1992.

_____. *Georgian Bay: The Sixth Great Lake.* Toronto: Clarke, Irwin & Company, 1978.

_____. *Wrecks and Rescues of the Great Lakes.* Lansing, MI.: Two Peninsula Press, 1994.

Brazer, Marjorie Cahn. *Well-Favoured Passage*. Marjorie Kahn Brazer, 1975.

Bruce Township Tales and Trails. Bruce Township Historical Society, 1984.

Bush, E., *Canadian Historical Sites: Occasional Papers in Archeology and History*. No. 9, Indian and Northern Affairs, 1975.

Campbell, William A. *Northeastern Georgian Bay and Its People*. Sudbury, Ontario: William A. Campbell, 1982.

Campbell, William A. *The French and Pickerel Rivers, Their Histories and Their People*. Sudbury, Ontario: William A.Campbell, 1992.

Correspondence Pertaining to Shortage of Provisions of Lightkeeper David McBeath: Public Archives of Canada, Registered Correspondence, Letters 50, 249, 641.

Correspondence surrounding George Collins: Public Archives Canada, Registered Correspondence, Letter 38796, 41060, 39040, 24, 394, 29:212, 213, 214.

Correspondence Surrounding John Brown: Public Archives Canada, Registered Correspondence, Letter 32618.

Correspondence surrounding the construction of Cove Isle Light: Public Archives Canada, Registered Correspondence Letter 33491.

Fillmore, S. and R. Sandiland. *The Chartmakers: The History of Nautical Surverying in Canada*. Ottawa: NC Press.

Folkes, P. *The Cove Island Light Station: Fathom Five Provincial Park*, 1972.

French River Lighthouse History: National Archives of Canada, RG42.

Fulton, Gordon. *Federal Heritage Buildings Review Office Building Report 90-189, 90-192 : Lightower, Fog Alarm, Dwelling Great Duck Island.*

Fulton, Gordon. *Federal Heritage Buildings Review Office Informal Building Report 93-058: Lighttower, Dwelling Lonely Island.*

Gateman, L. *Lighthouses Around Bruce County*. Chelsey, Ontario: Spinning Wheel Publishing, 1991.

Gonnsen, Kirk. *Cabot Head History Report*. Friends of Cabot Head, 1993.

Great Lakes Pilot Volume II, Ottawa: The Canadian Hydrographic Service, 1955.

Hammill, J.D. *Early History of Meaford and its District*. Ontario Historical Society Papers and Records, Vol. XIIII, 1920.

Hemming, R. *Ships Gone Missing: The Great Lakes Storm of 1913.* Chicago, Contemporary Books, 1992.

Hewers of the Forests, Fishers of the Lakes: The History of St. Edmunds Township. The Township of St. Edmunds, 1985.

Higgins, R. *The Wreck of the Asia: Ships, Shoals and a Great Lakes Survey*. Waterloo, Ontario: Escart Press, 1995.

Hyde, Charles. *The Northern Lights: Lighthouses of the Upper Great Lakes*. Lansing MI: Two Peninsula Press, 1990.

Inland Seas, 1945-1988.

Inland Waters: List of Lights, Buoys and Fog Signal, Canadian Coast Guard. Marine Navigation Services, 1995.

Kauffman, Carl. *Logging Days in Blind River*. Sault Star Printing, 1970.

Klotzbach, M. A. and P. Johnston. *Harbour Lights*. Kelowna: Klotzbach, 1990.

Knight, Stanley. *Pictorial Meaford*. Meaford: Stanely Night Ltd. 1992.

Kohl, Cris. *Dive Ontario Two!* Chatham, Ontario: Cris Kohl, 1994.

Landon, F. *Lake Huron*. Indianapolis: Dobb-Merrill Co., 1944.

Lefolii, Ken."The Slapstick Saga Of The S.S. Tropic Sea," *Maclean's*. May 19, 1962.

Lightkeepers' Logs 1979-1941 Janet Head,Gore Bay Museum.

List of Lights and Fog-Signals on the Inland Waters of the Dominion of Canada. Ottawa: Department of Marine and Fisheries, 1913.

MacDonald, J.E. *This Point of Land.* Sault Star Printing, 1978.

MacLeod, Rose. *Sarawak Saga.* Owen Sound: Richardson Bond & Wright Ltd., 1973.

MacLeod, Rose. *The Story of White Cloud, Hay and Griffith Islands.* Rose MacLeod, 1979.

Mattie, Joan. *Federal Heritage Buildings Review Office Building Report 90-204, 90-213, 90-214, 90-216: Four "Imperial Towers": Lighthouses at Lake Huron and Georgian Bay.*

Mattie, Joan. *Federal Heritage Buildings Review Office Building Report 93-211: Lighthouse at Lighthouse Point (also known as Big Tub Lighthouse).*

Mazur, Sandra. *Memories of My Lighthouse Days.*

McCuaig Ruth, *Our Pointe au Baril*. Ontario: Ruth McCuaig, 1984.

McMaster, Cindy. *Life of My Great Grandfather (George Collins).*

Mifflin, R. *The Light on Chantry Island*. Erin: Boston Mills Press, 1986.

Northcott, Bill. *Thunder Bay Beach.* Erin: The Boston Mills Press, 1989.

Parliamentary Sessional Papers, Kingston: George Desbarts & Thos. Cary. 1870-1917.

Pearen, Shelley. *Exploring Manitoulin*. Toronto: University of Toronto Press, 1992.

Rourke, Juanita. "Memories of Hope Island Light," *Free Press Herald*. Sept. 29, 1967.

Rourke, Juanita. "Reminiscences of a Midland Woman of Life on Hope Island Lightstation," *The Free Press*. June 28, 1974.

Rules and Instructions for the Guidance of Lightkeepers in the Dominion of Canada. Ottawa: Department of Marine and Fisheries, 1875 and 1905.

Sail Directions of the Canadian Shore of Lake Huron and Georgian Bay, Ottawa: Ministry of the Naval Service of Canada, 1919.

Sandell, Marion. *Keepers of the Light, Nottawasaga Island 1858-1983.* Collingwood and District Historical Society, 1993.

Schooner Days, 1933, 1938.

Stevens, John R. *Lighthouses of the Great Lakes.* Ontario National Historic Sites Service, Manuscript Report #94. National And Historic Parks Branch, Department of Indian Affairs and Northern Development, 1965.

Stonehouse, Frederick. *Wreck Ashore: The United States Life-Saving Service on the Great Lakes.* Duluth, Minnesota: Lake Superior Port Cities Inc., 1994.

Through the years: Manitoulin Geneological Society. 1987-1994.

Thurston Harry. *Against Darkness and Storm.* Nova Scotia: Nimbus Publishing Ltd., 1993.

Tobermory lighthouse information: Canadian National Archives, Registered Correspondence, File 21968K.

Warder, Maitland. *Footloose on the Bruce.* Owen Sound: Maitland Warder, 1994.

Williams, Lillian. *Memoirs of Griffith Island.* Meaford, Ontario: Lillian Thornley Williams, 1986.

ACKNOWLEDGEMENTS

This book was made possible through the assistance of the following organizations:

Huronia Museum, Midland, Ontario
Department of Canadian Heritage,
    Museum Assistance Program
The McLean Foundation
The Charles H. Ivey Foundation
Jackman Foundation

We would also like to extend our sincere appreciation to:
Barbara D. Chisholm, our editor, for her clear thoughts and tireless efforts; Jamie Hunter, Bill Smith for reprinting family photographs, Tracy Leonard, and the Board of the Huronia Museum; Heidy Lawrance, Kim MacKillop, and Nicola Hunt for their excellent and fastidious work; Christopher Baines for his energy and enthusiasm; Shawn Heissler for researching; Deborah Wise Harris for copy editing; Pat (Gumshoe) Johnston; Robert Square; R.W. Chisholm; the Wilson family; Jane Tasker; Ed Sluga; Steve Keil; Luca Di Nicola and Charles Harlton.

At the Canadian Coast Guard, special thanks go to: Edmund Lea, Randy Childerhose, Martin Aberhoff, Daniel Badger, Jack Kennedy, Glen Campbell, Robert Parr, and Glen Madigan; and at the Ministry of Fisheries and Oceans, to Sharon Ashley and Cindy Bertrand.

The following institutions have also provided invaluable assistance: Bruce County Museum and Archives, Collingwood Museum, County of Grey – Owen Sound Museum (Joan Hyslop), Federal Heritage Building Review Office (Terry Smyth), Friends of Cabot Head, Gore Bay Museum, Heritage Canada (Doug Franklin), The Little Schoolhouse and Museum, Heritage Centre Marine and Rail Museum, Marine Museum of the Great Lakes at Kingston, Parry Sound Public Library, Metropolitan Toronto Reference Library, National Archives of Canada (Marc Bisaillon, Diane Martineau, Marina Royo) Thessalon Public Union Library, West Parry Sound Museum.

The information could not have been compiled without the kind participation of the following individuals. While many people have contributed to the project, any errors or omissions found in the text are ours alone.

Badgeley: Marie Hall, Merle Solomon
Boyd Island: Lillian Boyd
Brebeuf: Mary Paradis, Joanne La Croix, Peter Shirriff
Bruce Mines: Merritt Strum
Bustards: Isabell Anderson, William A. Campbell, Dorothy Pillgrem, William Pillgrem
Byng Inlet Range: Jack Kennedy
Cabot Head: Ron Baker, Ann Bard, Stewart Burgess, Ken and Nancy Hopkins
Cape Croker: John Adams, Tracy Adams, Nancy Armstong, Juanita and Bev Keefe, Frederic Jerome Proulx, Carol Richardson
Cape Robert: Gerald Fowler, Mathew Matheson, Orton Rumley
Christian: Ken King, Mike Sandy
Clapperton: Norman and Elva Lloyd, Ray Corbiere, West Bay First Nations
Collingwood: Tracy Marsh, Patricia Miscampbell
Cove: Holly Dunham, Dora Spears, Robert Square, Jack

Vaughan, Don Wilkes, Hugh Campbell
Flowerpot: Danny Coultis, John Coultis, Mark Coultis, Archie Culham, Jim Rumley
French River: Robert Boudignon, William A. Campbell
Gereaux: Viola Barron, Bert Hopkins, Art Niederhumer, Stephen Wohleber
Giants Tomb: Rita Martin
Gore Bay: Stanley Johnson, George H. Thorburn, Nicole Weppler
Great Ducks: Madeleine Charlton, Marie Hall, Bert Hopkins, Raymond and Doreen Hughson, Juanita and Bev Keefe, Bill Lewis, Sandy McGillivray, George Purvis, Orton Rumley
Griffith: Rose MacLeod, Helene Weaver, Lillian Williams
Hope: Dorthea Arthur, Jerome Charlebois, Chuck Edwards, Bob Herron, David Hutchings, Achille Marchildon, Roland Muir, Bill Northcott, Jim Wallace, Howard Warner,
How Did They Work?: Pat Johnston, Glen Madigan
Janet Head: Stephen Fletcher, Stanley Johnson, George H. Thorburn, Nicole Weppler
Jones: (see Red Rock)
Kagawong: Lottie Chapman, Helen Croswell, Austin Hunt, Lois Linley, Norman Lloyd
Killarney East & West: Herbie and Margaret Burke, Alfred Delamordiere, Faye Delamordiere, Dorothy Hoyland, Edgar Loosemore, Brent Skippen, Merle Solomon
Lion's Head: Lottie Chapman, Maitland Warder
Little Current: Don Mackenzie, Sandy McGillivray
Lonely Island: John Adams, Frank Butler, Bert Hopkins, Dorothy Hoyland, Edgar Loosemore, Aldene Strand, Rosalind Zamiska
McKay: Merritt Strum, Eva Wing
Manitowaning: Jeanette Allen
Meaford: John Robert Hillis, Victor L. Knight, Dorothy Pillgrem
Michael's Bay: Richard Bowerman, William R. Ritching
Mississagi Strait: John McQuarrie, Joyce Sprack, D.N. (Joe) Sullivan, Helen Van Every
Nottawasaga: Almeda Archer, David Baird, Carolyn Irwin, Wilfred Johnson, Doris and Jim Keith, Tracy Marsh, Sandra Mazur, Jamie McMaster, Jim McNabb, Patricia Miscampbell, Marion Sandell, Kaye Thompson
Owen Sound: Andrew Armitage, Joan Hyslop, Dorothy Talford, Helene Weaver,
Pointe au Baril: J.W. Dickenson, Emmaline Madigan, Ruth McCuaig
Presqu'ile: John Corfe, Dorothy Vick, Helene Weaver
Providence Bay: Verna Haggith, Leland McIntyre
Red Rock, Jones, Snug Harbour: Don Christie, Craig d'Arcy, Pat Johnston, Doris Muckinheim, Charlie Parr, Verna Parr, Tina Quinn, Tom Sprunt, Dave Thomas
Snug Harbour (see Red Rock)
South Baymouth: Richard Bowerman, Lottie Chapman, Verna Haggith, Nancy and Danny Leeson, Ivan Sisson
Strawberry: Terry Gaffney, Don Mackenzie, Vicki Raisbeck, William R. Ritching
Thessalon: Mary Anne MacDonald
Tobermory (Big Tub): Holly Dunham, Pat McArthur
Westerns: Roberta Anderson, Alvin and Beth Brown, Ella Campbell, Bill Couling, Juanita and Bev Keefe, Doris and Jim Keith, Peter Ronn, Arnold and Lillian Wing, Alexander Younger
Why Were They Built?: Patrick Folkes
General shipping and lighthouses: Patrick Folkes, Chris Kohl, Norman Smith, Frederick Stonehouse, Wayne Supulski, Dave Thomas

And to all others who helped us along our way, thank you.

SITE INDEX

ABOUT THE AUTHORS

Barbara Chisholm, Russell Floren, and Andrea Gutsche are best known for films and books that search out and explore vanishing pieces of Canadian history. Their most recent project, *Ghosts of the Bay: The Forgotten History of Georgian Bay*, has quickly become a local favorite and Canadian bestseller. Their next book/film production, entitled *Superior: Under the Shadow of the Gods*, will focus on the dramatic history of Lake Superior's Canadian shores. Spring 1997 release.

Lynx Images Inc.

Established in 1988, Lynx Images is a film and book production company based in Toronto, Canada.

Recent Productions:	Ghosts of the Bay (1994)	Shoreline Living (1993)
	Toronto: Stories from the	Restoring the Balance (1993)
	Life of a City, Part 1: York (1994)	Mt. Pleasant Cemetery (1994)

For more information or a copy of the catalogue write:

LYNX IMAGES INC.
PO BOX 5961, STATION 'A'
TORONTO, ONTARIO M5W 1P4

Or contact our Web Site: http://www.lynximages.com